Domestic Violence, Islam and Gender in Indonesia

Based on extensive original research, this book explores how the Indonesian Anti-Domestic Violence Law is understood and applied in practice.

Drawing on an in-depth case study from the province of Aceh, the book canvasses informal and formal help-seeking avenues for domestic violence victims, including via religious and criminal courts. It is concluded that victim legal rights are currently not well understood or protected in practice, largely due to help-seeking processes being densely gendered and discriminatory against women. Most cases of domestic violence continue to go unreported; cases that are reported are generally mediated informally through *adat* (customary) justice avenues at the community level; and victims who seek help at the religious and criminal courts continue to face significant barriers to access to justice.

Providing an important overview of the current legal and socio-legal systems relevant to domestic violence in Indonesia, this book will be of keen interest to students and scholars of Islamic, gender and Asian studies.

Balawyn Jones is a Lecturer at La Trobe Law School, La Trobe University, Australia.

Asian Studies Association of Australia
Women in Asia Series
Editor: Louise Edwards
University of New South Wales

56. **Face-veiled Women in Contemporary Indonesia**
    Eva F. Nisa

57. **Women and Martial Art in Japan**
    Kate Sylvester

58. **Pious Girls: Young Muslim Women in Indonesia**
    Annisa R. Beta

59. **North Korea's Women-led Grassroots Capitalism**
    Kyungja Jung and Bronwen Dalton

60. **Women in Their Thirties in Japan: Life Course and Happiness**
    Kaori H. Okano

61. **Domestic Violence, Islam and Gender in Indonesia**
    Balawyn Jones

Domestic Violence, Islam and Gender in Indonesia

Balawyn Jones

Routledge
Taylor & Francis Group
LONDON AND NEW YORK

First published 2025
by Routledge
4 Park Square, Milton Park, Abingdon, Oxon OX14 4RN

and by Routledge
605 Third Avenue, New York, NY 10158

Routledge is an imprint of the Taylor & Francis Group, an informa business

British Library Cataloguing-in-Publication Data
A catalogue record for this book is available from the British Library

ISBN: 978-1-032-61356-7 (hbk)
ISBN: 978-1-032-61361-1 (pbk)
ISBN: 978-1-032-61364-2 (ebk)

DOI: 10.4324/9781032613642

Typeset in Times New Roman
by SPi Technologies India Pvt Ltd (Straive)

This book is dedicated to my family in Australia and Indonesia.

Syahrial dan Saani - *lon galak gata.*

Contents

Illustrations

Figures

Tables

Series editor's foreword

The contributions of women to the social, political and economic transformations occurring in the Asian region are legion. Women have served as leaders of nations, communities, workplaces, activist groups and families. Asian women have joined with others to participate in fomenting change at micro and macro levels. They have been both agents and targets of national and international interventions in social policy. In the performance of these myriad roles women have forged new and modern gendered identities that are recognisably global and local. Their experiences are rich, diverse and instructive. The books in this series testify to the central role women play in creating the new Asia and re-creating Asian womanhood. Moreover, these books reveal the resilience and inventiveness of women around the Asian region in the face of entrenched and evolving patriarchal social norms.

Scholars publishing in this series demonstrate a commitment to promoting the productive conversation between Gender Studies and Asian Studies. The need to understand the diversity of experiences of femininity and womanhood around the world increases inexorably as globalisation proceeds apace. Lessons from the experiences of Asian women present us with fresh opportunities for building new possibilities for women's progress the world over.

The Asian Studies Association of Australia (ASAA) sponsors this publication series as part of its on-going commitment to promoting knowledge about women in Asia. In particular, the ASAA Women's Forum provides the intellectual vigour and enthusiasm that maintains the Women in Asia Series (WIAS). The aim of the series, since its inception in 1990, is to promote knowledge about women in Asia to both academic and general audiences. To this end, WIAS books draw on a wide range of disciplines including anthropology, sociology, political science, cultural studies, media studies, literature, and history. The series prides itself on being an outlet for cutting edge research conducted by recent PhD graduates and postdoctoral fellows from throughout the region.

The Series could not function without the generous professional advice provided by many anonymous readers. Moreover, the wise counsel provided by Peter Sowden at Routledge is invaluable. WIAS, its authors and the ASAA are very grateful to these people for their expert work.

Louise Edwards (UNSW Australia)
Series Editor

Prologue

The following prologue is a compilation of real victim accounts collected during fieldwork in Aceh, Indonesia. The story of our hypothetical victim, Ibu (Mrs) Hayati, highlights some of the primary barriers that victims of domestic violence face when navigating access to justice in Indonesia.

October 2018, at home

Ibu Hayati sits on the veranda with her neighbours Ibu Dina and Ibu Risa.

'My husband will never agree to a divorce', says Ibu Hayati.

'You want to get divorced? … For what – to be a *janda* (divorcee)?',[1] Ibu Dina retorts.

'I can't take this anymore', Ibu Hayati responds, 'I keep praying that he will get better.'

'*Allah* would never give you a greater burden than you can bear',[2] says Ibu Risa softly, 'You have to be *sabar* (patient) *Kak*.'

Ibu Hayati nods and responds, '*Inshallah*', excusing herself to go and pick up her eldest child from school.

January 2019, in the village

The *Geuchik* (Head of the Village) sits across from Ibu Hayati furrowing his brow.

'It keeps getting worse', she says, 'I don't know what to do.'

Bapak (Mr) *Geuchik* shrugs. 'It's normal for couples to *cek-cok* (disagree) sometimes', he replies.

'It's not just disagreement though Bapak … I don't feel safe at home anymore and I am worried about the children.'

'You *should* think of your children', the *Geuchik* responds, 'they need a father to provide for them.'

July 2019, at the police station

Ibu Hayati sits next to Ibu Risa at the police station.

'There is nothing we can do', the officer explains. 'We don't have any evidence to charge him.'

'I saw it myself', Ibu Risa offers. 'He threatened to kill her – please, there must be something you can do. She even has texts on her phone, show them *Kak* –'

'It's just', the officer interrupts, 'that this kind of case … it's not that serious (*tidak berat*). With household problems, it's better to go P2TP2A[3] – they deal with cases like this.'

'Come on let's go', Ibu Risa says, taking Ibu Hayati's hand.

July 2019, at P2TP2A's office

Ibu Hayati hands the forms back to the P2TP2A secretary.

'Do you have anyone that you can stay with?', the secretary asks while looking over the forms.

'No, my mother and father live in a different province', Ibu Hayati replies. 'The *Geuchik* said that he can ask my husband to move out of the house so that my children and I can stay in the *kampung* (village), but I am worried that my husband will not listen.'

The secretary nods, 'It is probably best not to stay there if you think your husband might react badly to the divorce application.'

'He threatened to take the children if I file for divorce, I don't know what to do.'

'I understand, it's hard but you have to be strong Ibu. It's not okay for him to treat you like this – you have rights.'

December 2019, back at P2TP2A's office

Ibu Hayati sits in the waiting room at P2TP2A, looking at the 'Stop *Kekerasan* (Violence)' poster on the wall. 'Ibu Hayati', the secretary calls, 'Ibu Raihan will see you now.'

'Do you want the good news or the bad news?' Ibu Raihan asks.

Ibu Hayati ignores the question, 'I just need to know when I will be able to see my children again. I need to be with them.'

'The good news', Ibu Raihan continues, 'is that the enforcement proceeding for your divorce case has been listed for next month.'

'What does that mean?', Ibu Hayati asks.

'It means that we will be able to ask the Judge to enforce the original custody arrangement which was made when your divorce was finalised.'

'And in the meantime?'
'You just have to be *sabar* (patient) Ibu.'

Ibu Hayati's story starts with her being told to be *sabar* (patient) with the man who is abusing her and ends with her being told to be patient with the system that is failing to protect her. Even though Ibu Hayati is assured that she 'has rights', her experiences – including the police's dismissal of her report and her husband's non-compliance with the initial custody arrangement – illustrate that 'rights' can mean very little to victims of domestic violence in practice. Even in the case of Indonesia where specific legislation has been enacted to criminalise domestic violence, and even if victims of domestic violence are aware of their legal rights, victims face compounding barriers to access to justice when navigating State justice systems. Access to justice is further complicated for domestic violence victims in Indonesia – a majority-Muslim country – where the intersections between religion, gender, and law are highly contested. The word 'contested' here refers to the complicated ways in which religion, gender, and law interrelate and the ways in which women exercise their agency to challenge the construction of meaning at the intersection of these forces.

Notes

1 *Janda* means a woman who was married but is no longer married. It can therefore refer to widows, divorcees, or women who have been abandoned. For a full list of Indonesian terms, see Glossary.
2 '*Allah* does not burden a soul beyond that it can bear' – verse 2:286 of the *Qur'an*, commonly translated into Indonesian as an expression in response to hardship.
3 The Integrated Service Centre for the Empowerment of Women and Children (*Pusat Pelayanan Terpadu Pemberdayaan Perempuan dan Anak* – known as P2TP2A) is the primary organisation tasked with responsibility for coordinating State responses to domestic violence. P2TP2A is discussed in more detail in Chapter 3.

1 Introduction

In 2004, the Indonesian government passed Law No. 23/2004 *Undang-Undang tentang Penghapusan Kekerasan Dalam Rumah Tangga* (the Anti-Domestic Violence Law, also referred to in this book as 'the Law'). At the time of writing, domestic violence has been criminalised under the Law for over 20 years. However, there remain substantial barriers to the implementation of the Law, a lack of protection for domestic violence victims, and widespread impunity for perpetrators. According to a commissioner from *Komnas Perempuan* (the Indonesian Women's Commission) the Law is 'not yet fully operational, nationally or in regional areas.'

While most cases of domestic violence remain unreported, women who do report generally do so at the village level. The majority of reported cases are mediated informally through *adat* justice avenues. *Adat* is defined by Benda-Beckmann (2011) as 'a generic term to indicate an often undifferentiated whole constituted by the morality, customs, and legal institutions of ethnic or territorial groups'. Where customary mediation fails or where the case is especially serious, domestic violence cases may progress to religious (civil) law or criminal law avenues, parallel jurisdictions that have their own procedures. This book focuses on the exercise of religious (civil) jurisdiction by the *Pengadilan Agama* (Indonesian Islamic Courts) and the exercise of criminal jurisdiction by the *Pengadilan Negeri* (Indonesian State Courts).[1]

It is within the religious (civil) jurisdiction of the Islamic Courts that Islamic family law and divorce petitions are heard (Chapter 5) and in the criminal jurisdiction of the *Pengadilan Negeri* that cases are prosecuted under the Indonesian Criminal Code and Anti-Domestic Violence Law (Chapters 6 and 7). Domestic violence victims may apply for a divorce at the Islamic Courts or report violence to the police. If a victim reports to the police, only in rare situations are domestic violence cases prosecuted in the criminal jurisdiction of the *Pengadilan Negeri*. Victims who seek help from State legal avenues face many hurdles, including community stigma, victim-blaming, and cost and time burdens. This book investigates how victims who overcome these barriers to seek help from State institutions then face further barriers to access to justice within the State justice system, in particular due to gender bias and inadequate service provision.

DOI: 10.4324/9781032613642-1

The focus of this book is domestic violence at the intersection of Islam and gender. Indonesia has the world's largest Muslim population. The analysis in this book is based on fieldwork conducted in the Indonesian province of Aceh, a 98 per cent Muslim province located on the northern-most tip of Sumatra (Figure 1.1).

Aceh is one of the main provinces in Indonesia where 'sharia-isation' of the law has been documented. This makes Aceh the ideal case study for understanding the relationship between religion and gender in the context of domestic violence. This book seeks to answer the question of how religion and gender affect the implementation of the Anti-Domestic Violence Law in Indonesia using Aceh as a case study. In doing so, fieldwork conducted in Aceh is used to unpack community understandings of domestic violence, women's experiences of help-seeking, and legal system actors' attitudes towards domestic violence.

The findings of this book include that at the village level, domestic violence is generally not understood by the community in relation to the Law but rather by reference to local understandings of gender informed by religious interpretations. Hegemonic norms that embody patriarchal ideals about gender and marriage operate as a barrier to access to justice for women, particularly at the

Figure 1.1 Map of Indonesia and Aceh (Salim 2015).

community level. Community understandings of domestic violence are biased against women in a number of ways, including the perception of domestic violence as a private problem (or not a problem at all) and the justification of physical violence as 'disciplinary' or 'educative'. Further, restrictive gender norms relating to women often lead to victim-blaming or justificatory discourses about perpetrator behaviour. These discriminatory gender norms influence the implementation of the Law at every stage, including decision-making in religious (civil) and criminal jurisdictions by State actors. There are also diverse and competing religious interpretations with respect to gender and domestic violence within Aceh and across Indonesia.

In addition to legal pluralism involving formal State and informal *adat* systems, jurisdictional dualism between the Islamic Courts and the *Pengadilan Negeri* leads to many victims falling between the cracks in the State system. For example, the Islamic Courts tend to take a passive approach and rarely take domestic violence into account in decision-making. This is largely because Islamic Court judges feel that they do not have 'jurisdiction' to consider domestic violence. The book concludes that even though Islamic Court judges do not have jurisdiction to apply criminal provisions under the Anti-Domestic Violence Law, domestic violence still falls squarely within the Islamic Court's jurisdiction to the extent that it affects women's substantive divorce rights. As such, domestic violence should be taken into account by Islamic Court judges in deciding divorce applications. In addition to analysing the Islamic Court's approach towards domestic violence and divorce, 70 domestic violence cases decided by the *Pengadilan Negeri* (between 2013 and 2017) are examined. Based on this analysis, it is argued that *Pengadilan Negeri* judges are influenced by gender bias in exercising their discretion when deciding and sentencing domestic violence cases. For example, perpetrator sentences are often mitigated based on gendered, moralistic (as opposed to legal) justifications, leading to a failure to protect women's rights and a lack of perpetrator accountability.

Throughout this book, it is illustrated how the implementation of the Anti-Domestic Violence Law is affected by the operation of religiously-informed gender norms – from community understandings of domestic violence based on patriarchal ideas about gender – to gender bias in how judges exercise their discretion in domestic violence cases. Gender bias informs and produces institutional responses to domestic violence, compounding barriers to access to justice for women seeking support or exercising their legal rights. Overall, it is argued that due to compounding barriers to access to justice, the current implementation of the Law does not adequately protect victims of domestic violence or punish and deter perpetrators.

Overview of terminology and assumptions

The foundational assumptions underpinning the analysis in this book are outlined here to orientate the reader and are discussed in more depth in Chapter 3.

Assumptions about domestic violence

The phrase '*domestic* violence' is used in this book, as opposed to '*family* violence'. This is because in the Indonesian context the Law's application is not limited to those who have a familial relationship, rather it is the *household* (broadly defined) that is regulated by the Law. While some scholarship uses the phrase 'domestic *abuse*' rather than 'domestic *violence*', this book predominately uses the phrase 'domestic violence' as, linguistically, the Indonesian phrase *kekerasan dalam rumah tangga* (KDRT) translates to '*violence* in the household'.

This book adopts the feminist model of domestic violence as the analytical starting point. The feminist model is underpinned by the assumption that domestic violence stems from patriarchy and gender inequality. Patriarchy can be defined as societal or familial arrangements in which males predominantly exercise power. As described by Hill (2019):

> This perspective has been developed over decades of research and work with victims, in shelters, hospitals and courthouses, and the central assertion – that men who subscribe to rigid gender stereotypes are more likely to abuse their partners – is backed up by decades of research. Study after study finds that men are more prone to abusing if they've a) been socialised into rigid gender roles, b) believe that men are naturally superior or c) feel their masculinity or authority has been threatened, particularly if women have not complied with their gender-role expectations.

While patriarchy is not a complete explanation as to why individuals choose to use violence, its analytical significance is no longer seriously debated in feminist literature. As Kelly and Westmarland (2016) explain, over three decades of research on domestic violence establish it as 'a pattern of behaviours involving power and control, based in and reproducing gender inequality'. A core defining feature of patriarchy relevant to this research is that men, regardless of whether they individually have power, feel *entitled* to power. As will be illustrated in Chapter 7, men often choose to use violence if they feel that their power is being challenged in some way, are unable to fulfil masculine gender norms, or feel that they are losing control of their partners.

Although patriarchy, gender inequality, and gender norms are the starting point when discussing domestic violence, this account can be further complicated by taking into consideration the specific circumstances of the relationship between the victim and the perpetrator as well as broader socio-economic context in which they live. A number of factors may make individuals more prone to using violence or more vulnerable to experiencing violence.[2] Triggers for violence will be discussed further in Chapter 7.

Assumptions about gender

Gender – defined as the socially constructed meaning assigned to biological sex – varies according to time and place. It is assumed that constructions of gender are specific to (but not stagnant within) different contexts. The phrase 'gender norms' used in this book refers to *hegemonic gender norms* – ideas about and practices of gender that are dominant in society. Hegemonic gender norms exist alongside subversive or alternative gender norms. Further, although patriarchal gender norms may stem from, or be positioned within, the specific context of Aceh or Indonesia, these should not be viewed from a perspective of cultural essentialism. Rather, gender norms within Aceh and Indonesia should be understood as fluid, subject to contestation, and subject to change over time. Lastly with respect gender, the analysis in this book is underpinned by the assumption that a focus on gender is intrinsic or essential to analyses of domestic violence.[3] This is because, whether in Aceh, Indonesia, or globally, most victims of domestic violence are female and most perpetrators are male.

Assumptions about religion

An assumption underpinning the analysis in this book is that knowledge about both domestic violence and religion is required to effectively respond to domestic violence in faith-based communities.[4] Indonesia is well-known globally as having the largest Muslim population in the world, with approximately 87% of Indonesians identifying as Muslim. In addition to this, Indonesia is home to Christian, Hindu, Buddhist, and Confucian communities. Most of Indonesia's 38 provinces are Muslim-majority, with the notable exception of Bali, Papua, East Nusa Tengarra, and North Sulawesi. Whilst Indonesia is religiously and culturally diverse, as a majority Muslim country gender inequality and patriarchal norms are informed by and rooted in religious interpretations of Islam.

The case study of Aceh was chosen as the province has the largest Muslim majority in Indonesia. With 98% of Acehnese people identifying as Muslim, to be Acehnese and Muslim is largely seen as synonymous. Although the case study fieldwork was conducted in Aceh, the findings of this book relating to domestic violence law and policy are generally transferable across provinces. However, the generalisability of findings with respect to Islamic norms across provinces is contingent on whether a province is demographically a Muslim (or non-Muslim) majority. Further, if a point of analysis is specific to the Acehnese context, this is explicitly identified in the text. The book's findings with respect to religion, gender, and law more broadly can also be used as a comparative basis to inform analysis in other Islamic jurisdictions, such as Malaysia.

Assumptions about law

The focus of this book is the exercise of women's legal rights; however, the law does not operate in a vacuum. The implementation of the law is, in practice, influenced by the local context. Therefore, this book takes a socio-legal approach. Socio-legal approaches include analyses of the law that are linked to analyses of the social context in which the law exists and analyses of the part that the law plays in the 'creation, maintenance and/or change' of social norms.[5]

It is not assumed that the law is a neutral force, nor is it assumed that the law necessarily has utility for women. Rather, this book recognises that the law is itself gendered – for example, laws enact gendered norms into practice and gender bias exists within legal processes and institutions. Further, as the analysis throughout this book illustrates, for many victims of domestic violence the utility of the law is limited and engagement with the law is fraught. While analysing the legal system as it is (the status quo), this book also assumes that the law should, or could, have utility for women. This is not to say that women must or should engage with the legal system, but that the legal system should be available for women to engage with, should victims of domestic violence choose to do so. What this means in practice is mitigating barriers to access to justice as much as possible so that the utility of the law is increased for victims of domestic violence.

Access to justice

Access to justice is a central concept underpinning the book. Broadly, access to justice refers to the idea that claimholders should be able to 'seek and obtain a remedy through formal and informal justice systems', both by empowering claimholders to assert their legal rights as well as by holding the State accountable for the protection of these rights.[6] Indonesia has a pluralistic justice system consisting of both formal State systems and informal *adat* systems. As explained in Chapter 3, while Indonesian legal pluralism provides claimholders (in the context of this book, victims of domestic violence) a degree of choice in asserting their rights, due to overlapping or conflicting processes pluralism also often operates to obstruct victim access to justice and muddies accountability for the State in protecting victim rights. By applying the theory of bureaucratic violence (set out below), this book seeks to emphasise the responsibilities of State stakeholders under the Law in order to promote accountability for the protection of victim rights.

Method

The data analysis that informs this book was conducted using grounded theory methodology.[7] Grounded theory methodology uses inductive and abductive reasoning to develop theory from data based on lived experiences and local understandings. The methodology seeks to avoid essentialism by viewing knowledge as situated in a specific time and space. In addition, grounded theory was used to draw out theoretical implications from the data relating to the role of the State in protecting victims of domestic violence.

The primary fieldwork was conducted in Banda Aceh (the capital of Aceh) between 2017 and 2019. Forty interviews were conducted with local women's advocates, academics, government officials, staff from frontline women's services, police, prosecution, lawyers, community leaders, judges from the religious (civil) and criminal jurisdictions, and victims of domestic violence. There were four interview groups:

1 Interviews to contextualise domestic violence as an Indonesian women's rights issues – conducted with local women's advocates, academics, government officials, and staff from frontline women's services.
2 Interviews to understand the process that victims of domestic violence go through to seek State protection – conducted with police, prosecution, lawyers, community leaders, and staff from frontline women's services.
3 Interviews to explore judicial approaches towards domestic violence with judges from the Islamic Court and *Pengadilan Negeri*.
4 Interviews to highlight the perspectives of domestic violence victims.

In interview Groups 1 – 3, interviewees were contacted individually through a snow-balling approach. For interview Group 4, interviews with victims were organised through the Integrated Service Centre for the Empowerment of Women and Children (P2TP2A) – the primary government organisation tasked with responding to domestic violence. An open invitation advertised a call for interviews for victims of domestic violence who wanted to share their experiences seeking help through State or non-State avenues.[8]

In addition to these interviews, I analysed 70 domestic violence cases (decided between 2013 and 2017) provided by the *Pengadilan Negeri* in Banda Aceh.[9] The Court agreed to share this sample of cases for research purposes subject to the identifying details of defendants, victims, and witnesses being anonymised. The cases from the *Pengadilan Negeri* represent a significant number of women who, despite compounding obstacles, chose to engage with the State system to exercise their rights under the Law. In terms of the limitations of this dataset, the domestic violence cases prosecuted were overwhelmingly perpetrated by husbands against wives. In the domestic violence cases prosecuted at the *Pengadilan Negeri* between 2013 and 2017 in Banda Aceh, in 90% of the cases the perpetrator was the husband and the victim was the wife. Due to the dataset predominately consisting of domestic violence perpetrated by spouses, less commonly reported instances of child abuse, sibling abuse, and elder abuse are not addressed in this book. Further, due to the current scope of the Law, domestic violence protections do not apply to couples in *pacaran* (premarital) or same sex relationships.[10] Therefore the scope of this book is limited to examining domestic violence perpetrated by spouses within marital relationships recognised by the State.

Grounded theory recognises that researchers are not 'blank slates' and required me, as the researcher, to consciously reflect on my own potential biases to avoid imposing pre-existing ideas onto the data. This can also be described, methodologically, as an assessment of whether external theories demonstrate 'earned relevance', rather than forcing existing ideas onto, or simply assuming external theories fit, the data. An assumption underpinning the analysis in this book is that while some aspects of domestic violence are contextually specific (for example, local gender norms and local law), the core dynamics of domestic violence which are used to define and characterise this behaviour – based on decades of research globally – are largely transferrable across jurisdictions. As discussed in Chapter 3, the Indonesian legal and policy framework characterises domestic violence as a form of gendered violence underpinned by gender inequality, consistent with the feminist model outlined above.

In terms of positionality, it should be noted that I am an Australian-Muslim woman who was raised and lives in a Western context but speaks Indonesian and is connected to the Indonesian community via marriage. Most people in Aceh speak Indonesian and all interviews were conducted in Indonesian. For interviews with victims of domestic violence, I was accompanied by a female Acehnese translator to enable interviewees to speak Acehnese if they wished to do so.

Structure

Chapters 2–4 seek to orientate the reader in the relevant social, scholarly, legal and, policy contexts for the book. Chapter 2 outlines the case study context of Aceh Province. Chapter 3 positions the book in the relevant scholarly literature – at the intersection of religion, gender and, the law and sets out the legal and policy framework for domestic violence in Indonesia.

In Chapter 4, I analyse the barriers faced by victims attempting to seek help at the village level via *adat* avenues focusing on community understandings of gender and domestic violence, as informed by local religious interpretations. Chapter 4 illustrates that domestic violence tends to be ignored, minimised, or justified due to patriarchal interpretations of religious doctrines. Further, it is shown how – in identifying themselves as victims of domestic violence – women are naming the harm committed against them and, in doing so, implicitly or explicitly challenging the entitlement of men to use violence. Chapter 4 then canvasses victim perspectives on help-seeking. This section highlights the difficult decisions women are forced to make in domestic violence situations and the factors influencing their engagement with State systems, such as community norms and stigmas, economic considerations, and the presence or absence of support systems. Importantly in terms of help-seeking, many victims interviewed did not perceive it to be possible, preferable, or tenable to 'leave' domestic violence relationships.

Chapter 5 analyses the access to justice issues for victims pursuing divorce at the Islamic Courts, including the impact of unregistered marriages (*nikah siri*) and unauthorised divorces (*cerai liar*) on legal protections for women. In this chapter, I challenge the idea that the Islamic Courts lack jurisdiction to deal with domestic violence within the context of divorce proceedings and argue that the Islamic Courts must shift from a passive to active approach towards domestic violence in divorce cases. Chapter 5 argues that judges in the religious (civil) jurisdiction should actively identify domestic violence as relevant to mediation, the allocation of post-divorce rights, and the making of interim orders to protect women and children.

Chapter 6 analyses the processes and barriers for victims if they wish to report to police and act as witnesses for criminal prosecution. Although most cases of domestic violence are dealt with at the community level via *adat* processes, and victims who engage with the State generally do so by seeking a divorce at the Islamic Courts, the police act as the gatekeepers to the criminal justice system. Chapter 6 evidences a general reluctance on behalf of the police to investigate domestic violence cases, largely due to the operation of discriminatory gender norms as well as broader systemic issues, such as underfunding and a lack of training. Poor police practices create a bottleneck in terms of entry into the criminal justice system, impeding the State's potential to protect domestic violence victims. It is argued that the blatant failure of police to carry out their responsibilities under the Law constitutes an iteration of bureaucratic violence. The exception to this is arguably the Women and Children's Protection Unit within the police, which, although limited in its caseload, has a better understanding of domestic violence dynamics.

In Chapter 7, I analyse judicial approaches towards domestic violence cases at the *Pengadilan Negeri*, based on an analysis of 70 domestic violence cases (2013–2017). Despite the numerous barriers to access to justice set out in previous chapters, the cases prosecuted at the *Pengadilan Negeri* represent a significant number of women who sought to engage with the State system and exercise their rights under the Law. In Chapter 7, I analyse how the court treats different types of domestic violence (physical, psychological, sexual, and economic) and triggers for violence (such as challenges to male authority, jealousy, economic pressure, and custody disputes). This analysis illustrates how the court's approach to domestic violence is influenced by community understandings of gender and religion as canvassed in Chapter 4. For example, judges persistently overemphasise physical violence and lack an understanding of the broader dynamics of domestic violence.

The second section of Chapter 7 illustrates inconsistent judicial reasoning and sentencing disparities across the cases studied. Overall, the current judicial approach to sentencing is overwhelmingly carceral with judges rarely handing down non-custodial or alternative sentences that are provided for in the Law. This is partly because the State has failed to establish rehabilitation programs for domestic violence perpetrators, which undermines a significant part of the sentencing scheme under the Law. The analysis in the third section of Chapter 7 also highlights how conflicted many *Pengadilan Negeri* judges are when handing down custodial sentences in domestic violence cases, due to the negative impacts such sentences often have on victims and their children. However, judicial consideration of mitigating and aggravating factors remains densely gendered, including a tendency for male violence to be (morally) justified, leading to the mitigation of sentences even where there is no legal basis for doing so.

Benang merah (the red thread): State responsibility and bureaucratic violence

The *benang merah* (red thread) that ties this book together is the State's responsibility to protect victims of domestic violence and hold perpetrators accountable. Throughout this book, the barriers to access to justice for victims who seek to exercise their rights under the Law are analysed and the failures of the State to implement the protections promised in the Law are unpacked. Ultimately, this book emphasises the need for the State to be held accountable for its continued failure to protect victims or hold perpetrator accountable, fuelling a culture of impunity for domestic violence across Indonesia.

Throughout this book I develop a theory of *bureaucratic violence*. Bureaucratic violence describes structural violence committed by the State in the form of bureaucratic negligence. Bureaucratic violence is the harm done to victims by a system promising to provide help in law but failing to provide such assistance in practice. As I explain below, the provisions of the Law create a number of rights for victims and place correlative responsibilities on the State to fulfil these rights. Where victims have such rights, the failure of the State to fulfil legal promises is not benign because it, in fact, puts victims at an exacerbated and/or perpetuated risk of violence. I argue that State justice system stakeholders should, in theory (if not yet in practice), be held accountable for the distinct harms caused to domestic violence victims as a result of defaulting on their promises. In other words, the theory of bureaucratic violence seeks to establish a causal relationship between the failures of the State to operationalise laws relating to domestic violence and the harms experienced by victims of domestic violence. Throughout this book, I provide examples of bureaucratic violence including the failure to establish operational safe houses for domestic violence victims, the failure to establish rehabilitation programs for perpetrators, and the failure of State representatives (in particular, the police and judges of the Islamic Courts and *Pengadilan Negeri*) to appropriately carry out their responsibilities under the Law.

In the next section, I explain what I mean by the terms *bureaucratic* and *violence* before linking this theory to State accountability and the role of the State in protecting victims.

The 'bureaucratic' in bureaucratic violence

First, I have used the term 'bureaucratic' violence instead of 'State' violence because, in the Indonesian context, the phrase 'State violence' has connotations of direct, physical attack by the State. As discussed in Chapter 2, this is particularly so in the case study province of Aceh, which is a post-conflict area. The term bureaucratic is used to indicate a more indirect harm caused by the operation of government bureaucracy in implementing the Law across and within government departments. Bureaucracy is used in its ordinary sense to refer to State systems where government administration (including the allocation of government funds) is carried out by government officials, often in accordance with obscure or unnecessarily complicated procedures. Indonesia is well known for its inflated and inefficient bureaucracy, which includes a lack of coordination between levels of government and a resultant 'passing of the buck' for responsibility to implement laws between institutional stakeholders. For context, in Indonesia when legislation is implemented, the general practice is for the national government to be responsible for allocating the budget necessary for implementing the law and for the provincial or local government to be responsible for the allocation of land or physical infrastructure.

Second, with respect to bureaucracy as a form of structural violence, structural violence has defined by Winter and Leighton (2001) as violence that is:

> invisible, embedded in ubiquitous social structures, normalized by stable institutions and regular experience. Structural violence occurs whenever people are disadvantaged by political, legal, economic, or cultural traditions. Because they are longstanding, structural inequities usually seem ordinary – the way things are and always have been.

In the context of the Global South, Gupta (2012) analysed 'invisible' or 'implicit' violence 'taken for granted in the routinised practices of state institutions'. Specifically, Gupta argued that poverty in the Indian context can be theorised as a form of structural violence stemming from State policies and practices. In doing so, he challenged the idea that the State is not culpable for harm caused to citizens if they are passively 'allowed to die'. Like in the context of domestic violence in Indonesia, Gupta acknowledged that while there are government programs in place that attempt to assist citizens to a certain extent, 'no matter how noble the intentions of [these] programs, and no matter how sincere the officials in charge of them, the overt goal of helping … is subverted by … bureaucracy'.

Bureaucracy in this sense can be distinguished from the form-filling, box-ticking type of bureaucracy at lower levels of administration. Bureaucratisation of government procedures has been identified by many front-line service providers as impeding their ability to meet victim needs in a timely manner. While this type of bureaucratic inefficiency is tangentially relevant in that it may affect access to justice, this is not the kind of bureaucracy that is addressed within the theory of bureaucratic violence. Rather, I am talking about higher level bureaucracy across and within State departments and institutions, particularly a lack of coordination between the national and provincial governments that impedes implementation of the Law and has led to the failure of the State to protect domestic violence victims.

In the context of domestic violence, Douglas (2021) persuasively argued that victims experience not only direct harms at the hands of their abusive partners but also:

> injuries that come from the bureaucracies within institutions that do not respond to their needs and instead disrespect and mistreat them and further exacerbate their marginalization.

It is these injuries that the theory of bureaucratic violence seeks to capture, with a particular focus on the ways in which these harms materialise in the Indonesian context.

The 'violence' in bureaucratic violence

In this section, I argue that the failure of the State to fulfil its promises does not result in a type of 'neutral negligence' but causes unique forms of harm to victims of domestic violence. There are, at least, two kinds of harm that domestic violence victims potentially face if the State fails to provide protection as promised in the Law.

The first is an exacerbated risk of violence. It is well known in domestic violence literature that the risk of violence greatly increases in separation and post-separation contexts. In her recent study, Douglas (2021) found that:

> many women … reported that separation, and interacting with the legal system, marked a period of heightened danger and failed to deliver on the promise of safety for them and their children.

The analysis of criminal prosecutions under the Law (Chapter 7 of this book), documents a number of cases where women were assaulted when they attempted to pursue their rights or seek help. Therefore, it is not a stretch to say that if a victim engages with the State justice system on the premise of receiving assistance and protection and does not receive it, the State's failure to fulfil its promises is likely to result in an exacerbated risk of violence for the victim. For example, in the absence of operational safe houses (discussed below), the victim may literally have nowhere safe to seek refuge, opening her up to having to return home to her abuser or to another location where she may not be supported or safe or she may face homelessness. As Hill (2019) observes 'If women and children don't have somewhere to go, they are left with a set of dangerous options'.

With respect to the second form of violence – the risk of perpetuated violence – I argue that each time the State promises to help victims of domestic violence and fails to do so, it, first, loses the victim's trust and, second, emboldens perpetrators due to the lack of accountability. The State's failure to fulfil promises therefore potentially contributes to the victim's further isolation and abuse.[11] To provide an illustration, if you imagine that a victim coming to the State for help is metaphorically coming to the surface of the ocean and taking a breath then if, when she reaches out her hand, the State misses the opportunity to grasp it, the woman may not come to the surface again for a very long time, if at all. The second category of 'risk of perpetuated violence' is the sum of this lost opportunity, the dissipation of hope and trust on the part of the victim and the emboldening of abusers by the absence of accountability. This consistent with the UNDP's (2023) analysis of domestic violence in Indonesia which found that inadequate service provision contributes to victims becoming trapped in a cycle of silence and violence.

This is not to imply that engaging with the State system by 'going to the law' necessarily ensures women's safety long term. In fact, Douglas' (2021) study in the Australian context found that even years after first engaging with State justice systems, poor legal processes and stakeholder practices can exacerbate the danger of leaving an abusive relationship for women. Indeed, iterations of bureaucratic violence can be identified in the failures of State justice system processes over time; however, this chapter's analysis focuses on two examples. The first example – of safe houses – explores domestic violence victim's initial interactions with the State at one of the points of 'entry' to the system. The second example – of rehabilitation as a part of sentencing – focuses on one of the points of 'exit' from the system. Of course, in practice, multiple other incidents of bureaucratic violence exist along the spectrum from entry to exit as domestic violence victims engage or disengage with State systems.

Promises made by the state in the Law – the example of safe houses

In the next two sections, I provide examples of bureaucratic violence in practice. The starting point for this analysis is the identification of victim rights in the Law. Chapter 4 of the Law, 'Victim Rights', states that victims are entitled to protection, including healthcare and social, religious, and legal support. Chapter 5 of the Law, 'Obligations of the Government and Public', states that, first, the government is responsible for the efforts to prevent domestic violence. Second, in order to organise services for victims, the national government and provincial governments should make efforts to 'prepare and develop service program cooperation systems and mechanisms that are easily accessible to victims'. It is therefore clear in the Law that the State is responsible for the provision of care and protection of domestic violence victims.

Taking the example of safe houses, Chapter 6 of the Law makes these obligations even more explicit. For example, Article 16 states that within 24 hours after receiving a domestic violence report, police are obliged to provide the victim temporary protection. 'Temporary protection' is defined as including access to services as well as a protection order from the court. Article 22 provides that one of the services that victims are entitled to is assistance from a social worker. Social workers must, among other things, take the victim to a safe house or alternative dwelling. Again, the Law is explicit and places positive obligations on State stakeholders – stating that the services of a social worker must be conducted 'at a safe house belonging to the government, a provincial government, or the public'. 'Safe house' is further defined as a 'temporary dwelling used to provide protection to the victim', and 'alternative dwelling' is defined as 'a place for the victim to stay if she is forced to be separated from the perpetrator'.

The answer to the question of whether victims of domestic violence are entitled to access a safe house is yes. The answer to the question of who is responsible for such provision and protection is the State. During my fieldwork in Banda Aceh, some interviewees stated that there were no safe houses in Banda Aceh.

Other interviewees explained that there were, in fact, safe houses in the sense that there was a building that had been allocated for such a purpose (meaning the local or provincial government had allocated land and infrastructure). However, interviewees made it clear that no budget had yet been allocated by the national government for their operation. There was, for instance, no electricity or other amenities and no staff. This means that there were, in effect, no operational safe houses in Banda Aceh available for domestic violence victims.

A commissioner from the Indonesian Women's Commission (*Komnas Perempuan*) stated:

> If we are talking about implementation, we must also talk about infrastructural support. If the police do not have safe houses, and there are no other safe houses that can be accessed, how do they provide protection to victims?

The head of the Women's and Children's Protection Unit (*Bidang Perlindungan Perempuan dan Anak*) interviewed explained that it was common practice for women's advocates to 'bring victims back to our homes, often I have to take a victim home to provide protection because there are no safe houses'. This is just one example of the State failing to fulfil their positive obligations under the Law. This example from the case study province of Aceh is consistent with Mahfud and Rizanizarli's (2021) study of domestic violence, where they noted inadequate safe houses for victims and a lack of integrated crisis centres across Indonesia.

Establishing an operational safe house relies on coordination between different levels of government. As mentioned, in practice it would require the local or provincial government to allocate land and infrastructure and the national government to allocate a budget and pay staff to run the safe house; in the context of Banda Aceh, it is the latter that has not occurred. Perhaps this is not surprising when considered in the broader context of a political environment where the budget of the Ministry of Women's Empowerment and Child Protection (*Kementerian Pemberbayaan Perempuan dan Perlindungan Anak*) has been repeatedly cut and the Ministry is considered 'one of the weakest' in the national cabinet.[12] Ultimately it depends on political will whether at the national or provincial level. For example, in Eddyono et al.'s (2016) study of women's advocacy in Indonesia – women in East Java mobilised to advocate for the enactment of a subnational regulation of the implementation of the Anti-Domestic Violence Law. Based on a recognition that 'protecting and assisting victims is a state's responsibility', the 2005 regulation strengthened funding for the implementation of the Law from the subnational budget. After the enactment of the 2005 regulation, women's groups continued to advocate for improvements in the Law's implementation, including with respect to the provision of safe houses. A revised regulation was passed in 2012. Based on this example, it can be concluded that it is both possible and practicable for funding implementing the Law to come from subnational budgets instead of the national budget, if there is the political will to do so.

Promises made by the state in the Law – the example of rehabilitation programs

Building on the example of safe houses above, another example of bureaucratic violence is the failure of the State to establish perpetrator rehabilitation programs as required under Article 50(b) of the Law. Article 50(b) of the Law specifies that a judge may impose a sentence in the form of a 'ruling that the perpetrator undertake a counselling program under the supervision of a certain institution'. During an interview, judges from the *Pengadilan Negeri* confirmed that perpetrator rehabilitation programs have not been established in Banda Aceh, and, as a consequence, judges have never handed down sentences to this effect. According to judges interviewed, the responsibility for establishing such services lies with State institutional stakeholders outside the courts; however, no budget has yet been allocated by the national government. Services for court-mandated counselling are therefore another example of the implementation of the Law falling through the cracks of institutional responsibility (i.e., bureaucratic negligence).[13] As with the failure to establish operational safe houses, the failure to establish a court-adjacent system for perpetrator rehabilitation as required under the Law results in tangible harms for domestic violence victims.

For example, in criminal law cases applying the Law, the court stated that sentencing should aim to be 'corrective therapy for the defendant so that the defendant can realise the consequences of the deed he did and not repeat [such actions] again in the future' (see Chapter 7). However, the reality is that court-mandated counselling programs targeted towards perpetrators are currently non-existent. There was also no evidence of any domestic violence-related rehabilitation programs being run with perpetrator attendance as a condition of a suspended sentence or, alternatively, being run in State prisons as part of a carceral sentence. As one interviewee from a women's NGO (Ibu R) explained:

> If the husband goes to prison, after getting out there will likely be more violence because there is no education for the offender … and he may feel he was unfairly imprisoned.

As identified by the interviewee, without therapeutic intervention, it is common for perpetrators to conceptualise themselves as the 'victim' of criminal prosecution. It should of course be noted that even if these programs were established, the question of their effectiveness in terms of ensuring the safety and protection of domestic violence victims would still need to be evaluated on an ongoing basis.

While the content of the Law is promising in its inclusion of counselling for perpetrators, substantive barriers remain to successful implementation of these provisions. It is currently not possible for such orders to be executed by *Pengadilan Negeri* judges in Aceh. The lack of a system implementing, or making functional, the powers given to the court to impose orders for counselling as part of sentencing under Article 50(b) of the Law is particularly concerning considering that contemporary approaches towards domestic violence generally promote the inclusion of rehabilitation pathways for perpetrators instead of solely punitive approaches.[14] The example in Aceh is consistent with Rohaya et al.'s (2024) study where they noted a persistent 'lack of rehabilitation and reintegration programs for perpetrators' across Indonesia.

It can be concluded that due to bureaucratic negligence, current criminal justice processes do not adequately protect victims of domestic violence and, in fact, exacerbate risks to victim safety. At present, victims participating in criminal prosecutions do so at great personal risk, with little tangible protection in return. While the legal infrastructure for court-ordered rehabilitation programs as a sentence under the Law is in place, on-the-ground facilities and programs to carry out the promises of the Law have not yet been established by the State. To remedy this, it is crucial to develop perpetrator rehabilitation services to address the root causes of violence and attempt to break the cycle of violence.

Implications for state accountability

The reason I have drawn bureaucratic negligence and structural violence together in this way is to emphasise State accountability for the harms caused to victims (i.e., bureaucratic violence). I argue that the creation of legal rights and responsibilities by the State should not be assumed to result in positive, or even neutral, outcomes. Rather, in the context of domestic violence when the State fails to fulfil its legal obligations this results in unique types of harm. This has broader theoretical implications for human rights theory. Bureaucratic violence implicitly draws on concepts of international human rights law, including that the State has a responsibility to protect human rights and that domestic violence is a violation of women's rights. It is uncontroversial that State parties are responsible for acts or omissions that constitute gender-based violence against women under the Convention on Elimination of All Forms of Discrimination Against Women (CEDAW). Freedman (2021) explains:

> States' failure to protect women from violence is in itself a human rights violation, and that States must exercise 'due diligence' not only in not perpetrating violence against their citizens, but in actively protecting these citizens from abuse.

The theory of bureaucratic violence against domestic violence victims therefore seeks to identify the harms caused to victims by State negligence in implementing the Anti-Domestic Violence Law and to emphasise State responsibility for causing such harms.

The theory of bureaucratic violence also implicitly challenges the assumption that the State is a good or neutral actor in international law, even in cases where the State has explicitly enacted laws to implement CEDAW – such as Indonesia did when enacting the Law. Freedman explains that in order to combat domestic violence and seek redress for victims, it is 'necessary to push national governments to take more responsibility for protecting the human rights of their citizens'. The theory of bureaucratic violence seeks to do this by identifying and naming the harms caused by State failures to implement rights protections – in addition to and distinct from the harms caused by domestic violence perpetrators. Further, challenging the idea that enactment of a law is a neutral or positive action by the State, scholar Tapia argues that the 'law-centric state is delivering fewer and fewer services and offering more and more laws'.

From a more pragmatic perspective, the importance of developing the concept of bureaucratic violence against domestic violence victims is its ability to iterate a link between the State's responsibility to fulfil legal obligations and the specific kinds of harm that result when the State fails to do so. In establishing this link, the theory of bureaucratic violence may be invoked to promote State accountability and action. In practice, this would mean relying on the theory of bureaucratic violence to call on the State to allocate sufficient funding to fulfil the legal promises made to domestic violence victims under the Law.

In this chapter, I argued that the State's failure to implement the Anti-Domestic Violence Law does not result in a type of 'neutral negligence' but rather results in specific harms for domestic violence victims for which the State should be held accountable. Where the State's failure to protect victims of domestic violence as promised by the Law results in harm, I term these harms bureaucratic violence. I have argued that bureaucratic violence occurs when the State fails to protect victims or otherwise provide services as promised in the Law, and, as a result, victims are placed at an exacerbated risk of violence and/or a risk of perpetuated violence. The red thread of bureaucratic violence – and the State's roles and responsibilities relating to protecting victim rights and holding perpetrators accountable – continues throughout the book.

Notes

1 While the Islamic Courts are known across Indonesia as *Pengadilan Agama*, in Aceh these courts are known as *Mahkamah Syariah*. In Aceh, the Islamic Courts and State Courts exercise both criminal and civil jurisdiction. The jurisdiction of the *Mahkamah Syariah* includes marriage, inheritance, *shari'a* economy and Islamic criminal law: *Qanun* (Provincial Regulation) No. 10/2002 on *shari'a* courts.
2 For a discussion of these factors in the Indonesian context, see Hayati et al. (2014).
3 Regarding this assumption, see Amirthalingam (2005) and WHO (2010).
4 On this point see Aftab, Jones and Krayem (2024).
5 Schiff (1976).
6 UNDP (2010).
7 Regarding grounded theory methodology see generally Charmaz (2011), Clarke (2012), Birks and Mills (2015) and Glaser and Strauss (1967).
8 Ethics ID: 1749977. Note that interviewee data has been anonymised.
9 Only cases post-2013 were available due to the digitalisation of cases in that year. Pre-2013 cases were stored in hard copy by the court. Since 2013, most cases are accessible via the court website. However, domestic violence decisions are not shared online due to their sensitive nature.

10 Discussed further in Chapter 3. Note that in Aceh, pre-marital and same sex relationships are criminalised under Provincial Regulation No. 6/2014 relating to Criminal Law – known as *Qanun Jinayat*.
11 On this point see Goldblatt (2019) and Hill (2019).
12 Perdana and Hillman (2020). In the Acehnese context, Kamaruzzaman (2024) highlights that between 2020 and 2024, 'only 0.12% of Aceh's provincial budget was allocated to the Women's Empowerment and Child Protection Agency'.
13 Bureaucratic negligence affects coordination between the central and regional/local governments across a range of areas of law and service provision – colleagues and I have written about similar failures in the lack of establishment of accommodation and care for refugees under Presidential Regulation No. 125/2016: Suyatna et al. (2021).
14 See, for example, works by Bowen et al. (2003) and Day et al. (2010).

Bibliography

Aftab, Amira, Balawyn Jones and Ghena Krayem, 'The Contribution of Muslim Women Australia in the Domestic and Family Violence Space: Victim-Survivor Perspectives from the COVID-19 Pandemic' (2024) 15(7) *Religions* 772–784.

Amirthalingam, Kumaralingam, 'Women's Rights, International Norms and Domestic Violence: Asian Perspectives' (2005) 27(2) *Human Rights Quarterly* 697–698.

Aspinall, Edward, *Islam and Nation: Separatist Rebellion in Aceh, Indonesia* (Stanford University Press, 2009).

Bell, Charlotte and Dominiek Coates, *The Effectiveness of Interventions for Perpetrators of Domestic and Family Violence: An Overview of Findings from Reviews* (ANROWS Report, 2022).

Benda-Beckmann, Franz Von and Keebet Von Benda-Beckmann, 'Myths and Stereotypes about Adat Law' (2011) 167(2–3) *Bijdragen tot de Taal-, Land-en Volkenkunde* 167–195.

Birks, Melanie and Jane Mills, *Grounded Theory: A Practical Guide* (SAGE, 2015).

Bowen, Erica, Len Brown and Elizabeth Gilchrist, 'Evaluating Probation Based Offender Programmes for Domestic Violence Perpetrators: A Pro-feminist Approach' (2003) 41(3) *Howard Journal of Crime and Justice* 221–236.

Charmaz, Kathy, 'Grounded Theory Methods in Social Justice Research' in Denzin Norman and Yvonna Lincoln (eds), *The SAGE Handbook of Qualitative Research* (SAGE, 2011) 359–380.

Clarke, Adele, 'Feminism, Grounded Theory, and Situational Analysis Revisited' in Sharlene Hesse-Biber (ed), *The Handbook of Feminist Research: Theory and Praxis* (SAGE, 2012) 388–412.

Day, Andrew, Donna Chung, Patrick O'Leary, Donna Justo, Susan Moore, Ed Carson and Adam Gerace, *Integrating Responses to Domestic Violence: Legally Mandated Intervention Programs for Male Perpetrators* (AIC Report, 2010).

Douglas, Heather, *Women, Intimate Partner Violence and the Law* (Oxford, 2021).

Eddyono, Sri Wiyanti, Estu Fanani, Dini Anitasari Sabaniah, Yurra Maurice, Haiziah Ghazali, Juni Warlif, Sisillia Velayati and Farha Ciciek, *When and Why the State Responds to Women's Demands: Understanding Gender Equality Policy Change in Indonesia* (UNRISD, 2016).

Freedman, Jane, 'Domestic Violence through a Human Rights Lens' in John Devaney, Caroline Bradbury-Jones, Rebecca Macy, Carolina Overlien and Stephanie Holt (eds), *The Routledge International Handbook of Domestic Violence and Abuse* (Routledge, 2021) 68–78.

Glaser, Barney and Anselm Strauss, *The Discovery of Grounded Theory: Strategies for Qualitative Research* (Aldine, 1967).

Goldblatt, Beth, 'Violence against Women and Social and Economic Rights: Deepening the Connections' in Susan Rimmer and Kate Ogg (eds), *Research Handbook on Feminist Engagement with International Law* (Edward Elgar Publishing, 2019) 359–378.

Gupta, Akhil, *Red Tape: Bureaucracy, Structural Violence, and Poverty in India* (Duke University, 2012).

Hayati, Elli Nur, Maria Emmelin and Malin Eriksson, 'Challenges for a Local Service Agency to Address Domestic Violence - A Case Study from Rural Indonesia' (2014) 6(6) *Global Journal of Health Science* 214–225.

Hill, Jess, *See What You Made Me Do: Power, Control and Domestic Abuse* (Black Inc, 2019).

Kamaruzzaman, Suraiya, 'Acehnese Women: Crucial Role in Peacebuilding Overlooked, Discriminated by Local Regulations', *The Conversation* (24 December 2024) https://theconversation.com/acehnese-women-crucial-role-in-peacebuilding-overlooked-discriminated-by-local-regulations-246240

Kelly, Liz and Nicole Westmarland, 'Naming and Defining 'domestic violence': Lessons from Research with Violent Men' (2016) 112 *Feminist Review* 113.

Mackay, Erin, Althea Gibson, Huette Lam and David Beecham, *Perpetrator Interventions in Australia: Part One – Literature Review* (ANROWS Report, 2015).

Mahfud and Rizanizarli, 'Domestic Violence against Women in Indonesia: The Recent Domestic Violence Elimination Law Analysis' (2021) 15(4) *Fiat Justisia: Jurnal Ilmu Hukum* 385–398.

Montesanti, Stephanie and Wilfreda Thurston, 'Mapping the Role of Structural and Interpersonal Violence in the Lives of Women: Implications for Public Health Interventions and Policy' (2015) 15(100) *BioMed Central Women's Health* https://doi.org/10.1186/s12905-015-0256-4

Perdana, Aditya and Ben Hillman, 'Quotas and Ballots: The Impact of Positive Action Policies on Women's Representation in Indonesia' (2020) 7(2) *Asia & the Pacific Policy Studies* 158–170.

Putra, I Gusti Ngurah Edi, Putu Erma Pradnyani, Ni Wayan Putri Larassita Parwangsa, 'Vulnerability to Domestic Physical Violence among Married Women in Indonesia' (2019) 33(2) *Journal of Health Research* 90–105.

Reinke, Amanda, 'The Bureaucratic Violence of Alternative Justice' (2018) 4 *Conflict and Society* 135–150.

Rohaya, Nizla, Suartini, Mohammad, Prosper Maguchu and Gufroni, 'Unravelling the Legal Labyrinth: An In-depth Review of Domestic Violence Regulation in Indonesia' (2024) 24(1) *Jurnal Kajian Syari'ah dan Masyarakat* 77–90.

Salim, Arskal, *Contemporary Islamic Law in Indonesia* (Edinburgh University Press, 2015).

Schiff, David, 'Socio-legal Theory: Social Structure and Law' (1976) 39 *The Modern Law Review* 287–310.

Scott, Wallach Joan, *Gender and the Politics of History* (Columbia University Press, 1988).

Siegel, James, *The Rope of God* (The University of Michigan Press, 1969).

Suyatna, I. Nyoman, I. Made Budi Arsika, Ni Gusti Ayu Dyah Satyawati, Rohaida Nordin and Balawyn Jones, 'Assessment of the Responsibility of Local Governments in Indonesia for the Management of Refugee Care' (2021) *Asian Journal of Law and Society* 8 467–489.

Tapia, Silvana, 'Human Rights Penalty, the Inter-American Approach to Violence Against Women, and the Local Effects of Centering Criminal Justice' in Heather Douglas, Kate Fitz-Gibbon, Leigh Goodmark and Sandra Walklate (eds), *The Criminalization of Violence Against Women: Comparative Perspectives* (Oxford University Press, 2023) 231–248.

Turner, Mark, Eko Prasojo and Rudiarto Sumarwono, 'The Challenge of Reforming Big Bureaucracy in Indonesia' (2019) *Policy Studies* 43 333–351.
UNDP, '*Access to Justice in Aceh: Making the Transition to Sustainable Peace and Development in Aceh*' (Report, 2010).
UNDP, *Applying Behavioural Insights to Gender Justice in Indonesia* (Report, 2023).
Wahyuningroem, Sri Lestari, 'Peran Perempuan dan Era Baru di Nangroe Aceh Darussalam' (2005) 29(1) *Antropologi Indonesia* 93–101.
Winter, Deborah and Dana Leighton, 'Structural Violence' in Daniel Christie, Richard Wagner and Deborah Winter (eds), *Peace, Conflict, and Violence: Peace Psychology for the 21st Century* (Prentice-Hall, 2001) 99–104.
World Health Organisation, *Preventing Intimate Partner and Sexual Violence against Women: Taking Action and Generating Evidence* (WHO, 2010).

Laws and regulations cited in Chapter 1

Law No. 23/ 2004 regarding the Elimination of Domestic Violence (*Undang-Undang tentang Penghapusan Kekerasan Dalam Rumah Tangga*).
Provincial Regulation No. 10/2002 on *shari'a* courts.
Provincial Regulation No. 6/2014 relating to Criminal Law (*Qanun Jinayat*).

Interviews cited in Chapter 1

Interview with Bapak S (Lawyer) (Banda Aceh, 15 December 2017).
Interview with Ibu Commissioner (*Komnas Perempuan*) (Jakarta, 12 January 2018).
Interview with Ibu R (P2TP2A/*Balai Syura*) (Banda Aceh, 19 December 2017).
Interview with *Pengadilan Negeri* judges (Banda Aceh, 26 September 2018).
Interview with Ibu E (Head of the Women's and Children's Protection Unit) (Banda Aceh, 24 September 2018).

2 Case Study Context of Aceh, Indonesia

As outlined in Chapter 1, the analysis in this book adopts a feminist model of domestic violence which assumes that gender inequality plays a role in the perpetration, and justification, of domestic violence. Ideas around gender must then be understood as fluid and capable of re-definition over time for there to be the potential for change and progress towards relationships grounded in non-violence. To orientate the reader in the Indonesian context, this chapter provides an overview of how Indonesian (and Acehnese) gender norms have changed over time, focusing on the State's gender policies. Gender ideologies across Indonesia must be understood both in the context of national State policies and in relation to locally specific experiences.

This overview will commence in 1945, when Indonesia gained independence from the Dutch.[1] Between 1949 and 1957, post-independence Indonesia was a fledgling democracy headed by President Soekarno. According to Blackburn (2004), during this period of Parliamentary Democracy: 'no particular ideology of gender was imposed or inculcated by the [Soekarno] regime, with the consequence that organisations were free to advance their own agendas'.

However, the democratic experiment failed in 1957 when President Soekarno suspended parliamentary democracy for martial law and, in 1959, declared his dictatorial Guided Democracy regime, which lasted until 1965. Under Guided Democracy, there was a general lack of interest in women's issues. Explicit patriarchal policies designed to limit women's independence formally began under the New Order regime.

President Soeharto's New Order regime came to power after a coup that resulted in nationwide killings of hundreds of thousands of men and women, known as the 1965–1966 massacres. Anti-PKI (Indonesian Communist Party) massacres occurred across Indonesia, including in Aceh. The victims were targeted due to association with the PKI, particularly within the Chinese community. This period of violence was characterised by gendered violence against women and girls.[2]

During the New Order regime (1966–1998), Acehnese gender norms were significantly influenced by Indonesian State policies. The New Order promulgated

DOI: 10.4324/9781032613642-2

robust gender policies which positioned Indonesian women as boundary markers of 'Indonesian-ness' in the process of constructing the new national identity.[3] The central feature of this policy was *State Ibuism* defined by Suryakusuma (1988) as 'the domestication of Indonesian women as dependent wives who exist for their husbands, their families, and the state'. This policy was implemented through initiatives such as *Dharma Wanita* (the association of bureaucrats' wives) and *Pembinaan Kesejahteraan Keluarga* (PKK – Family Welfare Guidance), which were guided by five core principles. As outlined by Sunindyo (1996), these principles required a wife to:

1) support her husband's career and duties;
2) provide offspring;
3) care for and rear the children;
4) be a good housekeeper; and
5) be a guardian of the community.

Motherhood had formerly been broadly conceptualised in terms of kinship structures. The PKK stretched the concept even further so that *kaum Ibu* (*Ibu* meaning 'mother' and *kaum Ibu* meaning 'mothers' as a collective) mothered the fledgling Indonesian State and society. Their reward was limited to being considered a 'good Ibu', while the public sphere of 'power and prestige remained the privilege of men'.[4]

The policy distinguished between men and women based on their *kodrat*, with men as primary income-earners and women as child-rearers and housewives.[5] While the concept of *kodrat* is not necessarily inconsistent with gender equality, when combined with *State Ibuism* the notion of *kodrat* was used to exclude and restrict women (see Chapter 3 regarding *kodrat*). The restrictive femininity promulgated by the New Order policies influenced interpretations of religious doctrines and vice versa. *State Ibuism* also revived Dutch colonial ideals of the nuclear family, with women at home and men in the public sphere. However, most lower-class women continued to work outside the home under the New Order.

During the New Order, the highly controversial 1974 Marriage Law was passed. Article 31(3) of the Marriage Law states: 'The husband is the head of the family, the wife is the mother of the household'. Article 34 further provides:

(1) The husband shall protect his wife and provide for all necessities of life required in a family to the best of his ability.
(2) The wife shall manage the household to the best of her ability.

The Marriage Law – which remains in force today – explicitly legislates gendered roles within the household and entrenches heteronormativity as the hegemonic discourse.

Parker (2016) notes that:

> Much has been written by feminist and other scholars about the Marriage Law of 1974 and the many programmes and organisations that the New Order set up to implement its patriarchal gender ideology, its ideal of the new nuclear family and concomitant social agendas, particularly in family planning.

At the time the Marriage Law was passed it was seen as a significant achievement for the Indonesian women's movement. Among other things, the Marriage Law strengthened the rights of women by requiring husbands to go to the Islamic Court to seek divorce. Prior to the enactment of the Marriage Law husbands did not have to go to court to divorce their wives, which meant that there was no oversight or accountability for husbands during the divorce process (discussed in Chapter 5).

State Ibuism had far reaching and long-term consequences in terms of redefining the content of gender norms and the meaning of private/public spheres. For example, although the New Order promoted the inclusion of women in workforce industrialisation initiatives, in an increasingly patrifocal society women had to justify their participation in the public sphere in terms of *Ibuism*. In the late 20th century, this led to an acceptance of the dual role of women as both mothers and workers as long as women's involvement in economic and socio-political activities was 'couched in terms of benefiting the family'.[6] Arguably, the best outcome of the New Order's gender policies was the lowering of birth rates through family planning and education. This, combined with general development trends, meant that women married later, had fewer children, and had greater access to education. As a result, an increased number of women were able to pursue high education and enter white-collar, professional job markets.[7]

Within the current generation's lifetime, Acehnese people have survived civil conflict and military occupation by the Indonesian State (see Appendix 1). During the New Order, the Free Aceh Movement (*Gerakan Aceh Merdeka* – GAM) emerged. Formed in 1976, GAM fought an extended civil war for independence against the Indonesian government until 2005.[8] Within GAM, the male division of the army was named *Angkatan Gerakan Aceh Merdeka* (AGAM).[9] The female division was *Inong Balee* (commonly translated as guerrilla widows). GAM drew on the historical Acehnese tradition of female combatants, incorporating women into the military structure. As women had greater freedom of movement compared to men during the civil conflict, they played important strategic roles and were able 'to communicate information, deliver ammunition, weapons and food to GAM soldiers who stayed mainly in the mountains of Aceh'.[10] Although the *Inong Balee* were emphasised in GAM propaganda, leadership of the movement was male dominated. In contrast to GAM, the Indonesian government and *Tentara Nasional Indonesia* (National

Military of Indonesia – TNI) were patriarchal institutions and, although women still supported the war effort, labour division was highly gendered.[11]

The civil war continued under five different Indonesian presidents. After the New Order collapsed in 1998, a new political era began known as *reformasi* (reformation). During *reformasi*, the New Order gender ideologies were not explicitly dismantled, but there was an 'opening up of space for a diversity of images and representations' with respect to gender.[12] During this period of democratic transition women's groups organised to campaign on issues such as domestic violence. The influence of Islamic groups also grew rapidly and began to promote diverse discourses on family and gender.[13] Meanwhile, a number of different ceasefires failed to bring peace in Aceh and the civil war continued until 2005.

One of the worst periods of violence was between 1989 and 1998, when Aceh was declared a *Daerah Operasi Militer* (Area of Military Operations – DOM). The distinctive features of the TNI military violence were the uncontrolled nature of the violence (including forced disappearances, extra-judicial killings, rape, and torture) and the premeditated nature of the violence. Gross violations of human rights have been widely documented during the civil conflict and violence was distinctly gendered.[14] Although young men were more likely to be targeted for forced disappearances or extra-judicial killings (due to the presumption that they were GAM combatants), women were more likely to experience sexual violence. According to Siapno (2002), Indonesian troops instrumentalised 'sex and sexualisation to humiliate and control the local female population'.

While the Indonesian government had little sympathy for male victims, the testimony of female Acehnese rape victims before the National Commission on Human Rights (1998) caused outrage and criticism of the TNI. In their capacity as victims, women played a critical role raising awareness about the atrocities perpetrated in Aceh and advocating for a ceasefire. Drexler (2008) explains:

> Rape victims disrupted the New Order pattern of casting victims as enemies of the state and isolating them as political contaminants … These women symbolized the pure excess of military abuse of power and the profound injustice of violence in Aceh.

At times, it appeared that the Indonesian government did not control the TNI and it largely acted with impunity. However, the TNI were not the only perpetrators of human rights violations, GAM soldiers also perpetrated violence against civilians. There were also members of the TNI who pretended to be GAM. One of the barriers to prosecuting human rights violations was this dark pattern of violence.[15] By 2001, the TNI no longer solely targeted GAM but 'GAM/*Masyarakat*' (GAM/Society), effectively abolishing the distinction between combatant and civilian. This shift eliminated the possibility of there being 'innocent' victims and so military excesses were justified.[16]

Even for women who were not combatants, gender roles were effectively reversed during the civil war. When men were forced to flee, imprisoned, disappeared or died, women became the head of the household and community leaders. Women were responsible for both caring and economic obligations and it was women who had to provide for their families. It was also the women that went to the prisons and negotiated with the TNI for the release of their husbands and sons.[17] Women also bore the bulk of long-term burdens as single parents and heads of households. During interviews, it was clear that the long-term trauma of the civil war was ever-present in the advocacy work women do.

On 25 December 2004, a tsunami struck Aceh resulting in unprecedented destruction and loss of life. According to the Reconstruction and Rehabilitation Body's (2005) report, more than 130,000 people died, over 37,000 people were reported missing, and half a million people were displaced. Most Acehnese people believe that the tsunami was an act of God, 'either as divine retribution for the sins of the people, a test of their faith, or something pre-ordained'.[18] The tsunami compounded the impacts of the civil war, exacerbating already high levels of trauma and poverty, including the destruction of productive land, infrastructure, and human, financial and social capital.[19]

It is widely recognised that natural disasters and subsequent aid provision reproduce and entrench existing power inequalities, including gender hierarchies. The tsunami disproportionately affected women.[20] Although it is generally the case that gendered violence increases after a natural disaster, as Aceh was in a state of civil war before the tsunami struck violence did not increase in real terms. As discussed below, the tsunami was a catalyst for peace. Therefore, with the civil war coming to an end, violence decreased overall post-tsunami. Despite this, high levels of physical and sexual violence continued to be perpetrated against women. Multiple sources reported increased levels of domestic violence post-tsunami, particularly in the homes of ex-combatants.[21] Post-traumatic stress disorder, social dislocation, and unemployment were contributing factors to violence during the post-conflict era.

As mentioned above, during the civil war women's roles significantly expanded to include combatant, community leader, and head of the household. Meghdadi (2009) explains that when men returned home post-conflict:

> the clash between many women's new-found identit[ies] during conflict, and the threat this posed for men's status in the family, led to a significant increase in physical and sexual abuse in the home.

The Helsinki Peace Agreement between the Indonesian government and GAM was finalised on 15 August 2005. Although the tsunami is recognised as a catalyst for peace, talks between GAM, the Indonesian government, and an international mediator (Maarti Ahtisaari) were already underway to resolve the conflict before the tsunami struck. Further, the armed forces and civilian population were fatigued from decades of conflict and the majority of people wanted peace.[22] In broad terms the Helsinki Peace Agreement sought to end

GAM's insurgency against the central Indonesian government. It included a special regional autonomy arrangement delegating greater authority to the provincial government; the disarmament of GAM and re-integration of ex-combatants; greater ownership of provincial natural resources; permission to create provincial political parties (unique to Aceh); and the power to formally apply Islamic law. The latter power is exercised by local governments passing *Qanun* (the Acehnese term for *peraturan daerah* – local regulations) that reflect local Islamic norms. Although the Special Regional Autonomy arrangement in Aceh is unique, Aceh is not unique in its enactment of 'religiously inspired' regional regulations.

The negotiation process was densely gendered and driven by a masculinist agenda to the exclusion of women's interests. Only one woman, Shadia Marhaban, was involved in the Helsinki discussions as part of the Acehnese delegation. Later, another woman, Khairani, joined Marhaban on the drafting committee for the Law on Governing Aceh. Khairani has since openly criticised the drafting process as not recognising or valuing the contributions of the *Inong Balee*.[23] Although neglected in formal processes, outside the official peace negotiations Acehnese women made noteworthy contributions. For example, in 2000 and 2005, Acehnese women organised the Women's Peace Forums (*Duek Pakat Inong* Aceh I-II). At the 2000 Forum, over 400 women attended and produced a recommendation to the Indonesian government that the conflict be resolved through peaceful negotiations.[24]

During the conflict Aceh was closed to international assistance and media but post-tsunami thousands of foreign aid workers arrived. The initial emergency phase of the tsunami response was largely successful (for example, there were no major outbreaks of disease). However, as Afrianty (2015) notes, despite the benefits that international NGOs brought to Aceh, much of the post-tsunami aid work has been subject to criticism particularly in the long-term recovery phase. With respect to gender, hundreds of secular international NGOs promoted gender mainstreaming and gender-sensitive approaches to aid in Aceh. However, very few of these organisations engaged with religious perspectives in informing their approaches to gender in the Acehnese context. The assumption underlying this approach was that secularity equals neutrality, therefore the exclusion of religion ensured 'impartiality'.

The Western lens with which aid was provided tended to stereotype Acehnese women as '"oppressed Muslim women" in need of saving by outsiders.'[25] Siapno (2002) stresses the importance of women's history in Aceh to counter the relatively new discourse of Acehnese women as primarily 'victims', which has become dominant post-tsunami in international contexts. This approach led to community resentment of the top-down implementation of Western gender concepts. As discussed in Chapter 3, the term 'feminism' is viewed by locals as a foreign concept imported by Western NGOs, even if this concept has roots in local practice and beliefs.

Tsunami recovery approaches also lacked engagement with the post-conflict context. Schiller (2011) explains that reconstruction and reconciliation programmes operated on 'parallel tracks addressing post-tsunami recovery independently of post-conflict peacebuilding'. There was a vast imbalance in funding and organisational capacity between the tsunami and peace programmes. The coastal areas (such as Banda Aceh and Meulaboh) received the majority of tsunami aid, whereas the hinterland areas (such as Pidie and Bireuen, which were not affected greatly by the tsunami but were the most affected by decades of conflict) did not benefit from development projects. This distinction was not accidental. In the early stages of the tsunami response, the Helsinki Peace Agreement had yet to be finalised, and the conflict was still an active and sensitive issue. Initially the Indonesian government did not permit international organisations to provide aid to those affected by conflict, with relief efforts limited to tsunami survivors. It was not until August 2006 that organisations were directed to stop differentiating between tsunami and conflict areas.[26]

In addition to tensions between conflict and tsunami survivors, patterns of conflict evolved between GAM elites and rank-and-file combatants. Post-tsunami corruption and nepotism was rife among GAM elites who took over governance of the province. In the ensuing power-struggle, male rank-and-file combatants were almost completely forgotten by their war-time leaders.[27] The neglect of combatants was partly due to the fact that the number of combatants requiring reintegration assistance was underestimated in the Helsinki Peace Agreement.

Despite the fact that since the year 2000, photos and information about *Inong Balee* had been highlighted in media campaigns documenting women's roles within GAM, post-conflict GAM leaders attempted to minimise women's contributions to the civil war. The Helsinki Peace Agreement provided compensation for only 3,000 out of approximately 15,000 soldiers (excluding non-combatant strategic or support roles). Notably, women were completely excluded from the lists of ex-combatants when reintegration programmes were first created to provide compensation.[28] However, through the work of women's organisations, such as *Liga Inong Aceh* (the Acehnese Women's League), approximately 844 female combatants were eventually included in reintegration programmes.[29] Lee-Koo (2012) and Avonius (2012) also note that civilian compensation was limited to injuries with 'demonstrable loss' (for example, physical disability), effectively excluding victims of sexual violence.

Despite these weaknesses in the reconstruction and reconciliation process, the availability of substantial international aid, combined with reprieve from constant conflict, meant that the overall level of development improved. From 2005, Aceh's economy began to diversify and industrialise. There has been an accompanying increase in access to educational opportunities and professional employment in government and the private sector. Although both men and women enter the professional workforce in Aceh, according to Srimulyani (2013) it remains more common for women to work in informal vocations. There is also vertical and horizontal segregation of the work force, with women doing the vast majority of unpaid labour. Vianen (2006) states that women's workforce participation is discouraged in two ways, first, the discourse of women as wives and mothers entrenched by Dutch colonialism and *State Ibuism* means that women are domesticated to the home. Second, women as symbols of morality and religiosity are seen as needing protection from the 'outside world', which can be understood as an entrenchment of the private/public sphere dichotomy. The broader socio-economic changes associated with modernisation and industrialisation have led to the polarisation of gender roles and the minimisation of women's cultural authority.

Under the Helsinki Peace Agreement, Aceh's special regional autonomy status was strengthened by enactment of Law No. 11/2006 (Law on Governing Aceh), which followed Law No. 44/1999 on the Implementation of Aceh's Special Status and Law No. 18/2001 on the Special Autonomy of Aceh. In 1999, Aceh commenced implementation of Islamic legal norms in the form of regional regulations (*peraturan daerah*) known as *Qanun*. *Qanun* do not relate only to *shari'a* but cover a range of topics, including *adat* and women's empowerment.[30]

An-Na'im (2008) defines *shari'a* as Islamic teachings or values which are 'derived from God's revelations in the form of *Qur'anic* verses and *hadith* (the sayings of the Prophet)'. The way that *shari'a* is derived from the *Qur'an* and *hadith* is through *fiqh*. *Fiqh* (often translated as 'Islamic jurisprudence') is an interpretive process whereby humans construe or extract legal rules from the original sources. *Qanun* on religious topics are therefore not divine as they are a product of *fiqh* enacted as positive-State law by provincial government bodies, whereas *shari'a* is identified and developed by religious scholars. Therefore, when women's advocates critique *Qanun*, or argue that *Qanun* discriminate against women, they are not directly criticising *shari'a*, the *Qur'an* or *hadith*, but *fiqh* and the political process of drafting, enacting, or implementing *Qanun* more broadly.

Due to male-dominated political structures, the interpretative process of *fiqh* is largely informed by patriarchal perspectives. Afrianty (2015) explains that many problems with *Qanun* stem from 'the fact that women are neither considered nor included in the process of deliberating *Qanun* on religious matters, which has resulted in the neglect of women's interests'. On the other hand, as *Qanun* are a product of current interpretations made by religious scholars this means that there are 'possibilities for *Qanun* to be reformed, based on new interpretations'.[31] The difficulty that women's advocates face when critiquing patriarchal interpretations of Islam is that – due to the close relationship between *fiqh, Qanun*, and *shari'a* – criticism of *Qanun* can lead to advocates being accused of being blasphemous or un-Islamic.

As previously mentioned, Acehnese identity has long been rooted in Islamic beliefs, however it is only in the 21st century that the rapid 'shari'a-isation' of law has occurred. 'Shari'a-isation' refers to the increasing codification of religious laws. GAM initially rejected the introduction of *shari'a* law in Aceh on the basis that that it was merely a political strategy by the Indonesian government to weaken the separatist movement.[32] Despite this, the majority of

Acehnese people supported the implementation of *shari'a* law via *Qanun*. In a 2007 study conducted by *Insan Cita Madani* Foundation approximately 87% of respondents agreed that *shari'a* was the 'solution for problems facing society'. However, only 23% of respondents were satisfied with the implementation of *Qanun* in Aceh.[33]

Enhanced legal infrastructure to achieve implementation is only a partial answer to the question of why shari'a-isation has occurred. The more persuasive explanation relates to the (re-)construction of Acehnese identity post-tsunami and post-conflict. Lindsey et al. (2007) argue that the implementation of *Qanun* is a 'means of re-emphasising perceived traditional Acehnese values'. For example, there are *Qanun* which target gambling, drinking, *khalwat* (inappropriate association between males and females), Islamic dress standards, and adherence to religious rituals such as prayer and fasting.[34] By and large, the focus of Islamic law in Aceh is the socialisation of Islamic values through public education.[35] Although cases that are prosecuted are highly publicised – principally due to the fact that one of the (controversial) punishments for breaching *Qanun* is caning.

Afrianty (2015) argues that in Aceh the implementation of Islamic law discriminates against women. For example, Article 13(1) of *Qanun* 11/2006 requires Muslims to wear clothing that covers the *aurat* (parts of the body to be covered according to Islamic dress standards). In practice, women are subjected to greater levels of informal/community enforcement compared to men when it comes to Islamic dress. Although there is room for interpretation as to what 'Islamic dress' requires for both men and women, the provision is generally interpreted to include mandatory veiling. In Aceh, veiling has been widely interpreted as including a requirement that women wear *hijab* or *jilbab* (a headscarf which covers the head and neck but leaves the face exposed, as opposed to the *niqab* or *burqa*), but has also sometimes been interpreted as prohibiting women from wearing trousers.

Mandatory veiling has been described as 'an exercise in identity building with women holding a symbolic role in embodying cultural and national borders', a 'political shortcut to gain legitimacy by creating a symbol of Islam', a reactionary response to globalisation and the presence of foreign aid, and as symbolic protection.[36] Notably, the headscarf as an expression of Acehnese culture is contested, as historically although some women chose to wear a *selendang* (Acehnese-style loose headscarf), women were never required to wear a headscarf. In fact, the Arabic-style *hijab* or *jilbab* was not common in Aceh until the late 1990s, therefore, it has been argued that the requirement in the *Qanun* to veil is overly literal and decontextualised from Acehnese history and traditions.[37]

There is a tendency for contemporary veiling practices to be viewed narrowly as inherently oppressive, however, veiling can also be seen as an expression of women's agency.[38] Acehnese scholars, such as Nor and Inayatillah (2011), argue that the '*hijab* is not a symbol of oppression but one of devotion to Islam'. The explanation as to why Acehnese women wear *hijab* is more complicated than that they are 'forced to' by the enforcement of *Qanun*. Women veil for a range of reasons, including identity construction, gender performativity, protection from sexual harassment, to gain social capital, to increase social mobility; and/or out of a sense of religious or socio-cultural obligation.

In saying this, not all Acehnese women support the enforcement of veiling, which has been criticised as limiting women's personal choice as to whether or not to wear *hijab*. In fact, many activists argue that Muslim women should have the right to choose whether to veil or not. As explained by Afrianty (2015):

> With Islam and traditions strongly entrenched in the identity of Acehnese women, they insist on the need to reread and reinterpret the sources of Islamic law in reforming Islamic law. Acehnese women talk about equality and their rights in Islam, learn about women's role in the history of Aceh, discuss, debate and argue, making equality and women's rights in Islam their daily conversation.

Importantly, debates relating to gender in Aceh tend to focus on questions of interpretation of *fiqh* and, more broadly, the drafting, enactment, and implementation of *Qanun* as opposed to normative questions relating to *shari'a*. For example, it is rare for people to debate whether women *should* wear the *hijab* as a normative question, but it is debated whether women should *have to* wear the *hijab* and (if so) how enforcement should be approached. For example, Human Rights Watch (2010) has documented instances of violence against women by both vigilante groups and members of the former 'shari'a police'.[39] Acehnese women's advocate, Kamaruzzaman (2004) explains how in the mid-to-late 1999s, before there were formal legal bodies established to enforce *Qanun*, 'many people took the enforcement of Islamic law into their own hands'. She describes how during this time:

> women were subjected to various forms of violence. Some had their heads shaved, others were beaten or forced to march in public, pelted with tomatoes or eggs in the market, yelled at or had the tight clothing they were wearing torn or their jeans slashed to above the knees.

As the majority of Acehnese people are Muslim and support the implementation of *Qanun* (even if they are critical of its implementation), it is necessary for women's advocates to work within an Islamic framework.[40] Although religion is the dominant factor influencing the construction of contemporary gender roles in Aceh, it also intersects with factors such as politics, class, geography, and ethnicity. The question of why religious conservatism has increased in Aceh can only be answered by looking more broadly at the political context. As mentioned above, Aceh is the only province in Indonesia that is allowed to have its own, local political parties, distinct from the national political system.[41] Post-conflict the ex-GAM leaders transformed themselves into a political party, *Partai Aceh*, winning local elections in 2009. Although not running on an explicitly religious platform, according to Afrianty (2015) the majority of the elected parliamentarians were 'very conservative and many of them [held] strong views against women's equality and women's rights issues'.

Activists have also highlighted a lack of female political representation as an ongoing challenge for gender equality in Aceh.[42] As identified by Ibu R (an academic), the majority of politicians and policy makers are men who 'view women as embodying moral standards.' Protectionist political rationales can be understood as a form of patriarchal pushback or *domestifikasi* (domestication) of women post-conflict and post-tsunami. For example, the *jam malam* (curfew) imposed on women in Banda Aceh under *Instruksi Walikota* 2/2015 and the enforcement of restrictive dress policies under *Qanun* No. 11/2002. Nashriyah and Syahabuddin's (2015) study of masculinities in post-conflict Aceh found that local religious leaders continue to hold strong socio-political influence over the interpretation of Islam and 'tend to promote patriarchal views'.

Husin (2015) distinguishes between 'traditional' Acehnese *ulama* based in the *dayahs* (private religious schools) and 'white-collar' *ulamas* trained by the universities. Debates within and between 'traditional' *dayah ulama* and 'white-collar' *ulama* continue to define Acehnese Islam. The *dayah ulama* remain influential at the community level and the white-collar *ulama* generally having more influence over the development of law and policy. However, the white-collar *ulama* have limited influence outside urban centres, where the *dayah ulama* retain direct connection with rural communities.[43] In both *ulama* 'camps', almost all scholars are male, with female religious representation presenting a barrier to development of gender-equal religious interpretations and *Qanun*. The exception to this is the work of female *ulama* groups. Afrianty (2015) notes that the *dayah ulama* in particular have been hostile towards women's groups, accusing women's NGOs of working for 'Western interests to destroy Islamic values in Aceh and disrupt[ing] the implementation of Islamic law'.[44]

While acknowledging discrimination against women in the development and implementation of *Qanun*, Afrianty (2015) contextualises the implementation of *Qanun* in Aceh as having 'occurred alongside Indonesia's democratic reform and democracy' – providing opportunities for public discussion regarding women's rights and *Qanun*. Women's groups continue to actively challenge the development and implementation of *Qanun* in Aceh, with notable organisations including *Balai Syura* and Flower Aceh.

This chapter has sought to show how gender norms in the case study context of Aceh have been re-negotiated over time. This historical perspective assists to challenge stereotypes of Acehnese women as solely 'victims' of patriarchy and violence – with such representations becoming prevalent post-tsunami. Acehnese women have a long history of agency, including advocacy against, and manoeuvring within, patriarchal norms and structures. On the other hand, Aceh is still dealing with the aftermath of extended civil conflict, including trauma from gendered violence over many decades, and the consequences of women being sidelined during reconstruction and reconciliation processes. By identifying the social, economic, political, and cultural factors that have been significant in shaping gender historically, this chapter provides a basis for later chapters to identify factors that influence the implementation of the Law in Aceh today, as well as situating the case study context of Aceh within Indonesia's national policies relating to gender.

Notes

1 Note that there are extensive scholars works on gender in Indonesia that fall outside the scope of this book, in particular the history of Dutch and Japanese colonisation.
2 Melvin (2013) and Pohlman (2015).
3 Blackburn (2004) and Aspinall (2009).
4 Blackburn (2004). See also Sears (1996).
5 Oey-Gardiner (2002) and Blackwood (2005).
6 Saptari (2000). On this point also see Blackburn (2004), Srimulyani (2010), Afrianty (2015).
7 UNDP (2002), Blackburn (2004) and Afrianty (2015).
8 In relation to the civil war, see Drexler (2008), Aspinall (2009) and Waizenegger and Hyndman (2010).
9 *Agam* is the Acehnese word for boy. After 2002, AGAM was renamed *Tuentara Neugara Atjeh* (the Acehnese National Army).
10 Clavé-Çelik (2014).
11 See Suryakusuma (1988, 1996), Siapno (2002) and Blackburn (2009).
12 Robinson and Bessel (2002).
13 Robinson (2006), Grossmann (2014), Afrianty (2015) and Wieringa (2015).
14 Eye on Aceh (2004); Blackburn (2004), Drexler (2008), Aspinall (2009) and Melvin (2018).
15 Blackburn (2004) and Drexler (2008).
16 Blackburn (2004), Drexler (2008) and Grossmann (2014).
17 Siapno (2002, 2009a), Kamis and Mahdi (2006), Kamaruzzaman (2008) and Nor and Inayatillah (2011).
18 Feener (2012). See also Lindsey et al. (2007) and Siapno (2009b).
19 Afrianty (2015); Vianen (2006); Christoplos and Wu (2012).
20 Enarson (2000), Ferris (2010), Fitzpatrick (2012) and Jauhola (2013).
21 Felten-Biermann (2006), Vianen (2006), *Komnas Perempuan* (2007) and Reed (2009).
22 Morfit (2012) and Feith (2012).
23 Duguay (2006), Lee-Koo (2012), Afrianty (2015) and Jauhola (2016).
24 Kamaruzzaman (2008), Drexler (2008), Nor and Inayatillah (2011), Lee-Koo (2012) and Jauhola (2016).
25 Jauhola (2016) and Siapno (2011).
26 Waizenegger and Hyndman (2010), Zeccola (2011) and Jauhola (2013).
27 Grossmann (2011) and Ansori (2012).
28 Drexler (2008), Waizenegger and Hyndman (2010) and Clavé-Çelik (2014).
29 Reuters (2005), Kamaruzzaman (2008) and Jauhola (2016).
30 For example, *Qanun* 9/2008 *Adat dan Istiadat* (Customs and Ceremonies) and *Qanun* 6/2009 *Pemberdayaan dan Perlindungan Perempuan* (Empowerment and Protection of Women).
31 Afrianty (2015).
32 Bowen (2003), Duguay (2006), Milallos (2007) and Aspinall (2009).
33 Statistics from Johnson's (2007) report.

34 *Qanun* No. 13/2003 relating to *maisir* (gambling); *Qanun* No. 12/2003 relating to *khamar* (alcohol); *Qanun* No. 14/2003 relating to *khalwat* (inappropriate association between males and females); *Qanun* No. 11/2002 relating to *aqidah* (core religious beliefs) and *ibadah* (worship). See on this point Candraningrum (2007) and Feener (2012).
35 Regarding the implementation of *shari'a* in Aceh more broadly, see Feener (2012), Marhaban (2012), Jauhola (2013), Grossmann (2014) and Afrianty (2015).
36 Noerdin (2002), Schröter (2009), Feener (2012), Kusujiarti et al. (2015) and Jauhola (2016).
37 Siapno (2002), Jauhola (2013) and Taylor (2015).
38 For a discussion on this topic, see Hussain (2007) generally and in the Acehnese context Taylor (2015), Kusujiarti et al. (2015) and Jauhola (2020).
39 Note that in 2008, the formal enforcement agency formerly known as the 'shari'a police' (*Wilayatul Hisbah*) was dissolved into the general Public Order Enforcement Unit (known as Satpol PP).
40 While acknowledging that Muslim women's rights activists in Aceh are not a homogenous group, the majority of women's activists support the implementation of Islamic law in Aceh: see Grossmann (2011) and Afrianty (2015, 2020).
41 Chapter XI of Law No. 11/2006 (Law on Governing Aceh); also see Government Regulation No. 20/2007 on Local Political Parties in Aceh and *Qanun* No. 3/2008.
42 The notable exception to this is Ibu Illiza who – during the case study period – was the Deputy Mayor then Mayor of Banda Aceh: 9 February 2007–19 February 2012; 4 July 2012–17 February 2014 (Deputy Mayor); 17 February 2014–16 June 2014 (Acting Mayor); 16 June 2014–7 July 2017 (Mayor).
43 Afrianty (2015) and Schenk (2018).
44 Afrianty (2015) also notes that *Partai Aceh* 'could not win the election without the support of the traditional *Ulama* based in *Dayah* at the village level across the province', illustrating their influence in the political sphere.

Bibliography

Afrianty, Dina, *Women and Sharia Law in Northern Indonesia: Local Women's NGOs and the Reform of Islamic Law in Aceh* (Routledge, 2015).

Afrianty, Dina, 'Rising Public Piety and the Status of Women in Indonesia Two Decades After Reformasi' (2020) 8(1) *TRaNS* 65–80.

Aisyah, Siti and Lyn Parker, 'Problematic Conjugations: Women's Agency, Marriage and Domestic Violence in Indonesia' (2014) 38(2) *Asian Studies Review* 205–223.

An-Na'im, Abdullahi, *Islam and the Secular State: Negotiating the Future of Sharia* (Harvard University Press, 2008).

Ansori, Mohammad, 'From Insurgency to Bureaucracy: Free Aceh Movement, Aceh Party and the New Face of Conflict' (2012) 1(1) *Stability: International Journal of Security & Development* 31.

Aspinall, Edward, *Islam and Nation: Separatist Rebellion in Aceh, Indonesia* (Stanford University Press, 2009).

Avonius, Leena, 'Justice and the Aceh Peace Process' in Patrick Daly, Michael Feener and Anthony Reid (eds), *From the Ground Up: Perspectives on Post-Tsunami and Post-Conflict Aceh* (ISAS, 2012) 225–257.

Blackburn, Susan, *Women and the State in Modern Indonesia* (Cambridge University Press, 2004).

Blackburn, Susan, 'Violence' in Louise Edwards and Mina Roces (eds), *Women in Asia: Critical Concepts in Asian Studies* (Routledge, 2009) 194–219.

Blackwood, Evelyn, 'Gender Transgression in Colonial and Postcolonial Indonesia' (2005) 64(4) *Journal of Asian Studies* 849–879.

Boellstorff, Tom, '*Gay* and *Lesbi* Subjectivities, National Belonging and the New Indonesia' in Kathryn Robinson and Sharon Bessel (eds), *Women in Indonesia: Gender, Equity and Development* (ISAS, 2002) 95–96.

Bowen, John, *Islam, Law and Equality in Indonesia: An Anthropology of Public Reasoning* (Cambridge University Press, 2003).

Candraningrum, Dewi, 'Unquestioned Gender Lens in Contemporary Indonesia Shari'a Ordinances (*Perda Syari'ah*)' (2007) 45(2) *Al-Jami'ah* 289–320.

Cardozo, Mieke Lopes and Eka Srimulyani, 'Analysing the Spectrum of Female Education Leaders' Agency in Islamic Boarding Schools in Post-Conflict Aceh, Indonesia' (2018) 33(7) *Gender and Education* 847–863.

Christoplos, Ian and Treena Wu, 'Linking Relief, Rehabilitation and Development (LRRD) to Social Protection: Lessons from the Early Tsunami Response in Aceh' in Patrick Daly, Michael Feener and Anthony Reid (eds), *From the Ground Up: Perspectives on Post-Tsunami and Post-Conflict Aceh* (ISAS, 2012) 40–56.

Clavé-Çelik, Elsa, 'Silenced Fighters: An Insight into Women Combatants' History in Aceh (17th–20th c.)' (2014) 87 *Archipel* 273–306.

Drexler, Elizabeth, *Aceh, Indonesia: Securing the Insecure State* (Pennsylvania University Press, 2008).

Duguay, Philip, 'The Struggle for Women's Rights in Nanggroe Aceh Darussalam Province: A Look at History and Emerging Legislation' (2006) 26 *Singapore Law Review* 1–30.

Enarson, Elaine, 'Gender Issues in Natural Disasters: Talking Points and Research Needs', *Gender and Disaster Network* (3 May 2000).

Eye on Aceh, *We Are the Victims and the Witnesses: Women of Aceh* (Report, 2004).

Feener, Michael, 'Social Engineering through Shari'a: Islamic Law and State-Directed Da'wa in Contemporary Aceh' (2012) 19 *Islamic Law and Society* 275–311.

Feith, Pieter, 'Making Peace Agreements Effective: the Aceh Monitoring Mission Experience' in Patrick Daly, Michael Feener and Anthony Reid (eds), *From the Ground Up: Perspectives on Post-Tsunami and Post-Conflict Aceh* (ISAS, 2012) 214–224.

Felten-Biermann, Claudia, 'Gender and Natural Disaster: Sexualized Violence and the Tsunami' (2006) 49(3) *Development* 82.

Ferris, Elizabeth, 'Natural Disasters, Conflict and Human Rights: Tracing the Connections', *Brookings* (3 March 2010) https://www.brookings.edu/on-the-record/natural-disasters-conflict-and-human-rights-tracing-the-connections/

Fitzpatrick, Daniel, 'Between Custom and Law: Protecting the Property Rights of Women After the Tsunami in Aceh' in Patrick Daly, Michael Feener and Anthony Reid (eds), *From the Ground Up: Perspectives on Post-Tsunami and Post-Conflict Aceh* (ISAS, 2012) 114–131.

Giap, Tan Khee, Mulya Amri, Linda Low and Tan Kong Yam, *Competitiveness Analysis and Development Strategies for 33 Indonesian Provinces* (World Scientific Publishing, 2013).

Grossmann, Kristina, 'Women as Change Agents in the Transformation Process in Aceh, Indonesia' in Andrea Fleschenberg and Claudia Derichs (eds), *Women and Politics in Asia: A Springboard for Democracy?* (ISAS, 2011) 97–122.

Grossmann, Kristina, 'Muslim Female Activists and Sharia in Indonesia: Scopes of Acting in National and International Perspectives' (2014) 48(1) *Review of Indonesian and Malaysian Affairs* 95.

Human Rights Watch, '*Policing Morality: Abuses in the Application of Sharia in Aceh, Indonesia*' (Report, 2010).

Husin, Asna, 'Acehnese Women Struggle for Peace and Justice: Challenges and Opportunities' (2015) 6 *Islam and Civilisational Renewal* 318–335.

Hussain, Shakira, 'The Limits of Force Choice Discourses in Discussing Muslim Women's Dress Codes' (2007) 2(1) *Transforming Cultures eJournal* 1–15.

Jauhola, Marjaana, *Becoming Better 'Men' and 'Women': Negotiating Normativity through Gender Mainstreaming in Post-Tsunami Reconstruction Initiatives in Aceh, Indonesia* (PhD Thesis, University of Helsinki, 2010).
Jauhola, Marjaana, *Post-Tsunami Reconstruction in Indonesia: Negotiating Normativity through Gender Mainstreaming Initiatives in Aceh* (Taylor and Francis, 2013).
Jauhola, Marjaana, 'Decolonizing Branded Peacebuilding: Abjected Women Talk Back to the Finnish Women, Peace and Security Agenda' (2016) 92(2) *International Affairs* 333–351.
Jauhola, Marjaana, *Scraps of Hope in Banda Aceh: Gendered Urban Politics in the Aceh Peace Process* (Helsinki University Press, 2020).
Johnson, Troy, 'Voices from Aceh: Perspectives on *Syariat* Law' (Working Paper Series, No. 97, Southeast Asia Research Centre, 2007).
Kamaruzzaman, Suraiya, 'Women and syariah in Aceh', *Inside Indonesia* 79 (Jul–Sep 2004) https://www.insideindonesia.org/women-and-syariah-in-aceh-2
Kamaruzzaman, Suraiya, 'Agents for Change: The Roles of Women in Aceh's Peace Process' (2008) 20 *Accord* 70–71.
Kamis, Marzalan and Saiful Mahdi, 'Tsunami Response and Women' (Aceh Institute Report, 2006).
Komnas Perempuan, 'Experiences of Acehnese Women: Seeking and Accessing Justice from One Era to the Next' (Special Rapporteur for Aceh Report, 2007).
Kusujiarti, Siti, Elizabeth Miano, Annie Pryor and Breanna Ryan, 'Unveiling the Mysteries of Aceh, Indonesia: Local and Global Intersections of Women's Agency' (2015) 16(3) *Journal of International Women's Studies* 186–202.
Lee-Koo, Katrina, 'Gender at the Crossroad of Conflict: Tsunami and Peace in Post-2005 Aceh' (2012) 101 *Feminist Review* 59–77.
Lev, Daniel, 'On the Other Hand?' in Laurie Sears (ed.), *Fantasizing the Feminine in Indonesia* (Duke University Press, 1996) 191–204.
Lindsey, Tim, M. B. Hooker, Ross Clarke and Jeremy Kingsley, 'Shari'a Revival in Aceh' in Michael Feener and Mark Cammack (eds), *Islamic Law in Contemporary Indonesia: Ideas and Institutions* (Harvard University Press, 2007) 216–243.
Marhaban, '*Women in Post-Conflict Aceh: Participation in Socio-Economic and Political Processes*' (Research Paper, Weatherhead Centre for International Affairs 2012).
Meghdadi, Dina, 'Aftermath: Looking at Women's Roles in Post-conflict Transformation and Formal Peace Processes' (2009) 5 *Glendon Journal of International Studies* 127–139.
Melvin, Jess, 'Why Not Genocide? Anti-Chinese Violence in Aceh, 1965–1966' (2013) 3 *Journal of Current Southeast Asian Affairs* 63–91.
Melvin, Jess, *The Army and the Indonesian Genocide: Mechanics of Mass Murder* (Routledge, 2018).
Milallos, Theresa, 'Muslim Veil as Politics: Political Autonomy, Women and *Syariah* Islam in Aceh' (2007) 1 *Cont Islam* 289–301.
Mir-Hosseini, Ziba, 'Muslim Women's Quest for Equality: Between Islamic Law and Feminism' (2006) 32 *Critical Inquiry* 629–645.
Morfit, Michael, 'Managing Risk: Aceh, the Helsinki Accords and Indonesia's Democratic Development' in Patrick Daly, Michael Feener and Anthony Reid (eds), *From the Ground Up: Perspectives on Post-Tsunami and Post-Conflict Aceh* (ISAS, 2012) 179–213.
Nashriyah and Khairiah Syahabuddin (eds), *Masculinities in Post Conflict Aceh and Its Impacts on Violence Against Women* (PSW UIN Ar-Raniry, 2015).
Noerdin, Edriana, 'Customary Institutions, *Syariah* Law and the Marginalisation of Indonesian Women' in Kathryn Robinson and Sharon Bessel (eds), *Women in Indonesia: Gender, Equity and Development* (ISAS, 2002) 179–186.

Nor, Mohd and Inayatillah, 'Women's Marginalization from Public Spaces: The Case of Aceh' (2011) 27(4) *Asian Women* 55–79.

Oey-Gardiner, Mayling, 'And the Winner Is...Indonesian Women in Public Life' in Kathryn Robinson and Sharon Bessel (eds), *Women in Indonesia: Gender, Equity and Development* (ISAS, 2002) 100–112.

Parker, Lyn, 'The Theory and Context of the Stigmatisation of Widows and Divorcees (*janda*) in Indonesia' (2016) 44(128) *Indonesia and The Malay World* 7–26.

Pohlman, Annie, *Women, Sexual Violence and the Indonesian Killings of 1965–66* (Routledge, 2015).

Reconstruction and Rehabilitation Body (Badan Rehabilitasi dan Rekonstruksi), '*Aceh and Nias One Year After the Tsunami: The Recovery Effort and Way Forward*' (Report, 2005).

Reed, Sheila, '*Evaluation of United Nations Development Fund for Women, CIDA-Funded Project (2007–2009), Strengthening Women's Legal Rights in Aceh, Indonesia*' (Report, UNIFEM, 2009).

Reuters, 'Indonesia: Key points of Aceh peace agreement' (15 August 2005) https://reliefweb.int/report/indonesia/indonesia-key-points-aceh-peace-agreement-0

Rezaeian, Mohsen, 'The Association Between Natural Disasters and Violence: A Systematic Review of the Literature and a Call for More Epidemiological Studies' (2013) 18(12) *Journal of Research in Medical Sciences* 1103–1107.

Robinson, Kathryn, 'Muslim Women's Political Struggle for Marriage Law Reform in Contemporary Indonesia' in Amanda Whiting and Carolyn Evans (eds), *Mixed Blessings: Law, Religion and Women's Rights in the Asia-Pacific Region* (Martinus Nijhoff Publishers, 2006) 183–210.

Robinson, Kathryn and Sharon Bessel, 'Introduction to the Issues' in Kathryn Robinson and Sharon Bessel (eds), *Women in Indonesia: Gender, Equity and Development* (ISAS, 2002) 1–12.

Saptari, Ratna, 'Women, Family and Household: Tensions in Culture and Practice' in Juliette Koning, Marleen Nolten, Janet Rodenburg and Ratna Saptari (eds), *Women and Households in Indonesia: Cultural Notions and Social Practices* (Nordic Institute of Asian Studies, 2000) 19–25.

Saraswati, Rika, 'Justice and the Identities of Women: The Case of Indonesian Women Victims of Domestic Violence who have Access to Family Court' (2013) 1 *Forum on Public Policy: A Journal of the Oxford Round Table* 1–21.

Schenk, Christine, 'Islamic Leaders and the Legal Geography of Family Law in Aceh, Indonesia' (2018) 184 *The Geographical Journal* 8–18.

Schiller, Rachel, 'Reconciliation in Aceh: Addressing the Social Effects of Prolonged Armed Conflict' (2011) 39 *Asian Journal of Social Science* 489–507.

Schröter, Susanne, '*Cultural and Political Transformation in Aceh, Indonesia in the Wake of the Tsunami*' (German Science Foundation, 2009).

Sears, Laurie, 'Fragile Identities: Deconstructing Women and Indonesia' in Laurie Sears (ed), *Fantasizing the Feminine in Indonesia* (Duke University Press, 1996) 1–46.

Siapno, Jaqueline, *Gender, Islam and Nationalism and the State in Aceh: The Paradox of Power, Co-optation and Resistance* (Taylor and Francis, 2002).

Siapno, Jacqueline, 'Living Through Terror: Everyday Resilience in East Timor and Aceh' (2009a) 15(1) *Journal for the Study of Race, Nation and Culture* 43–64.

Siapno, Jaqueline, 'The Politics of Reconstruction, Gender, and Re-Integration in Post-Tsunami Aceh' in Malathi de Alwis and Eva-Lotta Hedman (eds), *Tsunami in a Time of War: Aid, Activism and Reconstruction in Sri Lanka and Aceh, Indonesia*(International Center for Ethnic Studies, 2009b) 163–190.

Siapno, Jaqueline, 'Shari'a Moral Policing and the Politics of Consent in Aceh' (2011) 1 *Social Difference Online* 17–29.

Siegel, James, *The Rope of God* (The University of Michigan Press, 1969).
Srimulyani, Eka, 'Islam, *Adat*, and the State: Matrifocality in Aceh Revisited' (2010) 48(2) *Al-Jami'ah* 321–342.
Srimulyani, Eka, 'Women, Micro-finance and Income Generation after the Political Conflict and the Tsunami in Aceh' (2013) 19(1) *Asian Journal of Women's Studies* 95–114.
Sunindyo, Saraswati, 'Murder, Gender and the Media: Sexualizing Politics and Violence' in Laurie Sears (ed), *Fantasizing the Feminine in Indonesia* (Duke University Press, 1996) 120–139.
Sunindyo, Saraswati, 'When the Earth Is Female and the Nation Is Mother: Gender, the Armed Forces and Nationalism in Indonesia' (1998) 58 *Feminist Review* 1–21.
Suryakusuma, Julia, *State Ibuism: The Social Construction of Womanhood* (Institute of Social Studies, 1988).
Suryakusuma, Julia, 'The State and Sexuality in New Order Indonesia' in Laurie Sears (ed), *Fantasizing the Feminine in Indonesia* (Duke University Press, 1996) 92–119.
Taylor, Reed, 'Syariah as Heteotopia: Responses from Muslim Women in Aceh, Indonesia' (2015) 6 *Religions* 566–593.
UNDP, *Indonesia Human Development Report 2001* (Report, 2002).
Vianen, Inge, '*Women, Gender and Work in Nanggroe Aceh Darussalam*' (Working Paper, ILO, 2006).
Waizenegger, Arno and Jennifer Hyndman, 'Two Solitudes: Post-tsunami and Post-conflict Aceh' (2010) 34(3) *Disasters* 787–808.
Wieringa, Saskia, 'Gender Harmony and the Happy Family: Islam, Gender and Sexuality in Post-Reformasi Indonesia' (2015) 23(1) *South East Asia Research* 27–44.
Zeccola, Paul, 'Dividing Disasters in Aceh, Indonesia: Separatist Conflict and Tsunami, Human Rights and Humanitarianism' (2011) 35(2) *Disasters* 308–328.

Laws and regulations cited in Chapter 2

Law No. 1/1974 Marriage Law.
Law No. 44/1999 on the Implementation of Aceh's Special Status.
Law No. 18/2001 on the Special Autonomy of Aceh.
Qanun No. 13/2003 relating to *maisir* (gambling).
Qanun No. 12/2003 relating to *khamar* (alcohol).
Qanun No. 14/2003 relating to *khalwat* (inappropriate association between males and females).
Qanun No. 11/2002 relating to *aqidah* (core religious beliefs) and *ibadah* (worship).
Law No. 11/2006 (Law on Governing Aceh).
Government Regulation No. 20/2007 on Local Political Parties in Aceh.
Qanun No. 9/2008 *Adat dan Istiadat* (Customs and Ceremonies).
Qanun No. 3/2008 on Local Political Parties.
Qanun No. 6/2009 *Pemberdayaan dan Perlindungan Perempuan* (Empowerment and Protection of Women).
Instruksi Walikota No. 2/2015.

Interviews cited in Chapter 2

Interview with Ibu Commissioner (*Komnas Perempuan*) (Jakarta, 12 January 2018).
Interview with a women's advocate from *Balai Syura* (Banda Aceh, 17 January 2018).
Interviews with Ibu R (a female academic at the State Islamic University Ar-Raniry) (Banda Aceh, 27 December 2017).

3 Situating the Law in the Context of Religion and Gender

Introduction

This chapter situates law in the context of religion and gender from an Islamic feminist perspective, then outlines the legal and policy framework regulating domestic violence in Indonesia. While acknowledging that law, religion, and gender intersect in complex and fluid ways beyond the scope of this research, this book focuses on three main intersections (Figure 3.1). First, gender norms are informed by the relevant socio-religious context; second, gender norms influence the drafting and implementation of the law; and third, the authority of State law competes with non-codified moral-religious interpretations. The operation of the law in Indonesia is densely gendered, with contextually specific gender norms informing both community and institutional responses to domestic violence.

As mentioned in Chapter 1, an assumption underpinning the analysis in this book is that a focus on gender is essential, or even intrinsic, to domestic violence research. The question then becomes: what influences constructions of gender? First, ideas about gender, including what marriage and the family unit look like, are informed by local context. As 87% of Indonesian people identify as Muslim, Islam plays a central role in informing gender roles and norms. Second, in Indonesia, the customs, traditions, or beliefs of ethnic groups – known as *adat* – inform ideas about gender. In Aceh, *adat* and Islam are conceptualised as almost inseparable, therefore religion and *adat* are analysed together in the case study context unless explicitly specified.[1]

When I say 'religion', I do not mean religion in an abstract doctrinal sense but Islam as it is understood and practised day-to-day by Indonesian people. As framed by Eidhamar (2018) in his study of attitudes towards domestic violence in Indonesia – the relevant question is 'not what the Qur'an actually says, but what Muslims say the Qur'an says'. A more apt descriptor may therefore be 'religious interpretations', 'religious practices', or 'religious traditions' as opposed to religion per se. Due to Islam being the cornerstone of Acehnese identity, I focus my case study analysis on religion as opposed to culture more broadly. This approach can also be understood as treating religion as a cultural identity marker or social practice. Whilst Acehnese cultural identity is

DOI: 10.4324/9781032613642-3

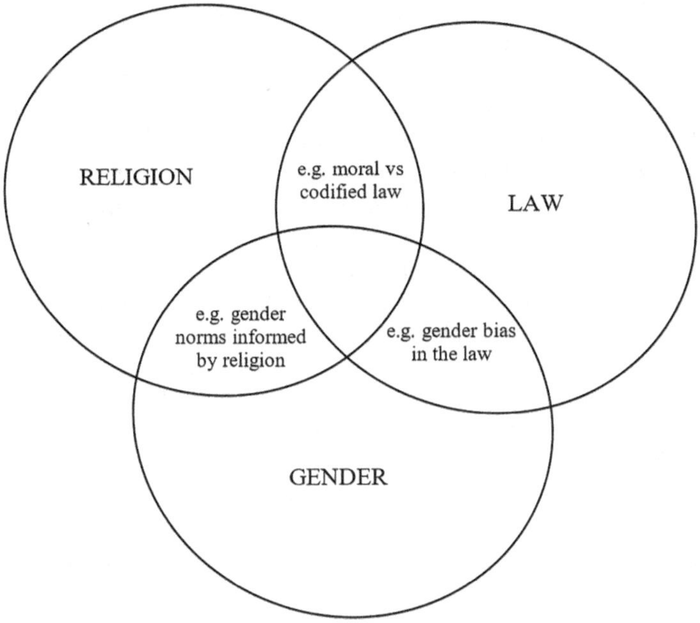

Figure 3.1 Broad intersections between religion, gender, and law.

Source: Author's own.

predominately built on understandings and practices of Islam, where other intersectional factors, such as politics and class, significantly impact local understandings of gender this is made explicit in the analysis.

Religion and gender

The gender norms reflected in this book are not set in stone but rather have changed throughout Indonesian and Acehnese history and will continue to change over time. In fact, the range of competing gender norms documented in this book challenge the idea that gender norms in Indonesia are homogenous. To assume homogeneity would be to assume that Indonesian people understand and perform gender in the same way, regardless of other intersectional factors such as age and ethnicity. Although this research concludes that patriarchal gender norms that are discriminatory against women are dominant, gender norms informed by religion continue to be contested. Many competing religious interpretations – ranging from feminist to patriarchal interpretations – of the *Qur'an* exist in Indonesia, in particular the interpretation of *Surat An-Nisa* verse 4:34 of the *Qur'an* as discussed in Chapter 4.

In analysing the relationship between gender and religion, particular attention is paid to feminist traditions in Indonesia and Aceh. With respect to terminology, I note that many Muslim women do not identify with the label 'feminist' as it is seen as an inherently Western. This is not to imply that there is any necessary inconsistency between feminist principles and practices and Islam in general, but that 'feminism' as a label may be perceived as having Western connotations.[2] Therefore where I use the term 'feminism', it is used in its broadest sense as any work which addresses gender inequality or discrimination against women.[3] There is a long tradition of women's advocacy within Islam, often referred to as 'Muslim feminism' or 'Islamic feminism'. This book contributes to existing scholarship from Muslim feminist authors, such as Abu-Lughod and Mahmood as outlined below.

As an Australian-Muslim scholar researching in the Indonesian context, I must answer the question posed by Abu-Lughod (2015) as to how we can 'acknowledge the seriousness of violence against women without contributing to the stigmatization of particular communities'? This book seeks to acknowledge the importance of identifying men's violence against women whilst avoiding reductively equating such violence with Islam or Indonesian culture. Mahmood (2012) clarifies that this should not be taken as suggesting that 'there is no violence against women in the Muslim world, but that it is the reductive character of this framing, one that orchestrates an entire chain of equivalences associated with Islam, that needs to be questioned'.

As outlined in Chapter 1, most feminist scholarship argues (or assumes) that patriarchy and gender inequality are core drivers of men's violence against women. While recognising that patriarchy and gender inequality exist in Aceh, Indonesian, and Muslim communities in general, Abu-Lughod (2015) notes that these communities do not have a 'monopoly' on violence against women. There is nothing innately *Islamic* about gender inequality or patriarchy, however the language which frames, justifies, and cloaks men's violence against women is context specific. As Indonesian narratives and conceptualisations of violence are predominately informed by Islamic understandings of gender it is essential to examine local religious interpretations and practices in order to understand the language in which patriarchy and violence are framed. As a baseline, knowledge about both domestic violence and religion is required to effectively respond to domestic violence in faith-based communities.

Within Islamic feminist frameworks, the distinction between sex and gender is complicated by the addition of the notion of *kodrat*.[4] Sex can be defined in relation to a person's body or anatomy and is usually ascribed as male or female at birth, while gender is the social construct built upon, or in relation to, sex. As explained by Scott (1986), due to gender being socially constructed, the terms 'man' and 'woman' are:

> at once empty and overflowing categories. Empty because they have no ultimate transcendent meaning. Overflowing because even when they appear to be fixed, they still contain within them alternative, denied, or suppressed definitions.

Common interpretations of Islam conceptualise men and women as inherently different by nature. In Indonesia, Islamic notions of innate God-given gender are prevalent. *Kodrat* is generally understood as the predetermined nature or fate/destiny of a person depending on their sex. Afrianty (2020) argues that dominant Indonesian interpretations of Islam promote 'separate roles for men and women grounded in biological differences that religion is said to consecrate'. As explained in Chapter 4, some Muslim feminists argue that *kodrat* can be defined as limited to biological sex, as opposed to including socially constructed gender norms. Many people reason that because you are a woman (based on your biological sex) you *must* perform certain gender roles (for example, cooking, cleaning, mothering) as it is your *kodrat* (gender destiny). Muslim feminists who distinguish between sex and gender are attempting to challenge gender essentialism or biological determinism and argue that just because you are a woman (based on your biological sex) this does not *necessarily* mean that you must perform socially constructed gender roles. It is, however, common for there to be a blurring between the categories of sex, *kodrat*, and gender. In practice, how many gender norms *kodrat* encapsulates as 'innately' linked to biological sex depends on local interpretations.

While the notion of *kodrat*, when combined with patriarchal practices and policies, is often used to exclude and restrict women, Mahmood (2012) persuasively argues that Muslim women are not merely passive victims who are subjected to external social impositions in terms of gendered norms. She argues that 'social norms are the necessary ground through which the subject is realized and comes to enact her agency'. Mahmood, adopting Butler's theory of performativity, states that:

> the reiterative structure of norms serves not only to *consolidate* a particular regime of discourse/power but also provides the means for its *destabilization*. In other words, there is no possibility of "undoing" social norms that is independent of the "doing" of norms; agency resides, therefore, within this productive reiterability.

As well as consolidation and destabilisation, Mahmood explains that norms are performed, inhabited, and experienced in a variety of ways day-to-day. The ways in which gender is embodied in the Acehnese context has been explored by scholars such as Siapno (2002) and Afrianty (2015, 2018), as outlined in Chapter 2.

In addition to the relevance of religion in terms of defining gender, the ways in which gender intersects with other characteristics and experiences must also be recognised, including, but not limited to, ethnicity and class. In the interviews for this book, the majority of respondents were Muslim women of Indonesian nationality and Acehnese ethnicity. Respondents ranged from low to high socio-economic class and all respondents were urban based (living in Banda Aceh at the time of interview, although some interviewees originated from rural areas). Further, respondent educational status (in terms of both State and religious schooling) varied widely.

Law and gender

The book's analysis is built upon, and informed by, an understanding of the relationship between religion and gender, however, most of the chapters relate to the operation of the law. As outlined in Chapter 1, law is not a neutral force but is itself gendered – both in terms of the gendered nature of enacted laws and the presence of gender bias within legal culture and institutions. The book contributes to the work of socio-legal scholars, such as Graycar and Morgan (2002) and Hunter (2013), who argue that the law cannot be viewed in isolation from broader social structures and systems due to the pervasive nature of gender within the law.

There are many critiques regarding the gendered nature of law, including, but not limited to, the framing of law from a masculine point of view, the legal subject as male, and the pigeon-holing of female legal subjecthood exclusively as victimhood. Some scholars even argue that the law is of little value to women in asserting their rights because it is an inherently patriarchal institution. For example, Peletz (2002) highlights the role of law in reproducing systems of inequality associated with gender. A clear example of gender bias in enacted laws can be found in the framing of the Marriage Law (Law No. 1/1974), which entrenches gender roles within the family. For example, Article 31(3) of the Marriage Law explicitly recognises husbands as the 'head of the household'. Further, the Marriage Law distinguishes between husbands and wives based on their gender roles with 'men as primary income-earners and women as child-rearers and housewives'.[5]

Chapters 4–7 evidence implicit and explicit gender bias in the approaches of *adat*, religious (civil), and criminal law systems towards domestic violence. Evidence of gender bias documented throughout this book is consistent with existing research on gender bias in the Indonesian courts. In Bowen's (2003) study of Islam and law in Indonesia, he found that social norms:

> shape decisions taken by judges, whose interests, perceptions, and norms derive from their own backgrounds in particular locales as well as their education in legal and religious traditions.

Further, Indonesian scholars such as Irianto and Cahyadi (2008), Nurlaelawati (2016) and Saraswati (2021) have also documented the presence of gender bias within State justice systems.

The criminal justice system in addressing violence against women. Another example of gender bias in legal practice is the under-use of general Criminal Code (*Kitab Undang-Undang Hukum Pidana - KUHP*) provisions to prosecute domestic violence prior to the enactment of the Anti-Domestic Violence Law. As discussed later in this chapter, despite the Criminal Code criminalising violence against spouses (albeit in a more limited form than under the Law), biases and discrimination in society weighed against the likelihood of these general criminal provisions being used in domestic violence contexts. Namely, because the household is considered to be a 'private sphere' under the control of the male head of the household, domestic violence is considered to be a 'private' issue and therefore intervention by the State is not appropriate. Eddyono et al.'s (2016) study of gender policy in Indonesia found that in line with the dominant idea of family harmony (*keluarga sakinah*) penalties under the Criminal Code were rarely applied. The location of domestic violence within the family has historically shielded this form of violence from scrutiny across jurisdictions. While the lack of prosecution under the Criminal Code highlights the importance of the enactment of the Law, this book's analysis illustrates how the implementation of the Law continues to be obstructed by gender bias in legal processes.

Religion and law

The law does not operate in a vacuum and, in some circumstances, has limited utility for domestic violence victims. One of the factors that affects the implementation of the Anti-Domestic Violence Law in Aceh is the prominence of moral-religious (non-codified) law. This is because the latter is often preferred by the community over State law. Whether positive (codified) or moral-religious law has authority over the area of family law is a debate that continues to challenge the legitimacy and boundaries of State authority. The boundary between positive State law and moral-religious law is discussed in Chapter 5. In addition to issues of authority, a primary barrier to implementation of the Law is a lack of socialisation. 'Socialisation' can be defined as the presence or absence of legal awareness, knowledge, or internalisation of relevant legal norms within the community. As revealed in fieldwork, community members generally have a limited understanding of domestic violence dynamics and victim rights under the Law. Even if the State better socialised the Law, a fundamental tension still exists between the norms enacted in the Law and gender norms informed by religious interpretations at the community level. The relationship between gender, religion, and law frames the analysis in this book. In the next section, the domestic violence legal and policy framework in Indonesia is outlined.

Legal and policy framework

For victims of domestic violence who engage with the State system, there are two main avenues for help-seeking or reporting: the State criminal jurisdiction and the religious (civil) law jurisdiction. In addition, there is the non-State avenue of *adat* dispute resolution, as in Figure 3.2.[6]

Domestic violence victims who seek help or report generally do so at the village level via *adat* justice. Where *adat* dispute resolution fails or where the case is considered especially serious, cases may continue to the Islamic Courts for divorce (Chapter 5) or be reported to the police (Chapter 6). Even if a victim reports to the police, only in rare situations do domestic violence cases continue to be prosecuted at the *Pengadilan Negeri* (Chapter 7). Most domestic violence cases that enter the State system are indirectly dealt with via divorce at the Islamic Courts.

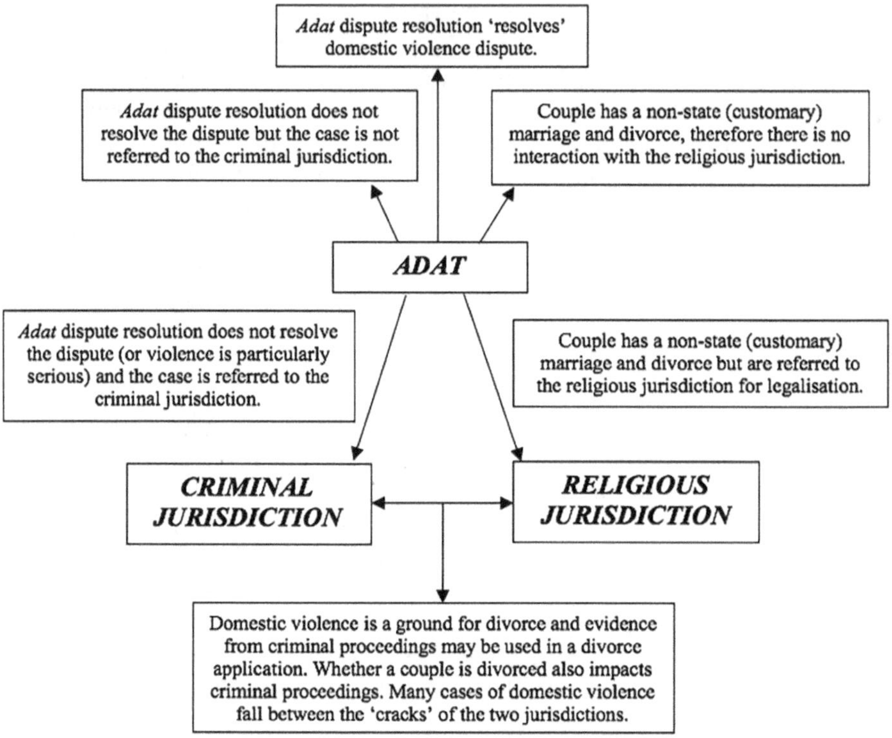

Figure 3.2 Relationship between State and non-State avenues.

Source: Author's own.

Criminal jurisdiction

Indonesia ratified the Convention on the Elimination of All Forms of Discrimination against Women (CEDAW) in 1984. A National Action Plan to Eradicate Violence Against Women was enacted in 1999, followed by a Zero Tolerance Policy in 2000. From 1997, LBH APIK (the Women's Association for Justice/Legal Aid Institution) mobilised the women's movement to campaign for the criminalisation of domestic violence. The women's movement lobbied the government for six years in what has been described as a monumental advocacy effort. Almost every aspect of the Anti-Domestic Violence Bill was controversial, including the definitions of 'household' and 'violence'. *Komnas Perempuan* and the Ministry for Women's Empowerment were at loggerheads with conservatives within the Ministry of Religious Affairs and TNI-Polri (the military and police) on several issues. It was necessary for campaigners to compromise on aspects of the proposed law to ensure the Bill would be passed, for example, the exclusion of non-married couples from the definition of household and not explicitly mentioning 'illegal polygamy' in the definition of psychological violence. As discussed below, polygamy is permitted in

Indonesia in limited circumstances (Articles 3–5 of the Marriage Law). Where 'illegal polygamy' is mentioned in this book, this refers to any polygamous marriage that is not registered under the Marriage Law. However, the inclusion of domestic workers in the definition of household and the provisions on marital rape and economic violence were successfully retained, as outlined below.

The Anti-Domestic Violence Law

In 2004, domestic violence was criminalised in Indonesia. The Law is a *lex specialis* (special law) that is more specific than the Criminal Code and the Marriage Law. Therefore, hierarchically, it should take precedence over the more general laws.[7] The relationship between the Law, Criminal Code, and Marriage Law is outlined below. As discussed in Chapter 7, there have been issues of interpretation, with some judges incorrectly continuing to preference the older, more general laws, rather than applying the specific provisions of the Anti-Domestic Violence Law.

The Law identifies household violence as a violation of human rights and human dignity, as well as a form of discrimination. Further, domestic violence contravenes the *Pancasila* (Indonesian State ideology) and the Constitution.[8] The Law aims to establish State protection from domestic violence through the legal system. This includes the prevention of violence, protection of victims, and prosecution of perpetrators by the State (Article 1(2) of the Law). The rationales underpinning the Law reflect State criminal law more broadly, namely *kepenjaraan* (retributive) and *pemasyarakatan* (literally 'socialisation', here a reference to prevention, deterrence, and reform) theories. The Law also states that victims are entitled to support and protection from both State and non-State actors, specifically healthcare and legal aid (Article 10). In addition to the Law, there are implementing regulations, which focus on establishing facilities for victim support and recovery, such as specific rooms at police stations and safe houses.[9]

Domestic violence is made a criminal offence by Article 44 of the Law. Domestic violence is defined in Article 1(1) as: 'any act against anyone, particularly women, bringing about physical, sexual, psychological misery or suffering, and/or negligence of the household … within the scope of the household'. The scope of the household is defined in Article 2(1) to include: the husband, wife, children, people who have a family relationship, and individuals working and living in the household. The definition of the household is in some respects broad – explicitly including domestic workers – and in other respects quite narrow, implicitly excluding couples whose relationships are not recognised under State law, such as ex-partners, unmarried couples (*pacaran*), and LGBTIQ+ couples. The Law is limited by hegemonic heteronormativity, underpinned by Islamic kinship relations – *mahram* (family relations) or non-*mahram* (marital relations). Further, as will be explained in Chapter 5, even couples that are married according to *adat*/religious ceremonies that are not registered with the State may fall outside of the scope of the Law.

Violence is further defined in Articles 5–9 of the Law as including:

(a) physical violence: an act bringing about pain, illness, or serious injury (Articles 5 and 6);
(b) psychological violence: an act bringing about fear, loss of self-confidence, or psychological suffering (Articles 5 and 7);
(c) sexual violence: forced sexual intercourse (Articles 5 and 8; see also the Explanation to Article 8); and
(d) economic violence/neglect of the household: the failure to provide livelihood, treatment or care or bringing about economic dependence by limiting and/or prohibiting an individual to work properly (Articles 5 and 9).

The Law's definition of domestic violence specifically includes psychological and economic violence in addition to physical and sexual violence. This is notable because, as discussed in Chapter 4, traditional conceptualisations of domestic violence have overwhelmingly tended to focus on physical (rather than non-physical) forms of violence. Further, the definition of economic violence explicitly recognises the element of control, with Article 9 criminalising 'bringing about economic dependence by limiting and/or prohibiting an individual to work properly thereby placing the victim under the control of the individual'. The framing of Article 9 recognises that domestic violence may involve elements of control and coercion.

While the Law recognises that forms of violence may be multiple and interrelated, in practice, community understandings of violence as non-physical are very limited. A representative from P2TP2A (Ibu A) explained during an interview that while victims of severe physical violence have access to the legal process, cases of psychological or economic violence are generally only considered in 'discourse', meaning that they are only given lip-service. In practice, cases of psychological and economic violence rarely reach court.

Further, despite the Law recognising various forms of violence, the nature of domestic violence remains difficult to encapsulate within a criminal law framework. The criminalisation of domestic violence can realistically only capture part of victim experiences. Hester and Westmarland (2006) argue that the nature of domestic violence as a pattern of behaviour does not fit within incident-based criminal law approaches – as follows:

> Domestic violence involves patterns of violence and abusive behaviour over time rather than individual acts. However, the criminal justice system is primarily concerned with specific incidents and it can therefore be difficult to apply criminal justice approaches in relation to domestic violence.

Therefore, beyond cases prosecuted at the *Pengadilan Negeri* under the Law, domestic violence requires an interdisciplinary and integrated response. Legal system responses to domestic violence, including criminal and religious (civil) law approaches, are only part of broader systems responding to domestic violence, including healthcare and economic support for victims. While an in-depth analysis of non-legal avenues falls outside the scope of this book, the fieldwork conducted highlighted a close relationship between the prevention of domestic violence and women's educational and economic empowerment. In practice, domestic violence cannot be viewed as a purely legal issue as it is deeply embedded in broader social-economic systems.

Relationship between the Law and the Criminal Code

The Law redefined the relationship between the State and the family unit. Before the enactment of the Law in 2004, the Criminal Code was interpreted and applied in a gendered way within a patriarchal culture so that crimes within the home were rarely prosecuted as public crimes would be. Violence within the domestic sphere was regarded as a 'private matter'. This was both explicit in the law and implicit in the legal culture, as exemplified by the former Criminal Code provisions (note that the Criminal Code was reformed in December 2022).[10] Article 285 of the former Criminal Code stated that 'Any person who forces a woman to have sexual intercourse *outside of marriage* shall be guilty of rape' (emphasis added). At the time the Anti-Domestic Violence Law was passed, if rape was committed by a husband against his wife this was not seen as requiring a criminal law response. Article 8 of the Law criminalised marital rape as a form of sexual violence. This provision was a significant achievement for the women's activists who lobbied for its inclusion. Recently in April 2022, the Indonesian Sexual Violence Bill was passed into law (Law No. 12/2022). The Sexual Violence Law addresses forms of sexual violence not previously criminalised by the Criminal Code or Anti-Domestic Violence Law, including forced marriage, forced contraception, forced sterilisation, online sexual violence, and sexual slavery. Article 4(2)(h) of the Sexual Violence Law cements the criminalisation of marital rape under the Anti-Domestic Violence Law.

Several articles in the Criminal Code encompass elements of domestic violence. Although, unlike the Anti-Domestic Violence Law, the Criminal Code provisions are 'neutral' and do not recognise violence as gendered. As the Criminal Code has recently been reformed, Table 3.1 sets out the relevant provisions before and after the amendments (noting that the new Criminal Code does not come into force until 2 January 2026).

Even though provisions of the former Criminal Code explicitly criminalised elements of domestic violence and could have been utilised to prosecute domestic violence before the enactment of the Anti-Domestic Violence Law – biases and discrimination inherent in society weighed against these general criminal provisions being used in the context of domestic violence.

Relationship between the Law and the Marriage Law

As mentioned above, illegal polygamy was initially explicitly identified as a form of violence in the Anti-Domestic Violence Bill, however, the reference was dropped as it was too much of a 'religiously sensitive issue'.[11] Despite this,

Table 3.1 Comparison between former and new Criminal Code provisions

Former Criminal Code provision	*New Criminal Code provision*
Maltreatment (Article 351).	Persecution (Article 466).
A spousal or familial relationship was an aggravating factor for maltreatment (Article 356).	Under the new provision, persecution of a spouse is no longer an aggravating factor (Article 470).
Adultery (Article 284).	Adultery (Article 411).
Abandonment (Article 304).	Abandonment (Article 428).
Verbal abuse as a form of violence was not criminalised under the former Criminal Code.	Verbal abuse in the form of 'threats of violence' is now criminalised (Article 157).
Marital rape was not criminalised under the former Criminal Code.	Marital rape is now included in the provision criminalising rape (Article 473).

Source: Author's own.

illegal polygamy is recognised as a form of psychological violence in practice. At first glance, this sits uncomfortably with Articles 3–5 of the Marriage Law, which permit polygamy by court order in limited circumstances, including the consent of both parties. However, on careful inspection, the Law operates as an indirect enforcement mechanism for the Marriage Law's limitations on polygamy, because if Articles 3–5 of the Marriage Law are not strictly followed then (illegal) polygamy is recognised as a form of domestic violence. Instances of illegal polygamy which constitute domestic violence include where the husband does not gain the permission of his wife before 'informally' taking a second wife or where the wife is under duress to consent to the taking of a second wife.[12]

In addition to the criminalisation of marital rape and illegal polygamy, the significance of the Anti-Domestic Violence Law compared to the Criminal Code and the Marriage Law is two-fold: its breadth and specificity. First, the Law's provisions are far broader than the Criminal Code and include prevention, protection, and recovery, in addition to criminalisation, as well as placing additional obligations on law enforcers, health, and social workers to meet victim needs. Second, the Law's specific conceptual emphasis on gender and the household shifts the focus of the law from public to private. The Explanatory Memorandum to the Law states that the existing criminal law was inadequate to deal with the special nature of domestic violence. Further, the Explanatory Memorandum explains how the Law goes beyond the existing criminal law to 'specifically provide for violence occurring in the household with criminal elements that [are] different from the prosecution [of] crimes provided for in the Criminal Code'. Unfortunately, sometimes domestic violence cases are still prosecuted under the Criminal Code, which undermines the protections afforded by the Law. Nursiti et al. (2006) found that legal practitioners commonly assume that the Criminal Code is sufficient to provide protection for victims. Further, Irianto and Cahyadi (2008) explain that it has been difficult to gain acceptance and understanding of the Law because the Criminal Code is well-known and dominant in policing. As discussed in Chapter 7, Criminal Code provisions are also sometimes relied upon in the alternative for charges of physical violence where a legal marriage cannot be proven.

Before enactment of the Law, the status quo was that the State did not interfere in the domestic realm, which was under the implicit and explicit authority of the male head of the household – husbands being legally recognised as the head of the household under Article 31(3) of the Marriage Law. By explicitly recognising violence in the household as a gendered social problem requiring a State criminal law response, the Law represents an important progressive 'intrusion' by the State into the 'private sphere' of the home.

As discussed in Chapter 4, one of the main issues with implementation of the Law is that 20 years since its enactment, socialisation of Law has not produced a significant shift away from the mindset that the household is a 'private sphere' under the control of the male head of the household. Through the enactment of the Law, the State was attempting to legitimise involvement in the domestic realm to protect women's rights. However, the community's understanding of 'domestic' affairs has resisted this re-definition of the public/private divide and has, to an extent, undermined the State's intention. The analysis in Chapter 4–7 of this book focuses on the implementation of the law, an area of scholarship known as rights enforcement – which includes interpretation and application of the law by community stakeholders, police, prosecution, and judges.

Relationship with Qanun

Since 1999, Aceh has implemented local regional regulations known as *Qanun* under the Special Regional Autonomy Arrangements.[13] Under Article 231(1) of the Law on Governing Aceh, the Acehnese government is responsible for the promotion and protection of women's rights and empowerment. The primary *Qanun* relevant to the implementation of the Law at the local level is *Qanun* 9/2008 *Adat dan Istiadat* (Customs and Ceremonies) – discussed below. The relevance of these *Qanun* are explained below. In terms of legal hierarchy, due to *Qanun* being lower in the official legal hierarchy than statutes (*Undang-Undang*) of the national legislature, such as the Law, the Criminal Code, and the Marriage Law, the statutes should prevail in the case of any inconsistency.[14] As mentioned in Chapter 2, while the Special Regional Autonomy Arrangement is unique to Aceh, provinces across Indonesia have the ability to pass local regulations which have the same status as *Qanun* in terms of legal hierarchy. According to *Komnas Perempuan*, there is a widespread issue with local regulations being passed that discriminate against women. Although these regulations contradict women's rights protections enshrined in national law and are therefore, in theory, not legally valid – in the absence of monitoring or enforcement such laws remain in force.

Religious (civil) jurisdiction

While the *Pengadilan Negeri* is the primary State institution responsible for addressing domestic violence under the Law, the Islamic Court (*Pengadilan Agama* – known as the *Mahkamah Syariah* in Aceh) is an important avenue for victims. In Triana's (2018) study, she found that Islamic Courts in Indonesia handled between 94 and 96% of domestic violence related cases, meaning these courts are at the forefront of the State's engagement with domestic violence. Further in the case study context, statistics from P2TP2A (Aceh) show that between 2014 and 2017, out of 332 reported cases, only 15% of these cases were finalised via criminal law avenues ('resolved' by the police, during prosecution, or by a decision of the *Pengadilan Negeri*). Comparatively, 30% of reported cases were finalised via family law avenues ('resolved' by the Islamic Courts). This means that the remainder of cases – a majority of approximately 57% – were 'resolved' via *adat* or non-State pathways. The word 'resolved' appears in inverted commas because cases may terminate for a variety of reasons (for example, reconciliation, either genuine or under duress), which do not necessarily correlate with the cessation of violence.

It is well-known that domestic violence victims commonly seek to divorce their husbands/perpetrators through the religious jurisdiction, rather than (or in addition to) reporting to the police. Considering the large number of domestic violence cases that are (indirectly) reported via the religious jurisdiction, the Islamic Courts have an important role to play in access to justice for victims.

The Marriage Law establishes that if either partner neglects their marital responsibilities, a complaint may be lodged with the Islamic Court. Under chapter VIII of the Marriage Law, a marriage may be dissolved through divorce, if there are 'sufficient grounds' and the court is unsuccessful in reconciling the parties (Articles 38(b) and 39). Sufficient grounds include adultery, addiction, desertion, cruelty, disability, and 'irreconcilable differences'.[15] The main grounds relevant to domestic violence are 'constant differences of opinion and quarrels between husband and wife' and 'serious cruelty or maltreatment endangering the other party'.[16] The word *penganiayaan* used in the Marriage Law, translated here as maltreatment, can also be translated as 'oppression' or 'battering'. The latter ground for divorce most closely aligns with physical domestic violence. A police or medical report documenting domestic violence could be used as evidence to prove this ground of divorce. However, this ground is rarely relied upon by women seeking divorce. Nearly all petitions for divorce are based broadly on 'irreconcilable differences' (Article 116(6) of the *Compilation of Islamic Law*), often as a euphemism for domestic violence.

In her 2018 study, Afrianty identified a number of reasons underlying women's divorce applications, including physical violence, verbal abuse, economic abandonment, and illegal polygamy. Despite this, she found that Islamic Courts tended not to engage with 'the criminal aspects of the case, even when it is clear that the reasons cited for divorce are physical and psychological violence'. This is due to the fact the judges presiding in the Islamic Courts do not have jurisdiction to consider State criminal law matters and therefore cannot directly apply the provisions of the Anti-Domestic Violence Law. Jurisdiction over State criminal law can be distinguished here from the Acehnese *Mahkamah Syariah*'s jurisdiction over Islamic criminal law (*Qanun Jinayat*). According to *Komnas Perempuan* (2015), the jurisdictional duality between the criminal and religious courts creates a culture of impunity for domestic violence perpetration. In Chapter 5, it is argued that Islamic Court judges do in fact have responsibilities to victims of domestic violence *within* the religious jurisdiction.

In terms of the relationship between the religious and criminal jurisdictions, whether a woman is divorced (or wishes to be divorced) can affect her decision to report to the police as well as affecting police responses to reports of violence. Further, as will be shown in Chapter 7, a victim's marital status can affect sentencing.

Integrated Service Centre for the Empowerment of Women and Children (P2TP2A)

P2TP2A is the primary organisation tasked with responsibility for implementing national and local regulations on the protection of women and children, including coordinating State responses to domestic violence. In practice, these integrated service centres conduct programmes ranging from legal aid and paralegal assistance to educational and economic empowerment programmes. There are P2TP2As in every province in Indonesia. However, the number of integrated service centres has been described by Puspawati et al. (2023) in their study of domestic violence in Indonesia as inadequate for the number of cases that must be handled by these services. In Aceh, the first P2TP2A unit was established in 2003 and there are now more than 20 centres across the province.

A number of studies have analysed the capacity and limitations of P2TP2A across Indonesia. Scholars – such as Rasyidah et al. (2011) and Agustin et al. (2019) – have noted that there remains a lack of coordination between P2TP2A and other government departments as well as limited integration between P2TP2A and the local community. The latter issue has led to a lack of community awareness about P2TP2A's activities and, relatedly, a lack of access to P2TP2A's services. A recent UNDP (2023) study concluded that many victims were not aware of P2TP2A's services or did not know how to access the services. The study also emphasised that as domestic violence service provision was not linear – even if victims contacted services, it is critical for the response from P2TP2A service providers to be continuous and engaged.

P2TP2A also faces many structural/institutional barriers to improving services such as limited infrastructure and funding. The management of P2TP2A (Banda Aceh) interviewed were well aware of these limitations. Despite these operational constraints, efforts to socialise the Law and empower women to seek help or report violence have resulted in an increase in reporting over time:

> Every year the number of domestic violence cases increases. In my opinion, this is because we have often carried out socialisation, perhaps women who have experienced domestic violence now dare to report ... the community understands that domestic violence can be reported to the police and that it violates the law.[17]

The interviewee is speaking here of P2TP2A, women's NGOs, and police efforts to educate the community about the Law. In addition to socialisation efforts, in interviews, P2TP2A staff explained their role in domestic violence cases predominately as information providers. P2TP2A staff provide victims information about the different avenues that victims may take but do not encourage them to take any particular avenue. This approach acknowledges that victims consider varying and complex factors when decision-making, as outlined in Chapter 4. As shown in Figure 3.3, these avenues include mediation at the village level; mediation at P2TP2A; counselling at P2TP2A; seeking a divorce at the Islamic Courts; and reporting to the police.

Figure 3.3 should not be read as implying that help-seeking is linear in any way. Victims of domestic violence may seek help from one or more avenues,

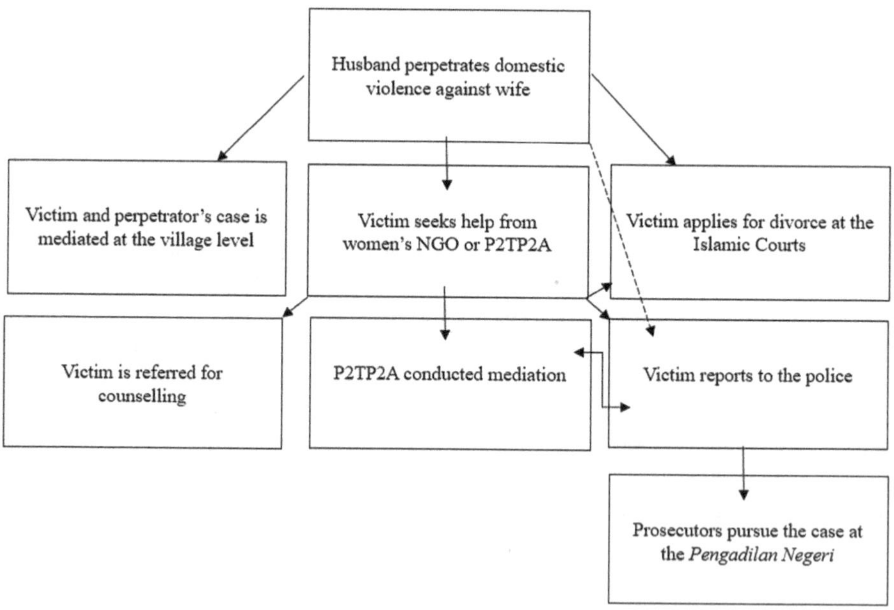

Figure 3.3 Overview of victim options when navigating the system.

Source: Author's own.

then withdraw from help-seeking – they may or may not seek help again in the future from the one or more avenues. In providing information to victims on the available avenues, P2TP2A staff give the victim an overview of relevant legal processes, including the likely cost and time burdens, as well as potential barriers that may be faced (for example, the requirement to obtain evidence if reporting via the criminal avenue). While P2TP2A may accompany or otherwise assist victims in seeking a divorce or making a police report, the primary in-house service provided by P2TP2A is mediation.

P2TP2A commonly facilitates mediation in coordination with family or *adat* and religious leaders. In such cases, P2TP2A facilitate the victim and perpetrator to produce a 'settlement letter' (*surat perdamaian*). According to the head of the Women's and Children's Protection Unit (Ibu E), while settlement letters are open to negotiation between the parties, many women ask for the husband to promise not to use physical, sexual, or psychological violence again and/or to financially support the household (i.e. promise not to commit economic violence). Even if the husband is not able to pay the full *nakfah* (spousal maintenance), including arrears, a compromise may be reached. It is also common during mediation for the victim to 'forgive' the perpetrator in order to 're-harmonise the household'. The exact content of P2TP2A mediations are confidential and fall outside the scope of this study, however, P2TP2A management indicated in interviews that each mediation was unique to, and guided by, the victims' preferences.

As P2TP2A mediation is not compulsory, the presence of choice, in theory, empowers the victim to navigate the system in a way that best serves her interests. The option of P2TP2A-facilitated mediation in domestic violence contexts may open an avenue for victims who do not wish to pursue avenues of assistance that are solely law-based (or may be accessed in addition to formal legal avenues). The option of a non-punitive avenue may meet some victim's needs, including women who do not wish to separate from their husband but want violence to end or women who want their husbands to be held accountable for violence but do not want him to be incarcerated (due to, for example, stigma or financial dependence).

On the other hand, there is a risk that mediation (that is conducted by staff who are not properly trained) may lead to a renewed cycle of abuse. A major concern is that if domestic violence victims are not sufficiently supported during mediation, mediation efforts will be undermined by 'power imbalances and dynamics of control which characterise many domestic violence relationships'.[18] It is well-documented that abusers often try to rationalise, minimise, deny, or trivialise their violence, so women's safety might be compromised if proper safeguards are not in place. Scholar Stubbs (2002) outlines how:

> A close encounter with the offender and the offender's supporters may hold little appeal for victims of domestic violence and may signal an opportunity for further abuse, especially emotional abuse. The risk of trauma may be compounded when victims participate [in mediation]

> from a sense of obligation or guilt. Offenders may exercise considerable control over victims who are intimates and victims often have learned to accommodate the interests of the offender as a survival strategy, or through fear of further violence.

Although P2TP2A staff members who facilitate mediation receive gender-sensitivity training, the involvement of family or *adat* and religious leaders in mediation can lead to a repetition of the stigmatisation that women face during village mediation (discussed in Chapter 4). P2TP2A practices, at best, have the potential to empower of victims by acting to equalise power between the parties. At worst, poorly implemented or monitored mediation practices may implicitly reiterate or perpetuate narratives of reciprocity, minimisation, or justification of violence (discussed further in Chapter 6).

Lastly, P2TP2A (Banda Aceh) works closely with local women's NGOs, the latter of which have played an important role historically and continue to lead women's advocacy efforts from the grassroots. Women's NGOs in Indonesia pioneered service provision for domestic violence victims and advocated for the national and local governments to enact the Anti-Domestic Violence Law. For example, Flower Aceh in Aceh and Rifka Annisa in Yogyakarta have a long history of providing services for victims of domestic violence. Although the role of women's NGOs is outside of the scope of this study, their critical contributions have been detailed in the other scholarly works including Eddyono et al. (2016) and Afrianty (2018).

Non-state avenues

The majority of domestic violence cases are resolved via non-State avenues, particularly *adat* dispute resolution at the village level. The popularity of *adat* justice is due, in part, to a cultural preference of harmonious dispute resolution, compounded by the multiple barriers to access to justice that deter or prevent women from engaging with the State system. *Adat* justice is based on community understandings, which may not be consistent with the Law or advance the achievement of women's rights. Community understandings can also be conceptualised as 'popular legal consciousness'. Silbey (2008) defines 'legal consciousness' as 'a reciprocal process in which the meanings given by individuals to their world become patterned, stabilized, and objectified'. However, due to poor socialisation of the Law, community understandings are not necessarily informed by the Law at all.

There is a wealth of existing literature on *adat* justice. In general, *adat* avenues are regarded as faster than State litigation pathways, with more immediate outcomes, flexibility, and affordability. Individuals may prefer to engage with *adat* avenues because these are more familiar, trustworthy, and less disruptive to social relations. Moreover, individuals may not practically have the option to engage with State systems, which may be inaccessible for people living in regional areas due to cost and distance. While State processes are more standardised, *adat* processes are highly contextual and differ from region to region (and even from village to village). This means that *adat* justice processes are often idiosyncratic and not transparent to outsiders. As the next section describes the *adat* processes documented during fieldwork in Banda Aceh the processes and terminology are specific to the case study context and are subject to change and nuance depending on the particular village in question.

At the village level in Aceh, domestic violence cases are generally reported to the wife of the *Geuchik* (village head), the wife of the *imam* (religious leader), the wife of a village elder or a female elder, who may, in turn, refer the case on to their husbands or up the (predominately male) chain of command. An interview with an Ibu *Geuchik* (wife of the head of the village) during fieldwork highlighted power imbalances within *adat* justice – this is supported by Graydon's (2016) study. Although women are involved in *adat* mediation processes, women's perspectives are often sidelined in village level decision-making. Further, the Ibu *Geuchik* stated that the village-level approach to domestic violence cases is generally non-interventionist.

Due to the fact that there is little oversight or accountability in *adat* justice structures, the outcome in any one case greatly depends on the approach of the village head which, in the words of a P2TP2A staff member (Ibu S), is 'sometimes fair, sometimes unfair'. For example, in a case studied in Chapter 7, the victim gave evidence that when domestic violence was reported to the head of the village, the *Geuchik* told the victim to reconcile with her husband and no longer 'make a fuss' (*tidak ribut-ribut lagi*).

Although there is a great degree of autonomy for individual *Geuchiks*, official guidelines on *adat* justice do exist. In Aceh, the Guidelines on *Adat* Justice state that in domestic violence cases, disputes should be mediated and that the consensus should be 'documented in a letter of agreement, highlighting the perpetrator's vow never to commit violent acts again'. If this agreement is breached the case should be referred to the police. As the primary objective of *adat* justice is to maintain social balance and harmony, the proceedings aim first and foremost to reconcile the parties. Further, the remedies available through *adat* justice are limited to advice, apology, or compensation. Ibu I (NGO worker) confirmed that:

> If there is domestic violence which *tidak berdarah-darah* (does not draw blood) that can be resolved at the village level. If it is not able to be resolved in the village, we can report it to the police or P2TP2A.

Tidak berdarah-darah is an expression which assesses seriousness. It literally means 'there is no bleeding' but the meaning is closer to 'if it is not serious', where 'seriousness' has an implied element of physicality.

An official from P2TP2A (Ibu R) elaborated:

> For the handling of domestic violence cases, we are currently improving the village infrastructure because usually under *Qanun* 9/2008 domestic

> violence cases are handled at the village level. Domestic violence is normal and a shame … We find in the villages often, because they consider domestic violence like that, peace is made [between the victim and perpetrator] but this also means that there is a great potential for violence to occur again.

In addition, the head of the Women's and Children's Protection Unit (Ibu E) highlighted that sometimes women do not want to engage in village mediation due to the perception that is 'does not guarantee justice' and because there is a risk of 'retaliation against the victim', especially if the perpetrator is related to the Head of the Village. This is consistent with the findings of Lestarini et al.'s (2021) study of *adat* approaches to domestic violence in West Sumatra which found that customary mediation prioritises harmony over safety, does not guarantee justice for the victim, and results in impunity for perpetrators.

Further, while the *adat* guidelines and *Qanun* mentioned above are specific to Aceh, the concerns raised by interviewees are consistent with research conducted by Syukur and Bagshaw (2013) in their research on *adat* mediation processes in Indonesia:

> It is questionable that the current models of community-based mediation [*adat*] available to separating couples in Indonesia can address the issue of domestic violence because they offer little opportunity for women – who comprise the majority of victims of domestic violence – to convey their interests or represent themselves. Traditional community-based mediation in Indonesia commonly focuses on reconciliation and is predominantly patriarchal and therefore tends to marginalize or subordinate women in the process of decision making. It may not be appropriate to try to reconcile couples where the violence is not acknowledged by the perpetrator and the victim continues to be fearful and intimidated, as domestic violence is a crime and continuing in the relationship would put the victim(s) in danger of further abuse.

Women may engage with *adat* mediation out of choice or necessity, for example due to insurmountable barriers to access to State systems. *Adat* justice exists as one of three alternative avenues for domestic violence victims. In raising these issues with *adat* justice, I do not seek to imply that *adat* avenues should necessarily be marginalised in favour of State systems. Rather, I argue that victims of domestic violence should not be forced to engage in village-level mediation if they do not wish to do so. Currently, women may, in practice, be barred from pursuing justice via State systems due to mediation at the village level being perceived as being compulsory. In a practical sense, engagement with *adat* justice is socially 'compulsory' due to community pressure. In that, if 'customary village mechanisms to resolve domestic violence disputes are bypassed, the victim may risk alienation from her community'.[19]

Specifically in the case study context, there is also an element of legal uncertainty regarding the scope of *Qanun* 9/2008 – which regulates the relationship between *adat* justice and the State system in Aceh. As discussed in Chapter 6, there are reports of police officers turning away women who wish to report domestic violence because they have not yet had their case mediated at the village level. Mediation at the village level is grounded in Article 13(3) of *Qanun* 9/2008, which states that *adat* leaders must have the opportunity to settle disputes at the village level.[20] Some people interpret this provision as meaning that village level mediation is a compulsory condition to be satisfied before accessing the criminal law system. However, this is a misunderstanding of the *Qanun* and potentially undermines State mechanisms for protection of domestic violence victims.

Although Article 13 of *Qanun* 9/2008 specifies that customary disputes include domestic disputes and disputes relating to families, this is a grey area because the jurisdiction of *adat* justice is limited to disputes in the household that are 'minor' or 'petty' in nature.[21] The Guidelines on *Adat* Justice in Aceh acknowledge that:

> the determination of jurisdiction in practice can become very complex as petty cases escalate into more serious crimes … Cases are referred to the police when the safety of any party is threatened – particularly common in cases of violence, and in cases involving vulnerable populations such as women or children.

Moreover, the Guidelines specifically state that *only* domestic violence that is non-physical in nature may be resolved at the village level, and then only if the relevant leaders are able to provide 'effective guarantees of protection' for the victim and if the victim prefers *adat* resolution. One of the principles underpinning *adat* justice in Aceh is voluntarism. Under the Guidelines, cases must be referred to the criminal justice system if parties refuse to settle their case through *adat* mechanisms. However, as flagged above, these guidelines are not followed in practice and many domestic violence victims are required to participate in *adat* dispute resolution due to a misinterpretation, or exaggeration, of *adat* jurisdiction.

It should be noted that the new Anti-Sexual Violence Law also impacts *adat* jurisdiction. Article 23 of the Anti-Sexual Violence Law clarifies that cases involving sexual violence cannot be resolved via restorative justice or alternative dispute resolution pathways – which includes *adat* mediation. Further, while each province in Indonesia has their own local laws regulating the relationship between *adat* and State law, it is likely that community preferences for *adat* mediation across Indonesia impact victim agency in choosing whether to engage with *adat* justice avenues when help-seeking.

Data on domestic violence

The precise incidence of domestic violence in Indonesia is not known, due to widespread under-reporting. CEDAW (2012) has identified under-reporting of domestic violence as a persistent issue of concern for Indonesia. As discussed in Chapter 4, there are a range of reasons why women choose not to report domestic violence or are unable to do so. Domestic violence data is therefore informed by the 'iceberg principle', that is, any statistic relating to reported cases of domestic violence is only the tip of the iceberg in terms of the actual violence experienced by women. Despite the majority of cases remaining unreported, statistics on domestic violence have utility in that they broadly reflect the scale of the issue.

At the time of writing, the most recent statistics regarding violence against women at the national level are available via the Online Information System for the Protection of Women and Children (SIMFONI-PPA). This data is collected by various organisations including P2TP2A, law enforcement officials and NGOs. In 2024, there were 12,244 instances of violence against women recorded nationally in SIMFONI-PPA. Over 90% of the perpetrators identified were male, and approximately half of these perpetrators were the husbands of the victims. The majority of reports related to physical violence, followed by psychological violence, sexual violence, and neglect. While these statistics relate to violence against women in general, domestic violence constituted the majority of reported cases.

The levels of domestic violence reported across Indonesia's provinces varies widely depending on the data collection method and time at which the data was collected (in particular due to difficulties collecting data during COVID19). Higher reporting rates in some provinces are much more likely to be due to greater socialisation of the law and better data collection methods, rather than higher levels of domestic violence in real terms. In the case study context of Aceh statistics can be accessed via *Jaringan Pemantau Aceh* (Aceh Monitoring Network – JPA). The domestic violence cases from the *Pengadilan Negeri* Banda Aceh studied in Chapter 7 were decided between 2013 and 2017. There are two JPA reports that relate to this period of time.[22] The JPA data will be briefly outlined below to provide context to the case study analysis in Chapter 7.

The JPA dataset provides statistics for Aceh province, including the capital, Banda Aceh, and regional areas. According to JPA, the highest number of domestic violence cases in the province were reported in Banda Aceh. This is likely due to greater responsiveness of service providers, better socialisation of the Law and higher community awareness compared to other areas, as opposed to a higher rate of domestic violence in real terms. In the 2013–2014 report, 356 cases of domestic violence were reported in Aceh Province and 478 cases were reported in 2015–2016. There were 1,144 instances of violence reported in 2013–2014 and 1,179 instances from 2015 to 2016. Data collected reflects the fact that domestic violence victims usually experience more than one form of violence simultaneously. This means that one case may be constituted by multiple instances of violence.

Most reported instances were of psychological violence (40% in 2013–2014 and 50% in 2015–2016). Reported psychological violence included verbal abuse, insults, threats, humiliation, lying, accusing the victim of having an affair, threatening divorce, or separating the victim from their child/ren. The reported instances of psychological violence are statistically higher than other forms of violence as psychological violence almost always occurs alongside, precedes, or follows physical, economic, and sexual violence.

Although reported instances of psychological violence are high, cases reported on the basis of psychological violence alone are rare. It is uncommon for a case to be reported without involving physical violence and most cases revolve around at least one instance of physical violence. The second highest number of reported instances involved physical violence (approximately 30% of reported instances in both 2013–2014 and 2015–2016). Reported physical violence included punching, slapping, kicking, chocking, smothering, throwing, stabbing, burning, and drowning. Victims generally initially report physical violence and when a victim seeks help frontline domestic violence workers will assist the victim to complete the report and, in doing so, often identify other instances/types of violence within the case, such as psychological violence.

The third highest reported type of violence was economic (approximately 22% in 2013–2014 and 10% in 2015–2016), which included neglect, being expelled from the home, being excluded from inheritance, being prohibited from working, excluded from control of property or having unreasonable restrictions placed on expenditures. In the period 2013–2014, 80% of economic violence reports involved household neglect (*tidak dinafkahi*) and from 2015 to 2016 it was over 90%.[23] Lastly, reported instances of sexual violence (6% in 2013–2014 and 8% in 2015–2016) included rape, sexual harassment, sexual acts the wife was not comfortable with, and forced prostitution. Cases included in the JPA statistics are not limited to victims/perpetrators in a spousal relationship, however in the vast majority of cases (approximately 85% of cases in both 2013–2014 and 2015–2016), the perpetrator was the husband and the victim the wife.

The second part of this chapter provided an overview of the different avenues through which victims may seek help, including P2TP2A and *adat* mediation, divorce via the Islamic Courts, and reporting violence to the police. While the analysis in this book focuses on the *Pengadilan Negeri* as the primary State institution responsible for implementation of the Law, I do not suggest that women should or must engage with legal avenues or the criminal justice system. As identified by Venning (2010), 'efforts to push Indonesian victims of violence to use the state criminal justice system will often not be in the survivor's perceived or real interests'. In the exercise of their agency, victims of domestic violence may choose to seek support from NGOs, mediate their dispute through *adat* avenues or P2TP2A, reconcile with or divorce their husbands instead of (or in addition to) reporting domestic violence the police. However, an assumption underlying this analysis is that all three avenues should be available to women so that their agency can be more fully and genuinely exercised. Where there are substantial barriers to engaging in the criminal justice system, making prosecution an untenable or unattractive option, this operates to limit women's options (similarly victims should not be forced to participate in *adat* mediation if they do not wish to). This book's focus on criminal justice therefore does not seek to imply that it is the only or best avenue of redress for victims of domestic violence, but that it is one of three interrelated avenues that should be available to victims if or when they choose to engage seek help.

Notes

1 *Adat ngon hukom lagee zat ngon siefeut* (Acehnese); *Adat dengan hukum seperti zat dengan sifat* (Indonesian translation); *Ethnic customs or practices and (religious) law are inseparable or intrinsically interrelated like a substance and its properties* (English translation). Further, Alfitri (2020) notes in her study of domestic violence that despite the diversity of *adat*, patriarchal culture prevails in most ethnic groups in Indonesia.

2 Abu-Lughod (2015) argues it is 'strategically dangerous to accept this cultural opposition between Islam and the West, between fundamentalism and feminism. This is because there are many people within Muslim countries who are trying to find alternatives to present injustices … who do not accept that being feminist means being Western, and who will be under pressure, as we are, to choose: Are you with us or against us?'.

3 Noting that the term 'equality' should not be interpreted to necessarily imply 'sameness' between men and women: see Merry (2006).

4 Note that although the concept of *kodrat* is not unique to Indonesian or Islamic contexts, the analysis in this book is limited to understandings within Indonesian Islamic teachings.

5 See also Article 79 (1) of the *Compilation of Islamic Law*. Alfitri (2020) argues that these provisions discriminate against women in contravention of CEDAW.

6 Figure 3.2 also outlines the relationship between non-State (customary) marriages and divorces and the Islamic Courts, which is discussed in Chapter 5.

7 The Indonesian legal principle of *lex specialis derogat lex generalis* means that 'if two inconsistent laws apply to the case at hand, the more specific of the two overrules the law of more general application': Butt and Lindsey (2018).

8 The *Pancasila* is the preamble to the *Undang-Undang Dasar Negara Republik Indonesia Tahun 1945* (Basic Law of the Republic of Indonesia Year 1945 – the 1945 Constitution), see limbs 2 and 5. Also see MPR Decision II/MPR/1978 concerning the Guide to Living and Practising Pancasila and Articles 28A, 28B, 28D(1) and (2), 28E, 28F, 28G, 28H, 28I, 28J and, 29 of the 1945 Constitution.

9 Implementing regulations at the provincial level vary widely across Indonesia. For example, in their study of access to justice for domestic violence victims, Sukendar et al. (2023) found that the Central Java Government has enacted at least 10 implementing regulations in relation to the Anti-Domestic Violence Law. However, such a level of political will has not been equally replicated across the country at the provincial level.

10 The Criminal Code will be referred to throughout as either the 'former Criminal Code' based on Law No. 27/1999 or the 'new Criminal Code' based on Law No. 1/2023 depending on which version of the Criminal Code is being referred to. If the provisions of the original and amended versions are the same, the act will simply be referred to as the Criminal Code without differentiation.

11 For a more detailed analysis of the drafting process for the Anti-Domestic Violence Bill see Shahirah Mahmood's (2018) study of gender-based violence and law in Indonesia.

12 Instances of illegal polygamy being treated as domestic violence are documented in the JPA *Annual Reports* and in the data provided to the author by P2TP2A (Banda Aceh).

13 See Law No. 11/2006 (Law on Governing Aceh), which followed Law No. 44/1999 on the Implementation of Aceh's Special Status and Law No. 18/2001 on the Special Autonomy of Aceh.
14 Article 7 of Law No. 12/2011 on Law Making. For more information see 'Table 2: Hierarchy of Law in Indonesia' in Suyatna et al.'s (2021) article.
15 The explanation to Article 39(2) of the Marriage Law outlines the reasons for divorce. Article 116 is the relevant equivalent in the *Compilation of Islamic Law* which is used for Islamic marriages.
16 Article 39(2) of the Marriage Law and Article 116 of the *Compilation of Islamic Law*.
17 Interview with the head of the Women's and Children's Protection Unit (Ibu E).
18 Hargovan (2005). See also on this point Hayden (2016).
19 Venning (2010).
20 Article 13(3) of *Qanun* 9/2008: '*Aparat penegak hukum memberikan kesempatan agar sengketa/perselisihan diselesaikan terlebih dahulu secara adat di Gampong atau nama lain.*' Confirmed in Interviews with Ibu I (NGO worker) and Ibu R (P2TP2A/*Balai Syura*).
21 *Keputusan Bersama Gubernur Aceh, Kepala Polisian Daerah Aceh dan Ketua Majelis Adat Aceh*, No. 189/677/2011 regarding *Adat* Justice in Aceh (Memorandum of Understanding between the Governor of Aceh, the Acehnese *Adat* Assembly, and the Police), [1]: 'Disputes that occur at the village level that are of a minor/petty nature (*bersifat ringan*), as referred to in Articles 13–15 of Aceh *Qanun* No. 9/2008 regarding customary law, must be resolved first through the *adat* law systems'.
22 JPA Annual Reports 2013–2014 and 2015–2016. At the time fieldwork was conducted, the 2017–2018 JPA Annual Report was not yet available. At the time of writing, the 2017-2018 was not accessible.
23 Note: '*tidak dinafkahi*' is a phrase that generally means husbands not providing spousal maintenance.

Bibliography

Abu-Lughod, Lila, *Do Muslim Women Need Saving?* (Harvard University Press, 2015).

Acehnese Adat Assembly (Majelis Adat Aceh), *Guidelines on Adat Justice in Aceh: For Adat Justice that is Fair and Accountable* (MAA and UNDP, 2008).

Afrianty, Dina, *Women and Sharia Law in Northern Indonesia: Local Women's NGOs and the Reform of Islamic Law in Aceh* (Routledge, 2015).

Afrianty, Dina, 'Agents for Change: Local Women's Organizations and Domestic Violence in Indonesia' (2018) 174 *Bijdragen tot de Taal-, Landen Volkenkunde* 24–46.

Afrianty, Dina, 'Rising Public Piety and the Status of Women in Indonesia Two Decades After Reformasi' (2020) 8(1) *TRaNS* 65–80.

Aftab, Amira, Balawyn Jones and Ghena Krayem, 'The Contribution of Muslim Women Australia in the Domestic and Family Violence Space: Victim-Survivor Perspectives from the COVID-19 Pandemic' (2024) 15(7) *Religions* 772–784.

Agustin, Retno, Indriyati Suparno, Samsidar and Bella Sandiata, 'Keterpaduan Layanan yang Memberdayakan: Hasil Asesmen P2TP2A di 16 Provinsi' (2019) 24(1) *Jurnal Perempuan* 53–65.

Ahmed, Leila, *Women and Gender in Islam: Historical Roots of a Modern Debate* (Yale University Press, 1992).

Aisyah, Siti and Lyn Parker, 'Problematic Conjugations: Women's Agency, Marriage and Domestic Violence in Indonesia' (2014) 38(2) *Asian Studies Review* 205–223.

Alfitri, 'Protecting Women from Domestic Violence: Islam, Family Law, and the State in Indonesia' (2020) 27(2) *Studia Islamika* 273–307.

Atmasasmita, Romli, 'Reformative or Retributive: A Preliminary Study of the 'Pemasyarakatan' System' (Paper presented at *International Trends in Crime: East Meets West, Australian Institute of Criminology Conference*, 10–13 December 1990).

Bennett, Linda, Sari Andajani-Sutjahjo and Nurul Idrus, 'Domestic Violence in Nusa Tenggara Barat, Indonesia: Married Women's Definitions and Experiences of Violence in the Home' (2011) 12(2) *The Asia Pacific Journal of Anthropology* 146–163.

Blackburn, Susan, *Women and the State in Modern Indonesia* (Cambridge University Press, 2004).

Blackwood, Evelyn, 'Gender Transgression in Colonial and Postcolonial Indonesia' (2005) 64(4) *Journal of Asian Studies* 849–879.

Bowen, John, *Islam, Law, and Equality in Indonesia: An Anthropology of Public Reasoning* (Cambridge University Press, 2003).

Bradley, Harriett, *Gender* (Wiley, 2007).

Butler, Judith, *Bodies that Matter: On the Discursive Limits of "Sex"* (Routledge, 1993).

Butt, Simon and Tim Lindsey, *Indonesian Law* (Oxford, 2018).

CEDAW, *Concluding Observations of the Committee on the Elimination of Discrimination against Women: Indonesia* (CEDAW/C/IDN/CO/6-7, 2012).

Crenshaw, Kimberlé, 'Mapping the Margins: Intersectionality, Identity Politics, and Violence Against Women of Color' in Martha Fineman and Rixanne Mykitiuk (eds), *The Public Nature of Private Violence* (Routledge, 1994) 93–118.

DP3AP2KB, 'Dasar Pembentukan P2TP2A [The foundation of P2TP2A]' http://dp3ap2kb.bandaacehkota.go.id/pusat-pelayanan-terpadu-pemberdayaan-perempuan-dan-anak-p2tp2a-kota-banda-aceh/

Eddyono, Sri Wiyanti, Estu Fanani, Dini Anitasari Sabaniah, Yurra Maurice, Haiziah Ghazali, Juni Warlif, Sisillia Velayati and Farha Ciciek, *When and Why the State Responds to Women's Demands: Understanding Gender Equality Policy Change in Indonesia* (UNRISD, 2016).

Eidhamar, Levi, "My Husband is My Key to Paradise'. Attitudes of Muslims in Indonesia and Norway to Spousal Roles and Wife-Beating' (2018) 29(2) *Islam and Christian-Muslims Relations* 241–264.

Geertz, Clifford, *The Interpretation of Cultures* (Basic Books, 1973).

Graycar, Regina and Jenny Morgan, *The Hidden Gender of Law* (Federation Press, 2002).

Graydon, Carolyn, *Valuing women in Timor Leste: the need to address domestic violence by reforming customary law approaches while improving state justice* (PhD thesis, The University of Melbourne, 2016).

Hargovan, Hema, 'Restorative Justice and Domestic Violence' (2005) 66(1) *Empowering Women for Gender Equity* 48–56.

Hayden, Anne, 'Reflections on Family Violence and Restorative Justice: Addressing the Critique' in Anne Hayden, Loraine Gelsthorpe and Allison Morris (eds), *A Restorative Approach to Family Violence* (Routledge, 2016) 211–220.

Hayden, Anne, Loraine Gelsthorpe and Allison Morris (eds), *A Restorative Approach to Family Violence* (Routledge, 2016).

Hester, Marianne and Nicole Westmarland, 'Domestic Violence Perpetrators' (2006) 66(1) *Criminal Justice Matters* 34–35.

Hunter, Rosemary, 'The Gendered 'Socio' of Socio-Legal Studies' in Dermot Feenan (ed), *Exploring the 'Socio' of Socio-Legal Studies* (Palgrave Macmillain, 2013).

Idrus, Nurul and Linda Bennett, 'Presumed Consent: Marital Violence in Bugis Society' in Lenore Manderson and Linda Rae Bennett (eds), *Violence Against Women in Asian Societies* (Routledge, 2003) 41–60.

Irianto, Sulistyowati and Antonius Cahyadi, *Runtuhnya Sekat Perdata Dan Pidana: Studi Peradilan Kasus Kekerasan terhadap Perempuan* (Yayasan Obor Indonesia, 2008).

Jamhuri and Rafi'ah, 'Upaya Meminimalisi Kasus KDRT di Aceh: Studi Kasus P2TP2A Provinsi Aceh' (2019) 3(1) *Jurnal Hukum Keluarga dan Hukum Islam* 89–115.

Jaringan Pemantau Aceh, *Catatan Dwi Tahunan Kekerasan Terhadap Perempuan di Aceh 2013–2014* [*Annual Report of Violence Against Women in Aceh* 2013–2014].
Jaringan Pemantau Aceh, *Laporan Catahu 2015–2016* [*Annual Report* 2015–2016].
Jaringan Pemantau Aceh, *Laporan Catahu 2017–2018* [*Annual Report* 2017–2018].
Jauhola, Majaana, 'Natural' Sex Difference? Negotiating the Meanings of Sex, Gender and *Kodrat* through Gender Equality Discourse in Aceh, Indonesia' (2012) 30 *Intersections, Gender and Sexuality in Asia and the Pacific* (online).
Katjasungkana, Nursyahbani, 'The Indonesian Family as a Contested Site of Women's Rights: Implementation of the Domestic Violence Act' in Maznah Mohamad and Saskia Wieringa (eds), *Family Ambiguity and Domestic Violence in Asia* (Sussex Academic Press 2013) 169–191.
Kelly, Liz and Nicole Westmarland, 'Naming and Defining 'domestic violence': Lessons from Research with Violent Men' (2016) 112 *Feminist Review* 113–127.
Komnas Perempuan, *Kekerasan terhadap perempuan: Negara segera putus impunitas pelaku* (Annual Report, 2015).
Komnas Perempuan, *Labirin Kekerasan Terhadap Perempuan: Dari Perkosaan Berkelompok Hingga Femisida, Alarm Bagi Negara Untuk Bertindak Tepat* (Report, 7 March 2017).
Kusujiarti, Siti, Elizabeth Miano, Annie Pryor and Breanna Ryan, 'Unveiling the Mysteries of Aceh, Indonesia: Local and Global Intersections of Women's Agency' (2015) 16(3) *Journal of International Women's Studies* 186–202.
Lacey, Nicola, 'Feminist Legal Theory and the Rights of Women' in Karen Knop (ed), *Gender and Human Rights* (Oxford University Press, 2004) 13–55.
Lestarini, Ratih, Dianwidhi Pranoto, and Tirtaweng Tirtawening, 'The Fault in Traditional and Formal Approaches to Domestic Violence: A Call for Reform in West Sumatra' (2021) 22(1) *Journal of International Women's Studies* 152–165.
Mahmood, Saba, *Politics of Piety: The Islamic Revival and the Feminist Subject* (Princeton University Press, 2012).
Mahmood, Shahirah, 'Adapting Human Rights: Gender-Based Violence and Law in Indonesia' in Mehrangiz Najafizadeh and Linda Lindsey (eds), *Women of Asia: Globalization, Development, and Gender Equity* (Taylor & Francis, 2018) 154–169.
McMaster, Ken, 'Restoring the Balance: Restorative Justice and Intimate Partner Violence' in Anne Hayden, Loraine Gelsthorpe and Allison Morris (eds), *A Restorative Approach to Family Violence* (Routledge, 2016) 93–106.
Mernissi, Fatima, *The Veil and the Male Elite: A Feminist Interpretation of Women's Rights in Islam* (Addison-Wesley, 1996).
Merry, Sally Engle, *Human Rights and Gender Violence* (University of Chicago Press, 2006).
Merry, Sally Engle, *Gender Violence: A Cultural Perspective* (Wiley-Blackwell, 2009).
Mir-Hosseini, Ziba, 'Muslim Women's Quest for Equality: Between Islamic Law and Feminism' (2006) 32(4) *Critical Inquiry* 629–645.
Mohamad, Maznah and Saskia Wieringa (eds), *Family Ambiguity and Domestic Violence in Asia: Concept, Law and Process* (Sussex Academic Press, 2013).
Najafizadeh, Mehrangiz and Linda Lindsey (eds), *Women of Asia: Globalization, Development, and Gender Equity* (Routledge, 2018).
Noer, Khaerul Umam, Siti Chadijah, Endang Rudiatin, 'There Is No Trustable Data: The State and Data Accuracy of Violence Against Women in Indonesia' (2021) 7(12) *Heliyon* (online).
Nurlaelawati, Euis, 'The Legal Fate of Indonesian Muslim Women in Court: Divorce and Child Custody' in Tim Lindsey and Helen Pausacker (eds), *Religion, Law and Intolerance in Indonesia* (Routledge, 2016) 353–368.
Nurmila, Nina, 'The Influence of Global Muslim Feminism on Indonesian Muslim Feminist Discourse' (2011) 49(1) *Al-Jami'ah* 33–64.

Nurmila, Nina, 'Polygamous Marriages in Indonesia and their Impacts on Women's Access to Income and Property' (2016) 54(2) *Al-Jāmi'ah: Journal of Islamic Studies* 427–446.

Nursiti, Eka, Kurnia Sari and Ria Fitri, *Laporan Penelitian Kajian Wanita: Implementasi Undang-Undang Nomor 23 Tahun 2004 di Kota Banda Aceh* (Fakultas Hukum Pidana Universitas Syiah Kuala, 2006).

Oey-Gardiner, Mayling, 'And the Winner Is... Indonesian Women in Public Life' in Kathryn Robinson and Sharon Bessel (eds), *Women in Indonesia: Gender, Equity and Development* (ISAS, 2002) 100–112.

P2TP2A, *Kondisi Mitra P2TP2A Pasca Terminasi: Pemetaan Awal dan Analisis Mitra* (Report, 28 December 2017a).

P2TP2A, *Kondisi Mitra P2TP2A Pasca Terminasi: Pemetaan Awal dan Analisis Mitra* [*Victim/Witness Condition P2TP2A Post Termination: Initial Mapping and Victim/Witness Analysis*] (Report, 28 December 2017b).

P2TP2A, 'Penanganan perempuan korban kekerasan di Aceh belum optimal' (3 October 2018) https://uptdppa.acehprov.go.id/berita/kategori/berita-harian/penanganan-perempuan-korban-kekerasan-di-aceh-belum-optimal

Pawestri, Tunggal and Tim Mann, 'Indonesia Finally Has a Law to Protect Victims of Sexual Violence. But the Struggle Is Not Over Yet.' (2022) *Indonesia at Melbourne* https://indonesiaatmelbourne.unimelb.edu.au/indonesia-finally-has-a-law-to-protect-victims-of-sexual-violence-but-the-struggle-is-not-over-yet/

Peletz, Michael, *Islamic Modern: Religious Courts and Cultural Politics in Malaysia* (Princeton University Press, 2002).

Puspawati, Ani Agus, Dewie Brima Atika, Rahayu Sulistiowati, Yudha Suchmasasi, and Laila Rahmawati, 'Analysis of the Implementation of Protection for Domestic Violence (KDRT) Victims in Indonesia' (Paper presented at 3rd Universitas Lampung International Conference on Social Sciences, 2 May 2023).

Rasyidah, Nurmasyithah, Ade Irma and Mira Fauziah, 'Optimizing the Function of P2TP2A in Aceh' (Symposium, 16–17 March 2011) https://perhotelan.undiksha.ac.id/wp-content/uploads/sites/88/2019/03/Symposium-Proceeding-Kementrian-Perempuan.pdf

Sadli, Saparinah, 'Feminism in Indonesia in an International Context' in Kathryn Robinson and Sharon Bessel (eds), *Women in Indonesia: Gender, Equity and Development* (ISAS, 2002) 80–91.

Saiful, Teuku, 'Gender Perspektif Dalam Formalisasi Syariat Islam di Aceh' (2016) 18(2) *Kanun Jurnal Ilmu Hukum* 235–263.

Saraswati, Rika, 'Gender Bias in Indonesian Courts: Is Perma No. 3 of 2017 the Solution for Gender-Based Violence Cases?' (2021) 10(2) *Laws* 1–16.

Scott, Joan, 'Gender: A Useful Category of Historical Analysis' (1986) 91(5) *The American Historical Review* 1053–1075.

Siapno, Jaqueline, *Gender, Islam and Nationalism and the State in Aceh: The Paradox of Power, Co-optation and Resistance* (Taylor and Francis, 2002).

Silbey, Susan, *New Oxford Companion to Law* (Oxford University Press, 2008).

SIMFONI-PPA, *(Sistem Informasi Online Perlindungan Perempuan dan Anak)* https://kekerasan.kemenpppa.go.id/register/login

Srimulyani, Eka, 'Islam, *Adat*, and the State: Matrifocality in Aceh Revisited' (2010) 48(2) *Al-Jami'ah* 321–342.

Stubbs, Julie, 'Domestic Violence and Women's Safety: Feminist Challenges to Restorative Justice' in Heather Strang and John Braithwaite (eds), *Restorative Justice and Family Violence* (Cambridge University Press, 2002) 42–61.

Sukendar, Muhammad Saifullah, Priyambudi Sulistiyanto, Luthfi Rahman and Hasan Asy'ari Ulamai, 'Women's Access to Justice: Mediation for the Victims of Domestic Violence in Central Java, Indonesia' (2023) 7(1) *Samarah: Jurnal Hukum Keluarga dan Hukum Islam* 602–628.

Suryakusuma, Julia, *State Ibuism: The Social Construction of Womanhood* (Institute of Social Studies, 1988).
Suyatna, I Nyoman, I Made Budi Arsika, Ni Gusti Ayu Dyah Satyawati, Rohaida Nordin and Balawyn Jones, 'Assessment of the Responsibility of Local Governments in Indonesia for the Management of Refugee Care' (2021) *Asian Journal of Law and Society* 1–23.
Syukur, Fatahillah Abdul and Dale Bagshaw, 'When Home Is No Longer "sweet": Family Violence and Sharia-Annexed Mediation in Indonesia' (2013) 30(3) *Conflict Resolution Quarterly* 271–294.
Triana, Nita, 'Progressivity of Judges in Domestic Violence Disputes Settlement in the Case of Divorce in the Religious Court' (2018) 2(1) *Jurnal Studi dan Penelitian Hukum Islam* 1–29.
UNDP, *Applying Behavioural Insights to Gender Justice in Indonesia* (Report, 2023).
Venning, Philippa, 'Marrying Contested Approaches: Empowerment and the Imposition of International Principles: Domestic Violence Case Resolution in Indonesia' (2010) 46(3) *The Journal of Development Studies* 396–416.
Wadud, Amina, *Inside the Gender Jihad: Women's Reform in Islam* (Oneworld Publications, 2006).
Wieringa, Saskia, 'Islamization in Indonesia: Women Activists' Discourses' (2006) 32(1) *Signs: Journal of Women in Cultural and Society* 1–8.
Wieringa, Saskia, 'Gender Harmony and the Happy Family: Islam, Gender and Sexuality in Post-Reformasi Indonesia' (2015) 23(1) *South East Asia Research* 27–44.
World Bank, *Village Justice in Indonesia: Case Studies on Access to Justice, Village Democracy and Governance* (Report, February 2004).
Yusdar, Yusdar, Amirullah Amirullah, Ruslan Ruslan, 'Efektivitas Pendampingan Penanganan Kasus KDRT oleh P2TP2A Kota Banda Aceh' (2020) 8(2) *Jurnal Pendidikan Kewarganegaraan Undiksha* 83–90.

Laws and regulations cited in Chapter 3

Law No. 23/ 2004 regarding the Elimination of Domestic Violence (*Undang-Undang tentang Penghapusan Kekerasan Dalam Rumah Tangga*).
Law No. 1/1974 Marriage Law.
Law No. 7/1984 regarding the Ratification of Convention on Elimination of All Forms of Discrimination against Women.
Law No. 39/1999 regarding Human Rights.
Law No. 44/1999 on the Implementation of Aceh's Special Status.
Law No. 18/2001 on the Special Autonomy of Aceh.
Law No. 11/2006 (Law on Governing Aceh).
Law No. 12/2022 regarding Sexual Violence.
Law No. 27/1999 (Former) Criminal Code (*Kitab Undang-Undang Hukum Pidana - KUHP*).
Law No. 1/2023 (New) Criminal Code (*Kitab Undang-Undang Hukum Pidana - KUHP*).
Qanun 9/2008 *Adat dan Istiadat* (Customs and Ceremonies).

Interviews cited in Chapter 3

Interview with Ibu A (Head of P2TP2A) (Banda Aceh, 3 October 2018).
Interview with Ibu I (NGO worker) (Banda Aceh, 19 December 2017).
Interview with Ibu N (academic and Ibu *Geuchik*) (Banda Aceh, 15 December 2017).

Interview with Ibu R (P2TP2A/*Balai Syura*) (Banda Aceh, 19 December 2017).
Interview with Ibu S (P2TP2A) (Banda Aceh, 21 December 2017).
Interview with Ibu I (head of the Women's and Children's Protection Unit) (Banda Aceh, 24 September 2018).
Interviews with P2TP2A management (Banda Aceh, 21 December 2017 and 17 January 2018).

4 Community Understandings, Victim Agency and Help-Seeking

Prologue to this chapter

January 2019, in the village

The *Geuchik* (Head of the Village) sits across from Ibu Hayati furrowing his brow.

'It keeps getting worse', she says, 'I don't know what to do.'

Bapak *Geuchik* shrugs. 'It's normal for couples to *cek-cok* (disagree) sometimes', he replies.

'It's not just disagreement though Bapak … I don't feel safe at home anymore and I am worried about the children.'

'You *should* think of your children', the *Geuchik* responds, 'they need a father to provide for them.'

July 2019, at P2TP2A's office

Ibu Hayati hands the forms back to the P2TP2A secretary.

'Do you have anyone that you can stay with?', the secretary asks while looking over the forms.

'No, my mother and father live in a different province', Ibu Hayati replies. 'The *Geuchik* said that he can ask my husband to move out of the house so that my children and I can stay in the *kampung* (village), but I am worried that my husband will not listen.'

The secretary nods, 'It is probably best not to stay there if you think your husband might react badly to the divorce application.'

'He threatened to take the children if I file for divorce, I don't know what to do.'

'I understand, it's hard. But you have rights and it's not okay for him to treat you like this – you have to be strong Ibu.'

(Source for the above: Author's own)

DOI: 10.4324/9781032613642-4

Introduction

This chapter outlines the main barriers faced by victims attempting to seek help at the village level via *adat* (customary) law avenues focusing on community understandings of gender and domestic violence informed by religious interpretations. This chapter concludes that domestic violence tends to be ignored, minimised, or justified by reference to patriarchal interpretations of religious doctrines, in particular based on *Surat An-Nisa* (verse 4:34) of the *Quran*. Against this background, the chapter then highlights victim perspectives, focusing on the factors that influence victim help-seeking. For example, how women make decisions about if, and how, to file for divorce or report domestic violence. The fieldwork data reveals how in some cases victims do not perceive it to be possible, preferable, or tenable to 'leave' domestic violence relationships, which challenges mainstream narratives in the domestic violence space that categorise help as contingent on victims leaving violent relationships.

The analysis in this chapter is based on 30 interviews conducted with victims (Table 4.1) and community and justice system stakeholders, including local women's advocates, academics, and staff from frontline women's services.

The majority of domestic violence cases in Indonesia are resolved via informal community dispute resolution or *adat* justice. Disputes resolved at the village level are dealt with by reference to community understandings, which are not necessarily consistent with the Law. Regardless of formal procedures or laws, in practice, when women identify themselves as victims of domestic violence, either by informally seeking help or formally reporting, they are subject to a political process of victimhood recognition and, relatedly, eligibility for care. To understand how key institutional stakeholders – police, prosecutors, and judges – understand their duties and responsibilities under the Law (Chapters 5–7), it is essential to first understand community conceptualisations of domestic violence. In saying this, many institutional stakeholders interviewed, such as lawyers and government officials, have nuanced understandings of the Law that are distinct from broader community understandings. As mentioned in Chapter 3, while socialisation efforts have been undertaken by the State and women's NGOs, many people still do not understand the Law or the dynamics of domestic violence.

In the first part of this chapter, I analyse community understandings of domestic violence. First, I consider how 'violence' and 'victimhood' are understood and how gender norms affect the process of victimhood recognition at the village level. The definition of violence is analysed in three parts: violence ignored, violence minimised, and violence justified. Further, I argue that a victim of domestic violence is only likely to be recognised and receive care if she is perceived to conform with locally specific gender norms. If a woman is perceived to have transgressed these norms, violence will likely be justified or excused. The recognition of victimhood directly informs the provision of care. If violence is not recognised (ignored, minimised, or justified), then victimhood is not recognised and the victim will likely not receive care.

Table 4.1 Victim survey data

Interviewee	*When did you first experience DV?*	*When did you first seek help?*	*Who did you first seek help from?*	*When did you next seek help?*	*Who did you next seek help from?*	*When did you next seek help from?*	*Who did you next seek help from?*	*How was your case finalised?*
Ibu Dewi	09/2018	09/2018	*Geuchik*	10/2018	Police	10/2018	P2TP2A/ Islamic Court	Divorce
Ibu Rumi	2013	03/2016	*Geuchik*	05/2016	P2TP2A	10/2016	Islamic Court	Divorce
Ibu Yati	2006	2014	Friends	03/2018	P2TP2A/*Geuchik*	11/2018	Islamic Court	Divorce (custody dispute ongoing)
Ibu Dian	2019	2019	Parents in law	2019	*Geuchik*	2019	Islamic Court	Divorce
Ibu Tia	2007	2008	Parents	2016	P2TP2A	2017	Islamic Court	Divorce
Ibu Nurul	2004	2010	Parents	2014	*Geuchik*	2018	Islamic Court	Divorce
Ibu Siti	2015	2018	Sibling	2018	P2TP2A/ workplace	2018	Islamic Court	Divorce
Ibu Yani	2006	2006	Parents in law	–	–	–	–	Stayed in relationship

Source: Author's own.

In the second part of this chapter, I reflect on how women exercise agency in the face of victimisation and highlight how women consistently act as agents in response to victimisation.

The law stops at the door – violence ignored

In Indonesia, violence within the domestic sphere is largely regarded as a private matter. Even in the face of explicit legal recognition that violence against spouses is a criminal offence, community understandings of violence and gender inhibit the recognition of violence in the domestic context. This is because the domestic realm is implicitly and explicitly under the authority of the male head of the household. As mentioned previously, gender roles within the family are entrenched in Article 31(3) of the Marriage Law, which formally recognises husbands as the head of the household.

A Commissioner from *Komnas Perempuan* stated that the extended family will often advise victims of domestic violence to 'make peace with the perpetrator' even if the violence is very severe. She explained that this is because:

> Domestic violence is considered the private business of the family, this culture is very thick/strong. Domestic violence being seen as a private issue is not only an issue in Aceh but in many places in Indonesia.

Understandings of the household as a private sphere under the control of the male head of the household stem from entrenched patriarchal culture. Domestic violence as a private issue also relates intricately to socially constructed gender roles and the concepts of *kodrat* (God-given or essential nature). As explained in Chapter 3, common interpretations of Islam conceptualise men and women as inherently different by nature. Quoting a domestic violence victim, Ibu I (an NGO worker) said:

> He is my leader in the house, in my religion. I may not disrespect my husband. I may not go against my husband … If I am hit [by my husband], this is surely my *kodrat*.

Kodrat can also be understood, in the quote above, as 'fate'. This fatalistic attitude can be contrasted against the explanation of *kodrat* by Ibu D (NGO worker), who explained that patriarchal interpretations of the *Qur'an*:

> give rise to the idea that the position of women must be secondary to men. So, the woman's nature is only to serve men … All this time, people think that women's *kodrat* is to cook – that's not the *kodrat*, it's the gender role and the role is interchangeable.

Further, Ibu K (an academic) explained that the only difference between men and women is their biological sex. Ibu D and Ibu K distinguished between *kodrat* as biological sex (*jenis kelamin*) and gender norms (*jender*) as a construct. Their understandings are consistent with the arguments of other feminists that *kodrat* refers only to the 'actual physical differences between women and men … and not to the social construct that is built on top of them'.[1] Although there is a distinction between *kodrat*, biological sex, and gender roles maintained by feminist academics and practitioners, it is common for community members to conflate these concepts. An example of this thinking given by Ibu I (NGO worker), is that:

> Cleaning the house and doing household tasks is the *kodrat* of women … not the gender role but the *kodrat*, women *must* do these things (as it is their nature).

The fieldwork findings show that the stigmatising and silencing of victims stems from the patriarchal positioning of men as the head of the household, and the imbuing of the concept of *kodrat* with restrictive gender norms. It is against this background that victims of domestic violence are stigmatised and silenced for seeking help outside the family sphere. One of the primary barriers that deters victims of domestic violence from seeking help or reporting is stigmatisation by their own communities. However, the stigma is not necessarily for being abused – it is for speaking out about being abused or, in other words, for challenging the authority of the male head of the household. Further, according to Eddyono et al.'s (2016) study in Indonesia *keluarga sakinah* (the idea of family harmony) 'validates any man's actions as right and obliges women to not expose their husbands' mistakes to the public'.

Reflecting the positioning of men as dominant in both public and private domains, respondents consistently indicated in interviews that, because of its domestic nature, domestic violence is seen as a private issue and only the 'business' of the male head of the household. It is on this basis that violence is ignored or silenced by village leaders if victims speak out about their husbands' abuse. The implicit authority over women by the male head of the household becomes clearer when compared to other circumstances where the happenings of a household are seen as the 'business' of everyone in the community. These include vigilante attacks where local villagers forcibly enter private households to apprehend people in cases of homosexual or *pacaran* (dating) relations.[2]

Village leaders and *adat* justice stakeholders are generally the first point of contact for victims of domestic violence seeking help outside of family or friends. When violence is explicitly or implicitly silenced based on community understandings of domestic violence as a private issue, this threatens to undermine the operation of the Law by acting as a barrier to access to justice and preventing the provision of care.

'Tidak berdarah-darah' – violence minimised

As outlined in Chapter 3, the Law recognises physical, psychological, sexual, and economic violence. In practice, however, community understandings of violence as non-physical are very limited. As a result, the reporting rates for psychological and economic violence are relatively low, since reporting of domestic violence is based on community understandings. If domestic violence is recognised at all at the community level – that is, if it is not ignored as a 'private issue' between husband and wife – then generally only severe physical violence is understood as violence by community members, despite the much broader scope of the legal definition.[3]

This over-emphasis on physical violence is reflected in the way that community members conceptualise physical violence as *berat* (heavy), *besar* (big), or *parah* (severe) as opposed to non-physical violence as *kecil* (small), *tidak serius* (not serious), or *tidak berdarah-darah* (not drawing blood). This distinction reflects a limited understanding of the dynamics of domestic violence as other than physical (or even visually apparent) violence. Many community members do not understand psychological and economic violence as constituting violence. This is consistent with studies conducted across Indonesia in which most respondents understood domestic violence to mean physical violence (see, for example, Venning (2010) and Bennett et al. (2011)).

In addition to community understandings that emphasise physical violence and minimise the seriousness of other forms of violence, physical violence is normalised. Ibu R (P2TP2A) stated that 'domestic violence is assumed to be normal.' In the same sentence, Ibu R clarified that while domestic violence is an ordinary occurrence, it is also *aib*, which in this context translates as a public shame or disgrace that carries stigma. This is consistent with the study of domestic violence in Indonesia by Nilan et al. (2014), which found that most victims 'felt their experiences were just a "normal" part of married life'.

An over-emphasis on physical violence has obvious negative consequences in practice. For example, Ibu A (P2TP2A) shared an anecdote in which a victim reported domestic violence to the police in January and in March, two months later, her case was listed for its first hearing at the *Pengadilan Negeri*. When she arrived on the day the judge looked at her and said: '*Loh ibu kan sehat hari ini* (well, you look fine today)'. This reflects a limited understanding of the dynamics of domestic violence as anything other than visual, bodily violence. It also illustrates that an over-emphasis on physical violence informs stakeholder understandings at both the State and non-State level. In Abdurrachman's (2017) study of domestic violence decisions in Indonesian courts he also found that 'Law enforcers tend to categorize domestic violence based on its physical evidence, while neglecting the fact that domestic violence always causes a double impact; the physical and the psychological'.

The next section discusses what happens if a woman comes forward with an allegation of domestic violence that is recognised by community leaders as sufficiently 'serious' to warrant the provision of care. Whether the woman will be recognised as a victim usually depends on whether the use of violence is perceived to have been justified.

'Just not in the face' – violence justified

If domestic violence is not ignored, silenced, minimised, or normalised, then it may still be subject to justificatory or excusatory rhetoric. Some respondents suggested that a degree of physical violence against women is allowed in local interpretations of Islam. This notion is sometimes described as 'within the borders of acceptable notions of fairness' (*di dalam batas kewajaran*) because the male head of the household has a responsibility to educate his wife and children. This type of rhetoric links back to gender roles and constructs of masculinity, for example, the husband's role as *imam* (religious leader) of the family. The fieldwork findings documented the belief that if the male head of the household believes that his wife is not conforming with her *kodrat* (or gender role), then he may use violence to 'teach her' and enforce compliance with these norms.

Ibu R (an academic), for example, highlighted that if women complain about violence, men will often say that physical punishment is not violence, it is a 'teaching method'. These beliefs are consistent with broader research conducted in Indonesia by Nilan et al. (2014) and Eidhamar (2018). Physical violence is often justified as being 'disciplinary' or 'educative' and therefore, in some cases, not recognised by the community as violence at all. These kinds of beliefs minimise the seriousness of violence and emphasise the reciprocity of violence, essentially blaming the victim for provoking violence.

Such interpretations generally stem from *Surat An-Nisa*, verse 4:34 of the *Qur'an*. Verse 4:34 is much debated within international, Indonesian, and Acehnese Islamic communities, and interpretations vary widely between *ulama* (religious experts). What is striking about these various interpretations is their arbitrariness. Arbitrary lines are drawn by *ulama* between 'legitimate' and 'illegitimate' uses of violence, usually in relation to variations in constructed gender norms. The aim of this section is not to find the 'correct' meaning of verse 4:34. For the purposes of the analysis, Eidhamar's approach will be adopted, which states that the relevant question is 'not what the Qur'an actually says, but what Muslims say the Qur'an says.' During my fieldwork many respondents were careful to clarify that they were not criticising or blaming Islam *per se*, but patriarchal interpretations of Islam.

Verse 4:34 of the *Qur'an* relates most directly to domestic violence. Most respondents in Eidhamar's study of Indonesian Muslim attitudes towards domestic violence directly or indirectly derived norms relating to gender roles and domestic violence from interpretations of verse 4:34. The relevant verse is often translated in Indonesia as follows:

> Men are the protectors and maintainers (*qawwamun*) of women, because Allah has given the one more (strength) than the other, and because they support them from their means. Therefore, the righteous women are devoutly obedient, and guard in (the husband's) absence what Allah

> would have them guard. As to those women on whose part you fear disloyalty and ill-conduct (*nushuz*), (first) admonish them (*fa'izuhunna*), (next) refuse to share their beds (*wahjuruhunna*), and last beat them (lightly) (*wadriduhunna*) – *Al-Qur'an*.

The first word that has a significant impact on gender relations depending on its translation is *qawwamun. Qawwamun* is commonly translated as 'maintainers', 'protectors', 'guardians', or 'leaders'. For example, the translation given by the Ministry of Religious Affairs of Indonesia is 'leaders'. The implications of these interpretation of *qawwamun* range from supporting the inherent supremacy of males over females to promoting conditional responsibility for husbands to provide financial maintenance to their wives. Some scholars assert that *qawwamun* is non-gender specific and 'women can also be called *qawwamun* ... if they have the skills and resources to lead in both the public and private spheres.'[4] Other scholars adopt a contextual reading of this verse – reading it in the original social context in which the verse was revealed. For example, Rofiah (2010) explains that the *Qur'an* states that men *were qawwamun* in the context of revelation but it does not state that men *should be qawwamun* – the phrase 'men are *qawwamun*' can therefore be read as 'a contextual statement and not a normative statement.' However, in the Indonesian context, *qawwamun* is generally interpreted to mean that men are the leaders of women, and implicitly, that women are therefore men's subordinates.

Second, the word *nushuz* is commonly translated as 'disobedience', 'rebellion against (male) authority', 'marital conflict', or 'adultery'. The translation of *nushuz* is significant because it is, arguably, the only basis on which violence may be used within a marriage according to Islam. Some scholars argue that *nushuz* does not mean 'minor' annoyances but only 'serious' misbehaviour that threatens the marriage. Interviewee Bapak S (Lawyer) stated that it is not uncommon for domestic violence perpetrators to attempt to justify their violence, with reasons such as: 'My wife didn't fulfil her household obligations' or 'my wife doesn't listen to me, so it wasn't really violence because I was just teaching her a lesson'. This type of rhetoric links back to gender roles and the constructs of masculinity and femininity.

References in fieldwork data to a 'lack of obedience' (for example, wives not cooking, cleaning, or caring for the children adequately) reflect the stretching of the concept of *nushuz* to cover minor annoyances, which align with the performance of locally specific gender roles or constructs of *kodrat*. This is consistent with Nilan et al.'s (2014) study of domestic violence 'provocations' in Indonesia which included:

> coming home late, being "weak", refusing to "serve" the husband, demanding more household income, working, neglecting household duties, being accused of having an affair, being angry over a husband's infidelity, and nagging.

Further, Putra et al.'s (2019) study of domestic violence in Indonesia documented the 'wife neglecting children', 'wife going out without telling the husband', 'wife arguing with husband', and 'wife refusing to have sex with husband' as reasons that community members may justify violence.

It is common for victim-blaming to occur when women identify themselves as victims of domestic violence. Community actors may seek to undermine a woman's claim of victimhood by making allegations that the woman did not conform to her *kodrat* and is therefore a 'bad woman' who deserved to be disciplined by her husband. Stringer (2014) explains how dominant 'definitions of victims, victimhood and victimization shape social, cultural, scholarly and legal responses to victims, and can do so in ways that are profoundly harmful and inequitable, thus constituting 'secondary' victimization'. In the Indonesian context, respondents from P2TP2A explained that:

Ibu S: Usually in our culture, if we report domestic violence, it is always the woman who will be brought into issue – the woman is not good/she was cheating/didn't look after the house.

Ibu R: It's the wife who is blamed because she has to take care of her family and husband. It is public opinion that it is the obligation of women to serve their husband and care for their children ... So sometimes there is the potential to be blamed, maybe because 'you don't play your role well enough.'

In relation to victim-blaming and the justification of violence, one victim of domestic violence explained her experience of village mediation as follows:

> After seeing the *Geuchik*, *imam* and both families, they reconciled us, after he had made mistakes, I was asked to apologise [to him], he was the one who was in the wrong, but I am the one who was asked to apologise. It happened four times where both my Mother and Father came all the way from their village to my place to reconcile us, even in their presence I was asked to apologise [to my husband] that *he made those mistakes because of me*. He was the one who had an affair with another woman, I am the one who was asked to give an apology [to him], *as if it was my weakness that he had an affair with another woman*. I apologised to him and I bowed to him, the more people asked me to apologise, the more it inflated his ego, he became even more insolent (emphasis added).

Instead of supporting victims to receive care, community members often attempt to discredit victim claims along gendered lines. As in the quotation above, many victims of domestic violence interviewed reported being victim blamed and having their reports of violence dismissed by others. Such secondary victimisation can implicitly be understood as a reaction to, or backlash against, a perceived threat to hegemonic gender norms, in particular the husband's role as the head of the household.

An Acehnese religious leader (Bapak M) stated that if *nushuz* occurs, then disciplinary violence may only be used conditionally after several steps have been taken, including giving advice and sleeping in separate beds. These 'steps' identified by Bapak M correspond to translations of *fa'izuhunna* (advice or intensive discussions) and *wahjuruhunna* (refusing to talk, sleeping in separate beds, or abstinence). Most interpretations of verse 4:34 require these steps to be performed chronologically, and only to progress to the next step if the previous step fails to resolve the dispute. Physical discipline is therefore often positioned as a 'last resort'. However, it is clear that, even if violence is interpreted to be subject to limitation, religious concepts such as *nushuz* can be manipulated and used as tools by men to legitimise the use of violence.

A 'literal interpretation' of the third step, *wadribuhunna* or *daraba* (to beat, strike, hit, chastise, or scourge) would permit husbands to use limited physical punishment if their wife is *nushuz*. Common limitations on physical punishment include: not being severe or violent; not leaving any physical mark (not bruising, causing bleeding, or breaking bones); not striking the face; striking only once or striking using an instrument such as a toothbrush or handkerchief; and chastisement. Some scholars argue that *daraba* should instead be interpreted as 'making a decision to initiate divorce', 'to go away', 'morally forewarn', or 'boycott', rather than as using physical chastisement.[5] However, dominant Indonesian translations 'understand the term *daraba* as indicating some kind of physical discipline of women/wives'.[6]

For example, Acehnese religious leader (Bapak M) explained that violence is restricted to 'blows that do not cause pain, let alone injuries' and only 'in parts [of the body] that do not cause disability and injury and … not in a visible place, like the face and hands.' Another respondent, Ibu N (Ibu *Geuchik*/wife of the head of the village), stated that 'a husband can discipline his wife, but not in the face.' Ibu N distinguished this from a case of 'true' domestic violence, reported to her in her capacity as Ibu *Geuchik*, where the wife was seriously injured after being punched, kicked, and slapped in the face and body. As with the concept of *nushuz*, it can be seen how ambiguity in interpretations of verse 4:34 ultimately allow perpetrators and community members to distort religious concepts to justify or excuse domestic violence.

There is also disagreement as to whether verse 4:34 is a command, recommendation, permission, or restriction. Some reformist scholars argue that the verse can be interpreted as a 'virtual prohibition' against the use of violence.[7] Such scholars often support alternative translations using *hadith* accredited to the Prophet Muhammad, including: 'it is shameful if a husband chastises his wife' and 'the best of you are those who are best to their wives'. For example, Ibu R (P2TP2A) stated that:

> We need to firstly remind people that the Islamic tradition and teaching are never about violence, and if we really grasp the essence of Islam, we should know that Islam does not promote violence. The community believe that it is fine to beat women when they do something wrong, this

> misunderstanding strengthens the justification to beat women as 'Islam allows this'. But we need to highlight that *our Prophet taught us how to treat our wives with kindness* (emphasis added).

Further, Ibu D (NGO worker) explained that:

> Although religious leaders teach us that denying our husbands is a sin and we will go to hell ... if you see the teachings of the Prophet Muhammad, the protection of women is extraordinary, contrary to the information we receive from religious leaders in the village (who are usually from the *dayah*).

This is consistent with Afrianty's (2018) study of domestic violence in Indonesia which found that people are being taught that 'in Islam, men/husbands have the right to discipline their wives, including through the use of violence.' Further, Alfitri's (2020) study found physical violence is widely considered as a legitimate method for husbands to 'educate' wives.

In Aceh, and in Indonesia more broadly, interpretations of *Surat An-Nisa* range from uninhibited male entitlement to use violence to a blanket prohibition on the use of physical violence. While Muslim feminists and advocates for gender equality tend to promote a the 'virtual prohibition' interpretation, many religious leaders in Indonesia interpret verse 4:34 to position males as leaders (and as superior to women) in both private and public realms and permit husbands to use limited forms of violence to discipline wives who are disobedient. This means that when victims report to village leaders at the community level, many women experience secondary victimisation.

In Indonesia, domestic violence is generally understood by community stakeholders as a private issue, physical in nature, and a normal part of married life that can be justified as a form of discipline if women are perceived not to have fulfilled their *kodrat* (or gender role). If a victim seeks help from her community, she may be ignored, stigmatised, or blamed. The fieldwork data illustrates how responses to domestic violence at the community level are heavily influenced by local understandings of gender and power, especially with respect to patriarchal interpretations of verse 4:34 of the *Qur'an*. Local constructions of victimhood distinguish between so-called 'good' women who comply with their *kodrat* and 'bad' women who do not, with only the former likely to be recognised as victims. The latter, who allegedly fail to conform with their *kodrat* in some way, are likely to be blamed for provoking the harm committed against them and subjected to secondary victimisation. These limited constructions of victimhood obstruct the provision of care.

A primary barrier to access to justice for domestic violence victims in Indonesia is the gap between the legal conceptualisation of domestic violence in the Law and community understandings of domestic violence. Without proper socialisation of the Law victims are not aware of their rights, the local community does not support victims in exercising their rights and may, in many instances, actively try to deter victims from reporting domestic violence. As will be discussed in Chapters 5–7, limited community understandings of domestic violence dynamics and the Law flow through to institutional stakeholders, such as police officers and judges, who, as institutional stakeholders, are inevitably influenced by their environment.

Victim agency and help-seeking

The above analysis of community understandings of domestic violence illustrates the complex nature of victimisation, where victims may be subjected to secondary victimisation by their communities when seeking help in relation to the primary perpetration of violence. Against this background, when women self-identify as victims of domestic violence, they are implicitly challenging the status quo, including notions of the acceptability of violence, women's place in the family, and the authority of husbands to use violence. By naming the harm committed against them, women challenge the entitlement of men to use violence and, in doing so, they simultaneously transgress gender norms that expect women to be passive and submissive to men's authority.

Analyses which equate victimhood with passivity and weakness and agency with strength and courage (known as 'victim feminism') fail to recognise that the act of identifying as a victim is itself an act of agency. Critiques of victim feminism are well-established in the literature, for example works by Schneider (1993), Mahoney (1994), and Connell (1997). The findings from the fieldwork support existing work which challenges a strict dichotomy between victimisation and agency, such as Dahl's (2009) work where she argues that to 'ask for victim status is not necessarily an abdication from agency, but can itself be a form of rewarding agency.' Further, Connell conceptualises victim agency as 'any measure of resistance and self-determination to regain control in her life, and in her attempt to stop the abuse she experiences'.

Although this chapter focuses on self-identification as a victim (help-seeking and reporting) as a form of agency, this example should not necessarily be positioned, akin to leaving the relationship, as the 'ultimate' expression of agency. Women seek help for many reasons, including awareness of their legal rights, empowerment through their religion, or because of an innate sense of injustice. There are also many reasons why women choose not to identify as victims, such as fear for their safety or a lack of tangible resources to support themselves and their children. Therefore, in some circumstances, it may also be an act of agency to choose not to identify as a victim. The element of choice is key and deprivation of the choice to self-identify is itself a form of victimisation that restricts women's agency.

In recognising a more complex relationship between victimisation and agency, this analysis adopts Schneider's approach of recognising 'the systematic nature of women's subordination and women's active efforts to resist such subordination'. Agency must be viewed within the frame of victimisation and vice versa, where a woman's choices may practically be constrained by oppressive structures. The victim's claims should not be viewed only in relation to the harm committed by the perpetrator, but also within the broader structural context, including both systems of oppression and systems of care. With respect to domestic violence, challenging a strict victim/agent binary is important because of secondary victimisation based on patriarchal religious interpretations that justify and excuse violence against women – where claiming victim status requires the continuing exercise of agency in response to continuing circumstances of victimisation.

An inherent tension in claiming victim status is that, in doing so, women transgress their gender role by challenging male authority, which often results in victim-blaming stemming from a perceived failure by the victim to conform with a woman's *kodrat* (or gender role). Complaints of domestic violence against a husband inherently contravene gender roles and norms that expect marital issues to remain private and not the business of anyone except the male head of the household. In this way, the politics of victimhood recognition and provision of care are often less a response to the original harm committed by the husband and more a reflection of broader gender norms and societal expectations.

Not all Indonesian women are victims of domestic violence and, of those who are, not all women choose to identify as victims. However, for those who do, identifying as a victim can be seen as a rejection of the legitimacy of patriarchal practices and attempted engagement with systems of care. In seeking acknowledgement of the harms committed against them, women self-identifying as victims call out domestic violence as a wrong and call on community and State actors to hold perpetrators accountable. Without recognition of victims in law and in practice, impunity for perpetrators of domestic violence persists and women do not receive access to the care they need and are entitled to.

If victims decide to seek help, they may do so by many avenues including community, civil (religious) law, or criminal law avenues. The decision-making processes that victims undertake in exercising their agency are discussed in the second part of this chapter based on interviews with victims. The next section highlights factors victims emphasised as influencing their decisions to seek a divorce or report domestic violence, including community norms and stigma, the significance of their children, economic considerations, and the presence or absence of support systems. The factors discussed are not exhaustive, but reflect the perspectives shared by domestic violence victims during interviews.

Community norms and stigma

In addition to community norms that dictate that domestic violence is a 'private matter', a 'normal' part of married life, and justifiable as 'disciplinary' violence (explained above), women making the decision whether to seek a divorce also face the stigma of becoming a '*janda*' (divorcee).[8] Ibu Commissioner (*Komnas Perempuan*) explained, with respect to *janda*, that 'there is still a negative stigma, many women feel they are better off remaining married even though they are unhappy rather than as divorcees'. While women legally have the right to divorce, the community conceptualisation of the family as a 'sacred' unit creates a social disincentive for women to initiate divorce.[9] In Parker's (2016) study of the stigmatisation of *janda* in Indonesia, she found that stigmas associated with divorce and *janda* status are distinctly gendered and built upon existing gender inequalities. In this way stigmas operate to re-enforce patriarchal power relations and compliance with gender norms. Further, Jamaluddin et al. (2015) in their study of divorce in Aceh, explain that:

> When the wife wants a divorce and proposes the divorce against her husband, it is seen as even worse than … divorce [from] husband to wife. This happens because there is still the belief among the society that the husband's position is religiously and culturally higher in rank than [the] wife.

These stigmas were reflected in the way that women spoke about navigating State and non-State systems when seeking help for domestic violence. In interviews victims spoke about fear, shame, and familial and community pressure, for example, saying, 'I was afraid/embarrassed (*takut malu*) of the reaction from family and neighbours'. In addition to the *janda* stigma, general rhetoric prioritising the integrity of the family unit (*keluarga sakinah*) discourages divorce and contributes to stigmatisation of victims who seek to separate from abusive husbands. Ibu Commissioner (*Komnas Perempuan*) observed that, in many places in Indonesia, there is the prevalent idea that:

> the integrity of the family must be maintained … this is an obstacle for victims, it's a cultural barrier. On the other hand people always assume that when victims report domestic violence that they are already divorced, that they want the household to be dissolved – this is also a barrier.

Victims also expressed fear of being blamed or being subjected to threats or intimidation if they reported violence. Related to this, victims have little faith that State responses to their reports will be effective.

The significance of children in decision-making

A primary factor influencing whether women report domestic violence or file for divorce is their children. Ibu Yati (a victim) stated that the 'first factor is thinking about the children'. This has many elements: the physical and psychological wellbeing of children; the ability to economically provide for children's needs; and the stigma or other consequences for children of divorce or due to the imprisonment of their father. For example, a victim explained, 'I could no longer bear it … but I love my children so much and they have many needs, I do not have the capacity to provide for them, so I am being patient'. Another victim stated:

> When I wanted to report to the police, my child says … if he [the husband] is in prison then we don't have any maintenance (*nafkah*), if we get divorced we at least have maintenance even if it's only once a year … So, I did not report it to the police because I was thinking ahead for my child.

It is not uncommon for women to wait until their children are grown (that is, old enough to go to school, boarding school, work, or marry) before reporting violence or filing for divorce. In the case of Ibu Dewi – she waited to file for divorce until she was able to enrol her children at a *pesantren* (traditional Islamic boarding school). She felt this kept her children safe because she did not want them to be cared for by their father and was unable to care for them herself as she had been hospitalised as a result of the domestic violence perpetrated by her husband. She recalled that when making the decision to divorce 'I was afraid, afraid for my children'.

Victims also exercise agency by strategically making decisions for their survival and minimisation of harm to themselves and their children. For example, Ibu Rumi (victim) decided to wait until her husband – who was an 'important person' working at the governor's office – lost his job. When he was working at the governor's office, she felt that her report would not be taken seriously due to him holding a position of influence. However, when he was fired, she said 'my heart was moved again, to take my rights, namely my children'.

Many victims expressed fear of losing custody of their children during divorce proceedings. Even though custody of minors generally falls to mothers, in one case, the mother (Ibu Tia, who worked at the Islamic Court) temporarily lost custody of her child due to a clerical error. In the words of Ibu Tia, there was a mistake in the letter from the *Mahkamah Syariah* and so the letter had to be amended (explained in the transcript below):

> *When she attended the interview, Ibu Tia was dressed neatly in an official government uniform. She spoke articulately. She made jokes about her husband. She outlined the Mahkamah Syariah process. She stopped speaking abruptly and cried – and then apologised – and continued talking about the battle for custody of her children, saying*:
>
> My husband tried to fault me. He said that *I* was violent and did not deserve to have custody. That I am not fit to take care of my child … that I abandon my child because I work. In my opinion, if I do not work my husband cannot fulfil the maintenance (*nafkah*) … My husband said he didn't give me permission to work, so why did I work? But custody still fell to me because I could provide proof for everything.

Ibu Tia's case provides an example of a mother's worst fears coming true with respect to losing custody of her children. However, in Ibu Tia's case the loss of custody was in error and she was able to regain custody of her children. As Ibu Tia worked at the courts, her level of familiarity of the Islamic Court systems assisted her to assert their rights to regain custody.

When women were interviewed, it was common for the interviewees to become emotional when talking about their children. Ibu Siti, for example, stated that her husband abused their children including making them do heavy labour and that as a result they became ill and fell behind in school. Another interviewee, Ibu Nurul, said that when she reported violence to the head of the village, the *Geuchik*'s advice was that she should stay with her husband for the sake of her children. However, she said that she could not stand to stay with her husband anymore as her children had also been beaten by him.

All interviewees, except one, had children with their abuser. While in some cases, women feel pressured to stay with their abusive spouses for the benefit of their children (for example, because of economic dependence), in cases where children were directly affected by violence women were on average more likely to try to leave the relationship to protect their children.

Economic considerations

It is well known that economic factors may present a barrier to women reporting or leaving abusive spouses. In cases where women are financially dependent on their husbands this may be a concrete obstacle to help-seeking, for example, everything from transport costs to attend court to application fees can prohibit women from applying for a divorce. There is also an attrition of access to justice by distance, with women living in rural or regional areas facing greater barriers than their urban counterparts in terms of time and cost for travel. However, one-off expenses that act as barriers to justice (such as application fees) do not come close to the broader economic barriers, in particular, the cost of providing for children long-term. For example, Ibu Nurul told her story about how her husband psychologically, economically, and verbally abused her for years, and each year the abuse worsened until the 'patience had long gone from my soul'. However, for over 13 years she stayed married as:

> I did not have a livelihood, and my husband was the one who worked to support my kids and their education. He provided sufficient food and shelter for me – just the bare minimum, enough to keep me alive, no more than that.

A lack of financial independence means that even if a woman wants to report her husband, the threat of her husband divorcing her or him being imprisoned is significant because either could render the wife and her children destitute. Women who cannot work because they have young children are especially vulnerable. Bapak S (Lawyer) explained in an interview that victims often do not wish to report violence to the police because 'if her husband goes to prison, there will be no one to financially support her'.

Interviewees highlighted the urgent need for alternative outcomes that provide 'win-win solutions' for victims of domestic violence, which do not 'save' people from violence only to leave them to starve. A lack of economic empowerment and security for victims is a pressing issue for short and long-term protection. Although domestic violence can occur in any household, women from lower educational and socio-economic backgrounds face greater barriers to accessing justice. On the other hand, in many cases of domestic violence there is either economic exploitation or abandonment, so there is little loss for women in separating from their husbands (at least in economic terms). In cases where husbands have already stopped financially supporting their wives, where wives are financially independent, and/or have strong family or community support, this factor may be less influential in decision-making. Just as women strategise to keep their children safe, they also develop strategies to deal with economic constraints. For example, Ibu Siti stated:

> My husband said he would never agree to divorce (*sampai mati*), he didn't want to mediate … but after my second child went to the *pesantren* (Islamic boarding school), there was only one more child at home and *Inshallah* (God willing) I could feed him.

Here the interviewee is referring to a system where her two eldest children would live at the *pesantren* and have their tuition and board paid for by their father. *Pesantren* are one of the cheapest options for education in Indonesia and, in this case, the woman was confident that her husband would pay the school fees through a child maintenance arrangement. As two of her children were old enough to go to boarding school, Ibu Siti felt she would be able to support the youngest child by herself and therefore felt ready to file for divorce. This is an example of how women navigate economic pressures, and how staying in an abusive relationship is not always 'passive' but may be a short-term strategy to gain security or safety long-term.

Further, one victim emphasised that community understandings of marital maintenance (*nafkah*) often prioritise financial support over other forms of support and care:

> Because the husband is the one who provides [financially] for the children, people consider that we [the wives] are the ones who make mistakes. But, with regards to … what we *feel*, they don't want to know. We, as wives, never get enough care … so, police officers presume that marriage is *only about material maintenance* (*nafkah lahir saja*) (emphasis added).

Some women distinguished between *nafkah lahir* (financial or material maintenance) and *nafkah batin* (non-material or emotional maintenance). The latter concept of *nafkah* encompasses ideas of emotional availability and intimacy.

The fact that many women raised non-material concerns around sex, love, and fidelity in interviews illustrates the emotional complexity of women's decision-making which spans far beyond pragmatic considerations such as finances. Indeed, domestic violence cases cannot be neatly categorised and must often be understood in light of the victim's love or emotional connection with the perpetrator, as well as the perpetrator's use of emotional manipulation or psychological abuse.

Support systems

One of the critical factors underlying women's decisions to report violence or file for divorce was the presence of a supporter, often a person from their family, their husband's family, their friends, village leaders, or an NGO or P2TP2A worker. Most victims interviewed first disclosed violence to friends, family, or to the head of their village, before participating in village mediation and/or reporting to P2TP2A. Many women noted that if they moved from their hometowns to live in the city with their husbands then they were isolated from their family support structures and, if this were the case, relied on their friendship circles for support.

Ibu Dewi stated that the *Geuchik* from her village supported her and testified as a witness in her divorce case. For Ibu Dewi, the divorce proceedings were smooth, and the divorce was finalised in about one month. In the interview, Ibu Dewi acknowledged that her case is not necessarily typical of women's experiences reporting at the village level:

> Because I had gone through all the stages in the village [mediation process], at the *Mahkamah Syariah* [Islamic Court] the process was not long, after one month I got the divorce, because the *Geuchik* himself wanted to be a witness. In my village it is like that, but it depends on the village head ... depending on the area, sometimes the village head will side with the perpetrator – so it's rather difficult in the village system, we are the victims, but we are the ones that are pressed (*ditekan*). If, for example, he [the perpetrator] is a person who is feared then he will be protected. That's why I feel it's quite difficult for us women.

In Ibu Dian's case – where her husband bound her hands, feet, and mouth before severely beating her – the husband's family supported her to divorce him and she continued to live with her in-laws while her ex-husband was ostracised by his own family. Her story is outlined in the transcript below:

> *She was the youngest by far and the only one of the victims who did not have children. She looked at the table as she recounted the violence committed against her by her husband. I asked her who supported her to divorce her husband. She said his family had supported her, as his family understood that she had* 'done nothing wrong at all'.

Ibu Yani (the only interviewee in the group who had not divorced her husband) also mentioned the influence of her parents-in-law:

> My legs were sewn together by my husband, who is a brutal man. I just kept quiet, never fought. It has changed in the last two years, but back then whatever was in his hand he would throw at me, once when he threw a glass and I was hit. I had to go to the hospital … After that there was no more violence because his parents talked to him and gave advice not to be brutal to your wife (*jangan kasar sama istri*).

As discussed above, many women experience pressure from their families and communities to reconcile with their abusers. On the other hand, the one factor that all interviewees had in common – besides all having taken action to seek counselling, mediation, report and/or divorce their husbands – is that they all cited at least one supporter they credited with giving them the strength to pursue their cases or otherwise seek help. In the first part of this chapter, I highlighted how community and kinship structures can operate to oppress victims. Women's perspectives about support systems therefore present a counter-narrative acknowledging the strength and support which can be provided by families and communities to domestic violence victims. One significant factor is that women who take action to assert their rights in domestic violence contexts rarely seem to do so alone. Whether it is a friend, family member, village leader, or NGO worker, the importance of the people who support victims cannot be underestimated. In a recent UNDP (2023) study, it was found that the only times that victims achieved their desired outcomes in domestic violence cases was 'when they were strongly supported and reaffirmed by the people they reached out to – this could be healthcare workers … or even family members providing social validation and financial support to separate from their abusive partners.'

On the other hand, if domestic violence victims face secondary victimisation, and are silenced or blamed by the people that they approach to seek help, this can further isolate them. Ibu K (academic) explained:

> If a domestic violence victim runs to the head of the village, and the head of the village says, "It is surely you who is in the wrong", then she may not be brave to run somewhere else [to report].

If women do not receive support, they may lose confidence in the people or institutions they have approached for help. In Blackburn's (2004) study she found low levels of trust amongst victims of gendered violence in the police force and judiciary. She elaborates that a lack of trust is based on the experiences of many victims who have been treated with a lack of understanding by State stakeholders which has tangibly worsened their circumstances. As discussed in Chapter 1, when State institutions have made promises, and have responsibilities, to assist victims but fail to do so, I argue that they commit a unique form of violence by perpetuating the victims' vulnerability to domestic violence and making victims less likely to seek help in the future.

Education and interpretations of Islam

Other factors that appeared to influence women's decision-making were their access to education and their personal interpretations of Islamic doctrines. First, advocates highlighted the importance of educational empowerment with NGOs and government working to increase women's access to information. While socialisation of the Law has been successful to an extent, as reflected in increased reporting rates over time, there continues to be community hostility towards socialisation efforts. This means that the taboo around reporting domestic violence remains pervasive. Ibu I (who works with a women's NGO conducting community education in rural villages) stated that male community leaders are generally suspicious of women's activities. Quoting comments made by men in the village, Ibu I stated:

> Why do you women want to come here and oppress us? … Why do you want to lecture us? Do you want to sit above us? Do you want to us to be divorced because women will have a higher economic status than us?

Education relates to both women's understanding of their legal rights and their sense of self-worth. Respondents often talked about women's *percaya diri* (self-confidence) touching on ideas of empowerment and self-help, arguing that women must be educated to counter internalised patriarchy and be empowered to make decisions for themselves. At the core of women's actions was often a sense of self-worth or confidence that made women feel 'brave' (*berani*) to stand up for themselves.

In addition to feeling confident or brave enough to report, many women also expressed feeling that they could no longer cope or had run out of patience. In response to being told to be '*sabar*' (patient) by family and community when seeking help, victims stated: 'I couldn't cope anymore, my patience was empty (*kesabaran saya sudah habis*)'; and 'I ran away from home because I couldn't cope anymore … he bound my hands and beat me so I decided to leave'.

Women also found strength in their faith and used it to empower themselves and justify their help-seeking. For example, commenting on husbands being the head of the household in Islam, Ibu Rumi (a victim) stated:

> We are looking forward, the future is waiting. Right now we have equal rights with men, there is no difference. Yes, men are still the head of the family, but women can work independently and live without a husband – *not without a leader but without a husband* (emphasis added).

While accepting that men are the head of the household, Ibu Siti (victim) emphasised that women do not need a particular man to be their husband. In other words, husbands as people are fallible and, if a husband is not acting as a proper leader should, he can be replaced. Further, Ibu Tia (victim) stated that:

> Actually in our religion, the role of women is not washing, cooking – the wife practically being made to be a maid ... If we truly consider Islamic *shari'a* – we must obey our husband *but what kind of husband*? If we do all the housework but when he comes home we are beaten and he is angry because the food is not good ... That kind of husband lacks understanding of the religion but *alhamdullilah* (thank God), we women understand it better. *I am not your maid!* (*Saya bukan pembantu kamu!*) (emphasis added).

Such statements made by women during interviews also create a counter-narrative to essentialist portrayals of Muslim women as 'passive' victims of their religion mentioned in Chapter 3. Although, dominant religious interpretations are patriarchal in Aceh and Indonesia, it is also clear that women have their own interpretations of Islam which they may use to justify and strength their help-seeking in domestic violence contexts.

Victims of domestic violence in Indonesia exercise agency in negotiating the political process of victimhood recognition. The ways in which women claim, or do not claim, victim status demonstrates the complex and subtle ways in which women traverse the terrain of patriarchal religious interpretations and community stigma. Claiming victimhood challenges the acceptability of domestic violence, societal expectations of women as passive and submissive, and the entitlement of men to use violence. However, for many victims, reporting violence or otherwise seeking help represents the beginning of a cycle of victimisation that requires women to persistently exercise agency in navigating the patriarchal politics of care.

On one hand, victim perspectives reflect how community norms and stigmas operate as a barrier to access to justice by deterring women from seeking divorce or reporting violence. On the other hand, victim perspectives provide counter-narratives to the arguments that families and communities generally do not assist victims of domestic violence and that religious interpretations are generally patriarchal. Victims highlighted the support they received from their communities and their own sense of empowerment and *percaya diri* (confidence) inspired by alternative, gender equal interpretations of Islam.

Victims also identified pragmatic and emotional factors, such as economic dependence and love for their children, in terms of strategising and decision-making in domestic violence contexts. A key take away from this chapter is that it cannot be assumed that women who report violence necessarily want, or are able, to separate from their husbands. Many victims simply want the violence to stop rather than the relationship to end. Above all, the second part of this chapter sought to highlight victim perspectives with respect to their decision-making processes when navigating help-seeking via *adat*, religious, and criminal law avenues.

Notes

1 Wieringa (2015). See also Nurmila (2011) on this point.
2 For example, see Kate Lamb, 'A Vigilante State': Aceh's Citizens Take Sharia Law into Their Own Hands' *The Guardian* (23 April 2018) and Max Walden, 'Four arrested in Aceh for Homosexuality, Face Caning' *Asian Correspondent* (3 April 2018).
3 Interviews with Bapak S (Lawyer) and Ibu R (P2TP2A/*Balai Syura*). As clarified in Chapter 3, if cases of domestic violence are reported via P2TP2A or partner organisations the statistical representation of incidents of psychological violence is higher as psychological violence is often identified by practitioners or women's advocates *within* a case – however, most victims only self-identify physical violence in the first instance.
4 Aisyah (2012). See also works by Dunn and Kellison (2010) and Nurmila (2011).
5 For a discussion on this point see Scott (2009), Dunn and Kellison (2010), Ibrahim and Abdalla (2010), Aisyah (2012) and Eidhamar (2018).
6 Eidhamar (2018).
7 For a discussion on this point see Scott (2009), Dunn and Kellison (2010), Ibrahim and Abdalla (2010) and Nurmila (2011).
8 *Janda* means a woman who was married but is no longer married. It can therefore also mean 'widow', while *janda cerai* specifically refers to a divorcee. In this chapter, I use *janda* consistently with the latter meaning.
9 Interview with Ibu R (P2TP2A/*Balai Syura*). This is supported by Jamaluddin et al.'s (2015) study of divorce in Aceh.

Bibliography

Abdurrachman, Hamidah, 'A Culture of Neglect: A Study in Indonesian Court Judgements Regarding Victims of Domestic Violence' (2017) 55 *International Annals of Criminology* 26–39.

Afrianty, Dina, 'Agents for Change: Local Women's Organizations and Domestic Violence in Indonesia' (2018) 174 *Bijdragen tot de Taal-, Landen Volkenkunde* 24–46.

Aisyah, Siti, 'Rereading Patriarchal Interpretations of the Qur'an from Hadith Perspective on the Eve of Law No. 23/2004 of the Elimination of Domestic Violence' (2012) 6(1) *Journal of Indonesian Islam* 48–75.

Aisyah, Siti and Lyn Parker, 'Problematic Conjugations: Women's Agency, Marriage and Domestic Violence in Indonesia' (2014) 38(2) *Asian Studies Review* 205–223.

Akhmadi, Asri Yusrina, Sri Budiyati and Athia Yumna, *Access to Justice: Empowering Female Heads of Household in Indonesia* (Research Report, 2010).

Alfitri, 'Protecting Women from Domestic Violence: Islam, Family Law, and the State in Indonesia' (2020) 27(2) *Studia Islamika* 273–307.

Bennett, Linda, Sari Andajani-Sutjahjo and Nurul Idrus, 'Domestic Violence in Nusa Tenggara Barat, Indonesia: Married Women's Definitions and Experiences of Violence in the Home' (2011) 12(2) *The Asia Pacific Journal of Anthropology* 146–163.

Blackburn, Susan, *Women and the State in Modern Indonesia* (Cambridge University Press, 2004).

Connell, Patricia, 'Understanding Victimization and Agency: Considerations of Race, Class and Gender' (1997) 20(2) *Political and Legal Anthropology Review* 115–143.

Dahl, Gudrun, 'Sociology and Beyond: Agency, Victimisation and the Ethics of Writing' (2009) 37 *Asian Journal of Social Science* 391–407.

Dunn, Shannon and Rosemary Kellison, 'At the Intersection of Scripture and Law: Qur'an 4:34 and Violence Against Women' (2010) 26(2) *Journal of Feminist Studies in Religion* 11–36.

Eddyono, Sri Wiyanti, Estu Fanani, Dini Anitasari Sabaniah, Yurra Maurice, Haiziah Ghazali, Juni Warlif, Sisillia Velayati and Farha Ciciek, *When and Why the State Responds to Women's Demands: Understanding Gender Equality Police Change in Indonesia* (UNRISD, 2016).

Eidhamar, Levi, "My Husband Is My Key to Paradise'. Attitudes of Muslims in Indonesia and Norway to Spousal Roles and Wife-Beating' (2018) 29(2) *Islam and Christian-Muslims Relations* 241–264.

Hudson, Barbara, 'Restorative Justice and Gendered Violence: Diversion or Effective Justice?' (2002) 42(3) *British Journal of Criminology* 616–634.

Ibrahim, Nada and Mohamad Abdalla, 'A Critical Examination of Qur'an 4:34 and its Relevance to Intimate Partner Violence in Muslim Families' (2010) 5(3) *Journal of Muslim Mental Health* 327–349.

Irianto, Sulistyowati and Antonius Cahyadi, *Runtuhnya Sekat Perdata Dan Pidana: Studi Peradilan Kasus Kekerasan terhadap Perempuan* (Yayasan Obor Indonesia, 2008).

Jamaluddin, Nanda Amalia and Laila Rasyid, 'Women and Divorce: Legal Justice Study of Societal and Judicial Perspective Toward Unrecorded Divorce in Aceh, Indonesia' (2015) 12 *US-China Law Review* 647–665.

Katjasungkana, Nursyahbani, 'The Indonesian Family as a Contested Site of Women's Rights: Implementation of the Domestic Violence Act' in Maznah Mohamad and Saskia Wieringa (eds), *Family Ambiguity and Domestic Violence in Asia* (Sussex Academic Press, 2013) 169–191.

Komnas Perempuan, *Labirin Kekerasan Terhadap Perempuan: Dari Perkosaan Berkelompok Hingga Femisida, Alarm Bagi Negara Untuk Bertindak Tepat* (Report, 7 March 2017).

Mahoney, Martha, 'Victimization or Oppression? Women's Lives, Violence and Agency' in Martha Fineman and Roxanne Mykitiuk (eds), *The Public Nature of Private Violence: The Discovery of Domestic Abuse* (Routledge, 1994) 59–92.

Nashriyah and Khairiah Syahabuddin (eds), *Masculinities in Post Conflict Aceh and Its Impacts on Violence Against Women* (PSW UIN Ar-Raniry, 2015).

Nilan, Pam, Argyo Demartoto, Alex Broom, and John Germov, 'Indonesian Men's Perceptions of Violence Against Women' (2014) 20(7) *Violence Against Women* 869–888.

Nurmila, Nina, 'The Influence of Global Muslim Feminism on Indonesian Muslim Feminist Discourse' (2011) 49(1) *Al-Jami'ah* 33–64.

Nursiti, Eka Kurnia Sari and Ria Fitri, *Laporan Penelitian Kajian Wanita: Implementasi Undang-Undang Nomor 23 Tahun 2004 di Kota Banda Aceh* (Fakultas Hukum Pidana Universitas Syiah Kuala, 2006).

Parker, Lyn, 'The Theory and Context of the Stigmatisation of Widows and Divorcees (*janda*) in Indonesia' (2016) 44(128) *Indonesia and The Malay World* 7–26.

Putra, I Gusti Ngurah Edi, Putu Erma Pradnyani, Ni Wayan Putri and Ni Wayan Putri Larassita Parwangsa, 'Vulnerability to Domestic Physical Violence Among Married Women in Indonesia' (2019) 33(2) *Journal of Health Research* 90–105.

Rofiah, Nor, *Memecah Kebisuan – Respon NU: Agama Mendengar Suara Perempuan Korban Kekerasan Demi Keadilan* (Komnas Perempuan, 2010).

Schneider, Elizabeth, 'Feminism and the False Dichotomy of Victimization and Agency' (1993) 38 *New York Law School Law Review* 387–399.

Scott, Rachel, 'A Contextual Approach to Women's Rights in the Qur'an: Readings of 4:34' (2009) 99(1) *The Muslim World* 60–85.

Stringer, Rebecca, *Knowing Victims: Feminism, Agency and Victim Politics in Neoliberal Times* (Routledge, 2014).
Sumner, Cate and Nani Zulminarni, '*Looking Back, Looking Forward: Women's Access to the Religious Courts of Indonesia*' (Policy Paper, 2018).
UNDP, *Applying Behavioural Insights to Gender Justice in Indonesia* (Report, 2023).
Venning, Philippa, 'Marrying Contested Approaches: Empowerment and the Imposition of International Principles: Domestic Violence Case Resolution in Indonesia' (2010) 46(3) *The Journal of Development Studies* 396–416.
Wieringa, Saskia, 'Gender Harmony and the Happy Family: Islam, Gender and Sexuality in Post-Reformasi Indonesia' (2015) 23(1) *South East Asia Research* 27–44.

Interviews cited in Chapter 4

Interview with Ibu A (Head of P2TP2A) (Banda Aceh, 17 January 2018).
Interview with Ibu Commissioner (*Komnas Perempuan*) (Jakarta, 12 January 2018).
Interview with Ibu D (NGO worker/Flower Aceh) (Banda Aceh, 22 January 2018).
Interview with Ibu I (NGO worker) (Banda Aceh, 19 December 2017).
Interview with Ibu K (academic and Head of Faculty) (Banda Aceh, 15 December 2017).
Interview with Bapak M (Religious Leader) (Banda Aceh, 23 January 2018).
Interview with Ibu R (P2TP2A/*Balai Syura*) (Banda Aceh, 19 December 2017).
Interview with Bapak S (Lawyer) (Banda Aceh, 15 December 2017).

5 Domestic Violence in the Islamic Courts

Prologue to this chapter

October 2018, at home

Ibu Hayati sits on the veranda with her neighbours Ibu Dina and Ibu Risa.

'My husband will never agree to a divorce', says Ibu Hayati.

'You want to get divorced? … For what – to be a *janda* (divorcee)?', Ibu Dina retorts.

'I can't take this anymore', Ibu Hayati responds, 'I keep praying that he will get better.'

'*Allah* would never give you a greater burden than you can bear', says Ibu Risa softly, 'You have to be *sabar* (patient) *Kak*.'

Ibu Hayati nods and responds, '*Inshallah*', excusing herself to go and pick up her eldest child from school.

December 2019, back at P2TP2A's office

Ibu Hayati sits in the waiting room at P2TP2A, looking at the 'Stop *Kekerasan* (Violence)' poster on the wall. 'Ibu Hayati', the secretary calls, 'Ibu Raihan will see you now.'

'Do you want the good news or the bad news?' Ibu Raihan asks.

Ibu Hayati ignores the question, 'I just need to know when I will be able to see my children again. I need to be with them.'

'The good news', Ibu Raihan continues, 'is that the enforcement proceeding for your divorce case has been listed for next month.'

'What does that mean?', Ibu Hayati asks.

'It means that we will be able to ask the Judge to enforce the original custody arrangement which was made when your divorce was finalised.'

'And in the meantime?'

'You just have to be *sabar* (patient) Ibu.'

(Source for the above: Author's own)

DOI: 10.4324/9781032613642-5

Introduction

Most domestic violence victims who engage with the State seek divorce in the religious (civil) jurisdiction, as opposed to reporting to the criminal jurisdiction via the police. The jurisdiction of the Islamic Courts is set out in the Marriage Law supplemented by the *Compilation of Islamic Law* (*Kompilasi Hukum Islam* or KHI).[1] The Islamic Court jurisdiction includes marriage, divorce, *shari'a* economy and, in Aceh, the *Mahkamah Syariah*'s jurisdiction includes Islamic criminal law (*Qanun Jinayat*).[2] The vast majority of cases heard by the Islamic Courts are divorce-related.

Divorce hearings are always proceeded by court-annexed mediation aimed to reconcile the couple.[3] If mediation does not resolve the case, the plaintiff must prove to the judge there are sufficient grounds for divorce. As explained in Chapter 3, while there are grounds for divorce that broadly correlate to domestic violence (including economic abandonment, verbal abuse and battery), the majority of divorces are based on 'irreconcilable differences'.[4] A female judge – interviewed as an institutional representative of the Islamic Court (*Mahkamah Syariah* Banda Aceh) – explained:

> Most cases of domestic violence are based on the reason of not being able to live in harmony. This category is very broad and, in fact, there are many cases in this category which are domestic violence, but maybe the wife doesn't say it is domestic violence.

The judge's explanation is consistent with Triana's (2018) study of divorce, which states that most domestic violence is 'hidden' in divorce cases handled by the Islamic Courts. In 2017, divorce paperwork at the Islamic Courts was amended to specifically list domestic violence as a reason for divorce. Despite clearer categorisation, applicants still largely rely on irreconcilable differences as the catch-all ground for divorce to avoid potential stigma and evidentiary issues associated with proving more complex claims.[5] Further, even when domestic violence is explicitly identified in divorce cases, judges tend to avoid engaging with allegations of domestic violence on the basis that the Islamic Courts do not have 'jurisdiction' to apply the Law.[6] This raises the question of what exactly the Islamic Courts' role is (or should be) in handling domestic violence cases?

While it is true the Islamic Courts do not have State criminal jurisdiction to penalise perpetrators under the Law, it is an oversimplification to say it has no role in addressing domestic violence. As discussed below, the proper identification of domestic violence in divorce cases is not only relevant as a ground for divorce but affects the distribution of divorce rights. The rebuffing of responsibility by the Islamic Courts illustrates a lack of interest in engaging with issues of domestic violence under the guise of a lack of jurisdiction. The reality is that within their own jurisdiction, Islamic Court judges have an important role in addressing domestic violence. This is because domestic violence affects both the substantive and procedural rights of women seeking divorce.

The prevalence of domestic violence in divorce cases continues to challenge the boundaries of criminal and civil matters. According to Ibu Commissioner (*Komnas Perempuan*) one of the biggest obstacles in terms of access to justice is that victims of domestic violence generally seek divorce via the Islamic Courts rather than pursue their cases in the State criminal jurisdiction. However, the Islamic Courts tend not to engage with domestic violence as it is considered to be a 'criminal law issue'. This strict dual jurisdictional approach fails to acknowledge the responsibility of both religious and criminal jurisdictions to deal with domestic violence. The passive approach of the Islamic Courts towards domestic violence has resulted in victim falling between the cracks between the two jurisdictions.

Continued passivity towards domestic violence in the religious jurisdiction has led to – what Afrianty (2016) describes as – 'a culture of impunity towards male violence'. The current Islamic Court approach towards domestic violence in divorce proceedings also does not address the root causes of violence and potentially perpetuates abuse. As Ibu Commissioner (*Komnas Perempuan*) explains, although a victim of domestic violence may leave an abusive relationship via divorce, divorce does not address the underlying problem (the husband's violence) and the husband may simply start a new (violent) marriage.

Compared to other avenues for domestic violence victims, the Indonesian Islamic Courts are well researched. In this chapter, I canvass existing literature on divorce in domestic violence contexts as well as interview data from the case study context to discuss: the impact of non-State marriage and divorce, the lack of domestic violence screening for compulsory mediation, the relevance of domestic violence to divorce proceedings and rights distribution, and issues with enforcement. The chapter concludes with reflections on how the system might be reformed to better meet women's needs and address domestic violence. As highlighted throughout this chapter, the failure of the Islamic Courts to engage with domestic violence has tangible consequences for victims and is an example of bureaucratic violence.

Non-state marriage and divorce

For a marriage to be recognised by the State under Indonesian law it needs to be registered with the State. Although a marriage under religious rites is recognised as valid under the Marriage Law, the State does not formally recognise marriages unless they are registered.[7] Unregistered marriages are known as *nikah siri* (literally 'secret marriages'). Similarly, a divorce can only be affected in a hearing at the Islamic Courts (Article 115 of the *Compilation of Islamic Law*). Divorce initiated by Muslim husbands is known as *talak*, while divorce initiated by Muslim wives is known as *khulu* or *cerai gugat*. While both husbands and wives can file for divorce at the Islamic Courts, according to Butt and Lindsey (2018), 'women bring twice as many applications for divorce in the religious courts as men, and are almost always successful'.

In conventional Islamic (Sunni) doctrines, *talak* is considered the 'absolute right' of men. Therefore, from the perspective of moral-religious law (that is, dominant interpretations of Islamic law which are not legally codified), the approval of the State is not required. Indeed, before 1974, in Indonesia a husband could legally divorce his wife simply by reciting the *talak* formula three times and registering the divorce. However, since the enactment of the Marriage Law, State law requires that, to be valid, *talak* must be spoken:

> in court and with judicial permission, which is granted only if, in earlier proceedings, the court decides the requirements for divorce are met. *Talak* uttered outside the court has no legal effect.[8]

Despite this, many husbands 'divorce' their wives via unauthorised *talak* known as *cerai liar* (literally 'wild divorce'). To formalise the divorce, the wife must then seek an official decision from the court. One of the victims of domestic violence interviewed was divorced by her husband outside of court (*cerai liar*). The wife was frustrated by the fact that she would have to bring the case to court herself even though, religiously, she believed they were no longer married. Nurlaelawati's (2013) study of Indonesian Islamic Courts confirms that 'women often have no choice but to go to court to petition for divorce or to request a divorce receipt or certificate'. Further, Jamaluddin et al. (2015), who conducted a study of *cerai liar* in Lhokseumawe, found that 'approximately 80 percent of incoming divorce cases are because the woman has been divorced at home'.

In an interview, Acehnese lawyer (Bapak S) explained that legal pluralism in Indonesia adds complexity to divorce proceedings. Bapak S differentiated between moral-religious divorce law and codified State divorce law – the latter being an interpretation of Islamic law (*fiqh*) *derived* (but distinct) from religious law (*shari'a*). In other words, Islamic Court judges apply a 'second-hand' version of Islamic law that is 'State-sanctioned' in the Compilation of Islamic Law. Sumner and Lindsey (2011) argue that as 'the substantive law applied by the courts deviates so significantly from the orthodox [Islamic] schools', this makes the State version of Islamic law in Indonesia 'largely symbolic'. Even if the couple believe they are religiously divorced, Islamic Court judges are legally bound to apply codified State law over moral-religious law in divorce proceedings.[9] Despite this, it is common for judges to give lip service to the moral-religious aspects of divorce. For example, the judge interviewed stated that 'in Aceh, we have to be very careful when resolving divorce cases, because even though it is lawful, divorce is hated by *Allah* (God)'.[10]

Although religious marriages must be registered with the State to be enforceable under the Marriage Law, the registration of religious marriages with the State is often viewed as unnecessary by the community. Lawyer (Bapak S) attributed poor engagement with the State related to divorce and marriage to a strong adherence to moral-religious law in Aceh. Religious leaders at the community level also continue to purport to officiate divorce proceedings in competition with the State and, as discussed in Chapter 2, religious leaders are influential at the community level. Therefore, community beliefs that men do not need to go to the Islamic Court to divorce remain a persistent barrier to socialisation of the Marriage Law and State regulation of marriage and divorce.[11]

In addition to bringing men's absolute discretion to divorce within the compulsory jurisdiction of the Islamic Courts, the Marriage Law expanded divorce rights for women. Before 1974, women's rights to divorce were strictly limited. Reform by the Marriage Law was considered a victory for women at the time it was passed. Despite law reform over 45 years ago, unregistered marriages and unauthorised *talak* continue to cause legal uncertainty, especially for women. Until recently, many couples in Aceh did not have registered marriages due to the absence of Indonesian State institutions in Acehnese communities during the civil conflict. Later, much official documentation in Banda Aceh and surrounding coastal areas was destroyed by the 2004 tsunami.[12] For example, many people do not even have birth certificates, which are required in order to obtain marriage certificates and marriage certificates are required to gain divorce certificates. Divorce certificates are generally used as evidence to obtain new identity cards that reflect an individual's updated marital status. As noted by Sumner and Lindsey (2011), without updated identity cards, women are likely to be ineligible for government services such as healthcare cards.

Further the rural-urban divide remains distinct, with the distance to and cost of attending court continuing to be prohibitive for many women living rurally, as well as people who are poor or do not have access to education or awareness of their legal rights. Jamaluddin et al.'s (2015) study found that 'nine out of ten female heads of households cannot access the court [to formalise] their divorce'. There are two inter-related issues: the failure of socialisation (people who actively reject, or passively fall outside of, the influence of the State) and the failure of accessibility (institutional and structural barriers to accessing State services). This said, there are a number of programmes aimed at increasing access for the rural poor including court fee waivers, expanded Circuit Court routes, and legal aid aimed at addressing these barriers particularly for female heads of household. As outlined by Sumner and Zulminarni (2018), Circuit Court programmes have now been set up across Indonesia to improve access to identity documents and marriage and divorce certificates in rural areas, including registration of un-registered marriages to facilitate the formalisation of divorces via State avenues. This programme has been praised as a critical contribution to bringing undocumented citizens into the State system, making them eligible for public services, including school enrolment for their children and the right to vote.

The obvious consequence of not registering marriages with the State or conducting unauthorised *talak* is that issues relating to marriage and divorce cannot be remedied through recourse to State law. Women whose marriages and divorces are not registered with the State cannot secure their rights through the courts and only have access to moral-religious or *adat* justice avenues. Jamaluddin et al. (2015) state in their study of unauthorised *talak* in Aceh that:

> It is almost certain that in every divorce imposed by a husband against his wife outside the court, her husband does not fulfill the obligation[s] for his wife as a result of the divorce, such as *nafkah idda[h]* (divorce stipend) … and the division of shared properties.

This is not to imply that couples who undertake non-State marriages are blanket 'victims' of *adat* or religious practices. As noted by Vignato (2012), there are strategic reasons why women choose to get married in this way, which are not necessarily related to a lack of socialisation or accessibility. For example, sometimes non-State marriages are utilised to legitimise otherwise informal relationships and avoid *adat* and religious sanctions for *zina* (extra-marital sex). While noting that in some contexts non-State marriage may be an example of women exercising agency, it must also be recognised that *nikah siri* is frequently employed by men to attempt to legitimise illegal polygamy. Many domestic violence victims interviewed mentioned their husbands were not faithful or engaged in illegal polygamy using *nikah siri*. Susanti (2022) also notes that there is a higher risk of gender-based violence against women in illegal polygamous relationships.

The continued prevalence of *nikah siri* and unauthorised *talak* undermine the legal protections for women under the Marriage Law and *Compilation of Islamic Law*. This is two-fold, because of people's trust in and reliance on religious leaders to the exclusion of the State and barriers to access to justice for women seeking divorce through formal State avenues. Although State-facilitated divorce has become increasingly accessible and socialised over time, the role and relevance of the Islamic Courts must be understood against this broader context. The following analysis of the Islamic Courts' approach to domestic violence in divorce cases can therefore be considered as only part of the solution to much broader socio-legal problems that married and divorced women face in Indonesia.

Court-annexed mediation

Even if domestic violence is identified in a divorce case, mediation remains compulsory. Islamic Court judges are obliged to mediate based on Supreme Court Regulation (PERMA) No. 1/2008 and No. 1/2016 concerning mediation and both parties must usually attend mediation in person. Before 2008, mediation was voluntary and rarely used. Despite mediation becoming compulsory in 2008, the majority of plaintiffs do not withdraw their divorce petitions post-mediation. Triana (2018) points out that it is not surprising that mediation at the court stage rarely leads to reconciliation as, in general, petitioning the courts is a last resort after other methods of mediation have failed (for example, informal mediation at the community level). Further, it is common for domestic violence victims to wait long periods before deciding to seek a divorce.

As identified by Syukur and Bagshaw (2013) and Tirtawening and Maryam's (2018) studies, a major issue with the court's current approach is that mediation is seen to 'fail' if a couple does not reconcile. Success being measured only in terms of reconciliation overlooks other outcomes that can be achieved in mediation (for example, agreement to the terms of a divorce settlement). In domestic violence contexts, mediation with such a narrow aim is likely only to unnecessarily pressure women to return to abusive relationships without addressing underlying issues. Syukur and Bagshaw (2013) also suggest that because of this approach agreements made by parties in mediation are often not considered by judges later in divorce proceedings.

The second issue with mediation is that there is currently no screening for domestic violence. Tirtawening and Maryam (2018) argue persuasively for the introduction of mandatory domestic violence screening for divorce mediation in Indonesia. According to Tirtawening and Maryam, screening would have three aims: to identify domestic violence, record domestic violence, and allow victims to be referred to relevant services. I would add that, because in many divorce cases domestic violence is 'hidden', screening would not only improve the visibility of domestic violence in the religious jurisdiction but would allow judges (and mediators) to adapt their approaches towards domestic violence in divorce cases to more adequately protect women and meet victim needs. Screening could potentially be the first step in moving from a passive to active approach towards domestic violence in the religious jurisdiction.

It has long been established in the literature that domestic violence greatly affects mediation and can compromise the safety and rights of women.[13] In some cases, domestic violence dynamics mean that mediation is not possible or advisable. At a minimum, domestic violence needs to be identified so that safeguards can be put into place to mitigate inequalities and prevent re-victimisation. As explained by Syukur and Bagshaw (2013), in cases where domestic violence is present there needs to be appropriate expertise and strategies, such as shuttle mediation to avoid victims 'being intimidated by the presence of the perpetrator'. This also raises the need for protection of victims of domestic violence during divorce proceedings as some women fear having to face their husbands in court. A Supreme Court Regulation (PERMA) No. 3/2017 states that judges have the authority (*ex-officio* or by request) to grant leave for women's testimony to be heard via distance audio-visual communication.[14] In theory, this regulation allows women not to attend court in person if: there is a physical or psychological condition such as trauma (based on a doctor's examination); the judge considers that it is necessary to guarantee the woman's safety; or the woman is in a victim or witness protection programme.

At present it cannot be assumed that all Islamic Court judges (or mediators) understand the dynamics and nature of domestic violence, which include power imbalances, coercion, and control. Across Indonesia there is a lack of adequately trained judges and mediators in terms of gender sensitivity or domestic violence training.[15] Syukur and Bagshaw's (2013) study found that most mediators are male and have not received training to recognise or address domestic violence. They also found that few Islamic Court judges have knowledge and/or experience handling disputes involving domestic violence.

This book supports the argument that screening is necessary to protect the rights of victims and argues that a failure to address domestic violence in the Islamic Court context – including the current lack of screening for domestic violence – constitutes bureaucratic violence. However, the exact nature of the ideal screening model requires further research. While in some jurisdictions, domestic violence cases automatically become ineligible for mediation, in other jurisdictions screening is used to gather information to determine eligibility for mediation on a case-by-case basis. For example, exceptions to ineligibility may be made if both parties are informed and agree to mediate and there are adequate safeguards in place. Regardless of the model implemented, Syukur and Bagshaw (2013) argue that, without reform, mediation will continue to be used by 'violent men to control their partners', making the courts complicit in the perpetuation of abuse. At a minimum, screening processes and further training for mediators should be introduced to actively address domestic violence within mediation processes. In our 2023 article, Aftab and I conduct a more detailed analysis on this point, concluding that mediation should not be compulsory at the Islamic Courts for cases that involve domestic violence.

Divorce in domestic violence contexts

While Nurlaelawati (2013) argues that, in Indonesia, the 'persistence of patriarchy' at the Islamic Courts acts as a barrier to access to justice for women seeking divorce, Butt and Lindsey (2018) describe the Islamic Courts as effectively providing 'divorce on demand' for women. Both statements are true to an extent. While statistically speaking approximately nine out of ten female plaintiff's divorce petitions are successful, divorce proceedings are by no means easy or straight-forward for women. On one hand, if the woman can illustrate sufficient grounds for divorce, then a divorce will most likely be granted. On the other hand, more difficult questions arise when resolving issues of post-divorce rights, particularly in the context of domestic violence.

A lot of uncertainty exists regarding the extent to which the Islamic Courts can take into account domestic violence and what consequences flow from the presence of domestic violence in divorce cases. As explained in Chapter 3, the aims of the Law are not limited to the criminalisation of domestic violence but also extend to prevention, protection, and recovery. The Islamic Courts' focus on the fact that it does not have criminal jurisdiction to punish perpetrators ignores the broader aims of the Law. In the religious jurisdiction, the occurrence of domestic violence must be identified and addressed to prevent the perpetuation of harm to victims. Tirtawening and Maryam (2018) highlight that an obstacle for domestic violence victims in the religious jurisdiction is a general 'lack of knowledge and understanding regarding [the] definition and parameter[s] of domestic violence'. The widespread misunderstandings of domestic violence at the community level and the lack of training for judges are compounding factors, although that will vary from judge to judge. For example, the Islamic Court judge interviewed for this book comprehensively understood domestic violence as encompassing physical violence, psychological violence, verbal violence, illegal polygamy, and sexual violence.[16]

Under the Marriage Law and *Compilation of Islamic Law*, the rights flowing from divorce are contingent on which party brings the action for divorce. If the husband petitions for divorce, the wife is generally entitled to receive *nafkah iddah* (maintenance) and *nafkah mut'ah* (a compensatory gift). The wife is usually entitled to *nafkah iddah* to cover living costs during the three-month *iddah* period post-divorce during which she cannot re-marry (Article 152 of the *Compilation of Islamic Law*). *Mut'ah* is a means-calculated 'gift' to compensate women for the divorce, usually in the form of money or property (Articles 149, 158 and 159 of the *Compilation of Islamic Law*). Despite this, Butt and Lindsey's (2018) study documented how many 'husbands ignore religious court orders to pay *iddah* and *mut'ah*'. If the wife brings the petition for divorce, she generally loses her entitlement to receive *iddah* and *mut'ah*. As discussed above, most divorce petitions are filed by women and most of these cases are brought by the wife due to unauthorised *talak* or domestic violence. In other words, although many women have little choice but to bring the petition themselves, they are effectively penalised for doing so.

However, Article 6 of Supreme Court Regulation (PERMA) No. 3/2017 potentially gives the Islamic Courts the power to order *iddah* and *mut'ah* even in cases of *cerai gugat* if there are extenuating circumstances, such as domestic violence.[17] The way in which PERMA 3/2017 creates an equal pathway for women to claim *iddah* and *mut'ah*, among other rights, is based on the principles of gender equality and non-discrimination.[18] Under the non-discrimination provision in Article 6 of PERMA 3/2017, if the judge considers that there are legitimate reasons behind the wife filing for divorce, she should not be penalised for bringing the petition.

The Islamic Court judge who was interviewed explained that under PERMA 3/2017 if the wife experienced domestic violence, judges have the authority to 'punish the husbands to pay *iddah* money to his wife … for a period of up to three months' – regardless of which party brought the divorce application.[19] The judge described the PERMA 3/2017 as a 'breakthrough in the law' to guarantee the rights of domestic violence victims. Before 2017, women were only entitled to *iddah* payments if they were directly divorced by the husband via court-sanctioned *talak*. The provision of *iddah* in cases of *cerai gugat* is therefore a significant development in the law. Further, its punitive or fault-based nature is notable with the interviewee stating that the wording of the verdict would be 'to punish the defendant to pay maintenance (*nafkah*)'.

However, it is not compulsory for judges to follow this interpretation of PERMA 3/2017. In the words of the judge:

> Despite the breakthrough in the law there are judges who hold on to the conventional/old *fiqh* books[20] [pre-PERMA 3/2017]. In those books, the women have no rights to maintenance in cases of *cerai gugat*. There are only a few judges that are brave enough to issue a verdict like the one I explained above. Probably, one out of ten judges would apply this new law in his/her verdict. Some of the factors that hinder the judges from sentencing the defendant to pay the *iddah* is that the defendant is from a low socio-economic background, the victim/wife does not ask for that money, and also there is a principle in the law that says "*non ultra petita*" which means that a judge may not approve something that is not being sued.
>
> However, judges who are good at making judgments would note in their verdict that it is the judge's decision upon consideration that the victim/wife should have the *iddah* period. There is jurisprudence for such a decision. As far as I know, *iddah* money is never asked for by the victims, but some judges put that into their verdicts because of the PERMA. However, there are only a few judges who follow that PERMA because it is a new one.[21]

The judge's interpretation of PERMA 3/2017 is supported by Triana's (2018) study of divorce at the Islamic Courts. Triana states that if the divorce is based on a husband's 'cruelty or violence, the Judge *ex-officio* could establish a living *iddah*, in the divorce process', which she describes as a 'civil sanction'. Triana's analysis makes it clear that the judge can make orders *ex-officio* – on their own motion – so it is unnecessary for the plaintiff to specifically ask for such an order to be made. Syukur and Bagshaw (2013) also mention in their study of divorce that *nafkah mut'ah* can be provided by Islamic Court judges 'as compensation for domestic violence'.

Therefore, it is not true to say that domestic violence is not relevant to divorce cases, as its incidence may affect the applicant's entitlement to substantive rights. However, it should be noted that it is an uphill battle for women to claim these rights, as many judges do not even order *iddah* and *mut'ah* in *talak* divorce cases, let alone *cerai gugat* cases. For example, in Butt and Lindsey's (2018) study they found that many Islamic Court judges 'pay no attention to ensuring that the property settlement adequately provides for the former wife and the children of the marriage'. Despite these challenges, this new interpretation of PERMA 3/2017 is a promising avenue for securing women's rights.

Literature often describes the Indonesian judicial approach as passive, including passivity towards the detection of domestic violence. This means that if women do not ask for the fulfilment of specific rights, such as *iddah* or *mut'ah*, judges are unlikely to proactively make such orders. The reference above to the *non ultra petita* principle goes some way in explaining why judges generally take a passive approach. However, as mentioned, the *ex-officio* principle gives judges' authority to make orders on their own motion.

The Islamic Court judge interviewed stated that it is the responsibility of a judge of first instance to check in 'as much detail as possible' the reasons why a woman has filed for divorce and that 'a good judge can dig relevant information from the applicant'. This indicates that the judge interviewed takes a more proactive approach compared to the generally passive judicial approaches highlighted in the broader literature. Further, she explained that it is important to look behind 'constant disputes' between the parties to understand why these occur and what they involve because women 'may lack knowledge, dare not report … do not understand or are not advised' about domestic violence and their substantive rights. In other words, domestic violence may be a relevant factor in the divorce, despite it not being explicitly identified in the application. As discussed in Chapter 4, there are many reasons why a woman may be unable or unwilling to advocate for their rights on their own. Further, it is very rare for women to be accompanied by a private lawyer; pro bono legal aid is often the only legal support women receive, and many do not even have that. As judges generally take a passive (or even conservative) approach, legal aid providers play a critical role in realising women's rights in divorce cases.[22]

In light of the passive attitude of the judiciary towards domestic violence, Naqiyah and Triana (2018) calls for Islamic Court judges to be progressive and courageous. I would argue that women's rights in divorce should not be viewed as optional extras but squarely within the Islamic Court judges' jurisdiction, role, and responsibility. In saying this, the achievements (and failures) of the Islamic Courts in providing access to justice to women outlined in this chapter must be understood in light of the structural difficulties that the courts face and the need for reforms which go far beyond the scope of this book.[23]

Post-separation violence and property division

When women report domestic violence or seek to divorce abusive husbands this can trigger men's violence. For example, victim (Ibu Nurul) stated that when she reported her husband to the *Geuchik* her husband 'destroyed all of the household items'. Another victim interviewed (Ibu Siti) said that when she filed for divorce her husband threatened her and said if she took the child, it would 'gamble her life' and that either she or her child would die.

While some village leaders will ask the husband to leave the family home, there are no strict rules or rights when it comes to who will maintain residence. In some cases, women may not want to continue to live at the family home so that their husbands will not know where they are living, due to threats of violence or child abduction. In the case of Ibu Dewi (victim), after reporting the violence to the *Geuchik*:

> I asked the *Geuchik* who had to leave the house … the *Geuchik* answered 'actually the one who has to leave the house is the husband, not the wife', but my husband remained persistently stubborn, he felt that this was his house, his children … that I could leave the house, fine!

> I was ready for all the consequences, I took my office clothes and other things that I needed, I left the house and stayed at the village *imam's* house, starting from that day (eight months ago) until now I have not returned to the house … The advice from the village leaders was that one of us must leave the house, but my husband didn't want to leave, so I had to go.

Islamic Court judges rarely consider protection against the risk of post-separation violence or the right to reside in the family home during the divorce process. However, as argued by Naqiyah and Triana (2018), judges have *ex-officio* authority to make decisions that include conditions such as that 'the husband is not allowed to live in the same house with his victim'.

Many women raised the issue of housing during interviews. Ibu Siti noted that the time from when she first left the house until the end of the divorce process was about six months. Women who have no other choice but to move from their houses to escape violence may face homelessness if they do not have sufficient support from social or kinship networks. Further, as raised in Chapter 1, there are no operational safe houses for domestic violence victims in Aceh, therefore, the right to maintain residence (if women choose to do so) is an important issue that is currently routinely overlooked during divorce proceedings.

Custody

Domestic violence is also relevant to custody. Butt and Lindsey (2018) note that in Indonesia Islamic Court judges 'rarely award joint custody, preferring to grant exclusive custody to one parent'. Mothers are generally granted custody for children (under 12 years old or before puberty). Once children reach puberty, they can choose which parent will have custody. Although post-divorce both parents remain legally obliged to provide for any children of the relationship, non-custodial fathers often ignore the Court's orders relating to child support.[24]

Decisions regarding custody should take into consideration the best interests of the child. For example, parents who are violent or drug users can be deemed inappropriate by the Court. However, the Islamic Courts have also made some controversial decisions regarding when a parent is 'inappropriate'. Butt and Lindsey (2018) cite the examples of working mothers who are sometimes 'denied custody on the presumption that employment might leave inadequate time to care for the child'. If a mother is deemed 'inappropriate', custody will likely go to a close female relative on the mother's side before it goes to the father (Article 156(a) of the *Compilation of Islamic Law*). As mentioned in Chapter 4, in the divorce case of Ibu Tia, her husband argued that she had abandoned their child because she worked, as well as making other allegations against her. Despite this, the judge still ultimately granted her custody.

One of the greatest fears raised during interviews with domestic violence victims was the risk of losing custody of their children when filing for divorce. Many victims interviewed stated that when they filed for divorce, their husbands initially took the children to be raised by their 'younger wives' (second wives through illegal polygamy). Even during the divorce process, which often takes several months, women felt distressed at being temporarily separated from their children. In Ibu Yati's case, after the court decided that she should have sole custody, her husband was non-compliant causing the matter to be referred to the police. At the time of the interview, she was still waiting for a second decision from the Islamic Court to enforce the first decision (discussed further below).

A major issue that needs to be addressed by Islamic Court judges is the right for women to maintain custody *during* divorce proceedings, especially in domestic violence cases where even temporary custody by perpetrators potentially poses a threat to the children, and, at a minimum, causes immense distress to mothers. The failure of the Islamic Court to actively address domestic violence in divorce proceedings, particularly in relation to custody, not only causes ongoing stress for women and children but places them at an exacerbated risk of harm in separation and post-separation contexts.

Enforcement of Islamic Court decisions

Lastly, the enforcement of Islamic Court decisions is poor. To pursue enforcement, a separate application must be brought to the court for an enforcement order (Articles 195–196 of the *Compilation of Islamic Law*). Through enforcement proceedings the court has several options to compel compliance, such as the seizure and sale of property to pay debts (Articles 197, 200 and 225 of the *Compilation of Islamic Law*). As Butt and Lindsey (2018) explain, the 'need to obtain a separate order for execution adds, unnecessarily, to the time, complexity and costs of legal proceedings'.

Ibu Commissioner (*Komnas Perempuan*) explained that a common example of non-compliance is when couples divorce and the children are cared for by their mothers. In these cases, 'the father often feels like he no longer has financial obligations, and as many women are not economically independent, this becomes an obstacle'. This is especially so for men from lower socio-economic backgrounds or those who are self-employed. The exception to the rule is where a husband works as a civil servant, as child support can then be deducted directly from the husband's government salary.

During interviews, the most emotionally charged examples of non-compliance related to custody rather than post-divorce economic rights. Ibu Yati stated that:

> When I sued for divorce, it took several months to process, I did not live with my children during this time, when I asked P2TP2A to help me take back my children, they told me to be patient first and wait for court

> decisions. Now there have been decisions but my husband still does not give my children back so that it must be handled by the police. I am still waiting for the second decision [enforcement proceedings]. Now for my child, the impact is a psychological disorder.

This illustrates not just the time and cost burdens of enforcement proceedings, but the overlooked emotional and psychological harm suffered by women and children due to the separate proceedings for enforcement.

Conclusion

This chapter emphasised the roles and responsibilities of the Islamic Courts with respect to domestic violence. Despite the ongoing prevalence of non-State marriages and divorces (which fall outside the protection of the Law),[25] the Islamic Courts remains one of the most important strategic State institutions for combatting domestic violence. This is because, for marriages and divorces registered with the State, the majority of domestic violence victims seek divorce at the Islamic Courts rather than reporting violence to the police. The relevance and impact of domestic violence at all stages of the Islamic Court proceedings – from mediation to enforcement – demonstrates that the Islamic Courts urgently need to proactively address domestic violence. The current approach of Islamic Court judges – that is, avoiding engaging with domestic violence on the basis that they do not have criminal jurisdiction to punish perpetrators under the Law – ignores victims' needs and perpetuates a culture of impunity for perpetrators. As argued throughout this book, the negligence of the Islamic Courts cannot be described as benign but is a form of bureaucratic violence.

With respect to recommendations for reform, first, the failure to screen cases for domestic violence compromises the safety of victims. Mandatory screening should be introduced to identify domestic violence and develop appropriate strategies to protect women's rights in such cases. Screening would represent a first step in shifting the approach of the Islamic Courts from passive to active.

Second, the identification of domestic violence has the potential to substantively alter the distribution of rights during divorce. While the Islamic Courts has been known to grant 'divorce on demand' to women, I questioned in this chapter whether the bare minimum of granting a divorce itself is praiseworthy when women receive very few other legal rights, particularly in domestic violence contexts. Further, if a victim of domestic violence files a divorce petition to escape violence (*cerai gugat*) they still face being penalised under the Marriage Law. PERMA 3/2017 has created an avenue for judges to make orders for *nafkah iddah* and *mut'ah* to compensate victims who are forced to bring divorce applications, such as in cases of domestic violence. These civil sanctions aim to counter discrimination against women in the religious jurisdiction. Unfortunately, such orders have only been implemented by a progressive minority of judges. The majority of the judiciary retain a conservative approach to the allocation of divorce rights. In light of an overwhelmingly passive judicial approach towards these issues, the role of legal aid and women's advocates remain crucial to ensuring that women are informed and empowered to assert their rights.

Third, it is clear that further training programmes specific to domestic violence should be established and funded for Islamic Court judges. Further training programmes which educate judges about the nuances of domestic violence would assist in addressing issues, such as post-separation violence and its impact on custody and rights to maintain residence, both during and after trial. Last, although it is outside the scope of this chapter, structural barriers to access to the Islamic Court and enforcement of Islamic Court decisions urgently need to be addressed through wider reforms.

Notes

1 Marriage Law 1974 and *Compilation of Islamic Law* 1991 (the compilation was enacted through Presidential Instruction No. 1/1991).
2 Law No. 11/2006 (Law on Governing Aceh). Divorce proceedings for non-Muslims in Indonesia are heard by the *Pengadilan Negeri.*
3 Supreme Court Regulation No. 1/2008 and No. 1/2016 regarding court mediation procedures.
4 Article 39 of the Marriage Law; Article 19 of the Government Regulation No. 9/1975; Article 116 of the Compilation of Islamic Law.
5 On this point see Alfitri's (2020) study.
6 This has been documented more broadly in Indonesia by Afrianty (2018) and Katjasungkana (2013).
7 Article 2 of the Marriage Law; Articles 5–6 of the *Compilation of Islamic Law*; Articles 2–9 of the Government Regulation No. 9/1975.
8 Butt and Lindsey (2018).
9 See Sumner and Lindsey (2011). It should also be noted that while all Islamic Court judges are Muslim, judicial appointments to Islamic Courts operate on a rotating basis so that judges periodically move from region to region to sit on different courts around Indonesia.
10 See also Bowen (2003) who explained that even though Islamic Court judges apply positive law based on the Marriage Law and *Compilation of Islamic Law*, 'Islamic judges s[ee] divorce as a moral issue and marriages as sacred'.
11 On this point see Schenk's (2018) study – where she describes the interaction between *adat*, religious, and State laws in the area of family law in Aceh as a 'deadlock'. See also Sumner and Lindsey (2011).
12 Not all Acehnese communities were affected by conflict and tsunami but many communities were affected by one or the other. See Schenk (2018) and Vignato (2012).
13 See generally Pearson's (1997) report and, in the Indonesian context, Tirtawening and Maryam (2018) and Syukur and Bagshaw (2013).
14 Article 10 of Supreme Court Regulation (PERMA) No. 3/2017.
15 Although there have been pilot training programmes, these are not yet mainstream or widely implemented.
16 Triana (2018) notes that some Islamic Court judges have begun to reference the Anti-Domestic Violence Law in their judgments.
17 Article 6 of PERMA 3/2017 is translated as follows: 'Judges adjudicating cases that women face in the law should (a) consider gender equality and gender stereotypes in statutory regulations and unwritten laws; (b) interpret statutory regulations and/or

unwritten laws so that they can guarantee gender equality; (c) explore legal values, local wisdom, and the sense of justice that lives in society to ensure gender equality, equal protection, and non-discrimination; and (d) consider the application of ratified international conventions and treaties related to gender equality'.

18 For a discussion of PERMA 3/2017 more broadly, see Saraswati's (2021b) paper.

19 Note that the imposition of an order for punitive *nafkah* is not limited to domestic violence cases.

20 As discussed above, *fiqh* are interpretations of Islamic law, so the 'old *fiqh* books' referred to here are traditional reference materials that Islamic Court judges sometimes rely on when interpretating the provisions of the *Compilation of Islamic Law*: Syarif (2021).

21 Despite rhetoric in support of making such orders, in Yusuf et al.'s (2023) study of divorce and domestic violence, their research team were not able to location any decisions handed down by the Islamic Court in Banda Aceh that actually ordered *iddah* or *mut'ah* support in a divorce brought by the wife due to domestic violence.

22 During fieldwork, respondents highlighted the importance of the pro bono legal aid services for domestic violence victims delivered through paralegal programmes run by P2TP2A.

23 Sumner (2019).

24 Butt and Lindsey (2018), with reference to Article 41(a) of the Marriage Law. See also Nurlaelawati (2013).

25 In their 2024 report *Komnas Perempuan* recommended that women in unregistered marriages should be recognised as falling within the scope of the Anti-Domestic Violence Law.

Bibliography

Afrianty, Dina, 'Why Divorce Doesn't Work for Indonesian Women' (2016) *Indonesia at Melbourne* https://indonesiaatmelbourne.unimelb.edu.au/why-divorce-doesnt-work-for-women/

Afrianty, Dina, 'Agents for Change: Local Women's Organizations and Domestic Violence in Indonesia' (2018) 174 *Bijdragen tot de Taal-, Landen Volkenkunde* 24–46.

Afrianty, Dina, 'Protecting Women from Domestic Violence: Islam, Family Law, and the State in Indonesia' (2020) 27(2) *Studia Islamika* 273–307.

Aisyah, Siti and Lyn Parker, 'Problematic Conjugation: Women's Agency, Marriage and Domestic Violence in Indonesia' (2014) 38(2) *Asian Studies Review* 205–223.

Alfitri, 'Protecting Women from Domestic Violence: Islam, Family Law, and the State in Indonesia' (2010) 27(2) *Studia Islamika* 273–307.

Astor, Hilary, *Guidelines for Use if Mediating in Cases Involving Violence against Women* (National Committee on Violence against Women, 1992).

Bowen, John, *Islam, Law and Equality in Indonesia: An Anthropology of Public Reasoning* (Cambridge University Press, 2003).

Butt, Simon and Tim Lindsey, *Indonesian Law* (Oxford, 2018).

Irianto, Sulistyowati and Antonius Cahyadi, *Runtuhnya Sekat Perdata dan Pidana: Studi Peradilan Kasus Kekerasan terhadap Perempuan* (Yayasan Obor Indonesia, 2008).

Jamaluddin, Nanda Amalia, and Laila Rasyid, 'Women and Divorce: Legal Justice Study of Societal and Judicial Perspective Toward Unrecorded Divorce in Aceh, Indonesia' (2015) 12 *US-China Law Review* 647–665.

Jones, Balawyn and Amira Aftab, 'Inside Indonesia's Religious Courts: An Argument for Domestic and Family Violence Screening and Exemption from Compulsory Mediation' (2023) *Oxford Journal of Law and Religion* 1–15.

Katjasungkana, Nursyahbani, 'The Indonesian Family as a Contested Site of Women's Rights: Implementation of the Domestic Violence Act' in Maznah Mohamad and Saskia Wieringa (eds), *Family Ambiguity and Domestic Violence in Asia* (Sussex Academic Press, 2013) 169–191.

Komnas Perempuan, *Catatan Tahunan Kekerasan Terhadap Perempuan Tahun 2023* (Report, 7 March 2024).

Naqiyah and Nita Triana, 'Reconstruction of Integrated Legal System for Protecting the Victims of Domestic Violence in Divorce Cases' (2018) 54 *SHS Web of Conferences* 1–7.

Nurlaelawati, Euis, 'Muslim Women in Indonesian Religious Courts: Reform, Strategies, and Pronouncement of Divorce' (2013) 20(3) *Islamic Law and Society* 242–271.

Pearson, Jessica, *Divorce Mediation and Domestic Violence* (Research Report, 1997).

Saraswati, Rika, 'Accommodating the 'Best Interests of the Child' in Custody Disputes in the Indonesian System/s of Family Law' (2021a) 35(1) *International Journal of Law, Policy and the Family* https://doi.org/10.1093/lawfam/ebab011

Saraswati, Rika, 'Gender Bias in Indonesian Courts: Is Perma No. 3 of 2017 the Solution for Gender-Based Violence Cases?' (2021b) 10(2) *Laws* 1–16.

Schenk, Christine, 'Islamic Leaders and the Legal Geography of Family Law in Aceh, Indonesia' (2018) 184 *The Geographical Journal* 8–18.

Sumner, Cate and Tim Lindsey, 'Courting Reform: Indonesia's Islamic Courts and Justice for the Poor' (2011) 4(1) *International Journal for Court Administration* 3–16.

Sumner, Cate and Nani Zulminarni, 'Looking Back, Looking Forward: Women's Access to the Religious Courts of Indonesia' (Policy Paper, 2018).

Susanti, Laras, 'Another Marriage Law Controversy: Is Reform Overdue?' (2022) *Indonesia at Melbourne* https://indonesiaatmelbourne.unimelb.edu.au/another-marriage-law-controversy-is-reform-overdue/

Syarif, Nurrohman, 'The Discourse and Practice of Islamic Family Law in Indonesia' (2021) 58(1) *Psychology and Education* 5201–5212.

Syukur, Fatahillah Abdul and Dale Bagshaw, 'When Home Is No Longer "sweet": Family Violence and Sharia-annexed Mediation in Indonesia' (2013) 30(3) *Conflict Resolution Quarterly* 271–294.

Tirtawening and Rini Maryam, 'The Urgency of Applying Domestic Violence Screening Mechanism for Divorce Mediation in Religious Court' (2018) 30(1) *Mimbar Hukum* 140–154.

Triana, Nita, 'Progressivity of Judges in Domestic Violence Disputes Settlement in the Case of Divorce in the Religious Court' (2018) 2(1) *Jurnal Studi dan Penelitian Hukum Islam* 1–29.

Vignato, Silvia, '"Men come in, men go out": Single Muslim Women in Malaysia and Aceh' (2012) 18(2) *Social Identities* 239–257.

Yusuf, Nasruddin, Nur Azizah and Faradila Hasan, 'Feminist Analysis of Judges' Considerations for Post-Divorce Domestic Violence Victims in Medan and Banda Aceh Religious Courts' (2023) 20(2) *Al-'Adalah* 283–308.

Laws and regulation cited in Chapter 5

Law No. 23/ 2004 regarding the Elimination of Domestic Violence (*Undang-Undang tentang Penghapusan Kekerasan Dalam Rumah Tangga*).

Law No. 1/1974 Marriage Law.

Government Regulation No. 9/1975.

Presidential Instruction No. 1/1991 (*Compilation of Islamic Law*).

Law No. 11/2006 (Law on Governing Aceh).

Supreme Court Regulation No. 1/2008 regarding court mediation procedures.

Supreme Court Regulation No. 1/2016 regarding court mediation procedures.
Supreme Court Regulation No. 3/2017 on adjudicating cases in relation to women facing the law.

List of interviews cited in Chapter 5

Interview with Ibu Commissioner (*Komnas Perempuan*) (Jakarta, 12 January 2018).
Interview with Bapak S (Lawyer) (Banda Aceh, 15 December 2017).
Interview with Cate Sumner (Online, 8 August 2019).
Interview with a female Islamic Court judge (Banda Aceh, 25 September 2018).

6 Domestic Violence, Policing and Prosecution

Prologue to this chapter

July 2019, at the police station

Ibu Hayati sits next to Ibu Risa at the police station.

> 'There is nothing we can do', the officer explains. 'We don't have any evidence to charge him.'
>
> 'I saw it myself', Ibu Risa offers. 'He threatened to kill her – please, there must be something you can do. She even has texts on her phone, show them *Kak* –'
>
> 'It's just', the officer interrupts, 'that this kind of case … it's not that serious (*tidak berat*).
>
> With household problems, it's better to go P2TP2A – they deal with cases like this.'
>
> 'Come on let's go', Ibu Risa says, taking Ibu Hayati's hand.
>
> (Source for the above: Author's own)

Introduction

Most cases of domestic violence are mediated at the community level and victims who engage with the State generally do so by applying for a divorce at the Islamic Courts. However, the primary State institution responsible for the implementation of the Law is the *Pengadilan Negeri*. For a case to reach the *Pengadilan Negeri*, domestic violence must first be reported to and investigated by the police and then pursued by the prosecution. This chapter analyses the role of the police and prosecution in implementing the Law. Reporting domestic violence to the police is the entry point for victims to the State criminal system. There is, however, a general reluctance on the part of the police to investigate domestic violence cases, largely due to gender bias and a lack of understanding of the Law. Current police practices create a bottleneck in terms of entry into the State system, impeding victim protection and accountability for perpetrators.

DOI: 10.4324/9781032613642-6

It is well established in the broader scholarly literature that policing in Indonesia suffers from issues, such as corruption, inadequate training, low community trust, and a lack of representation of women.[1] As such, these issues are not canvassed in great detail, instead this chapter focuses on women's experiences with frontline police and the *Unit Pelayanan Perempuan dan Anak Polresta* (the Women's and Children's Protection Police Unit, known as the 'PPA Unit'). The PPA Unit's practices and procedures, at best, represent the forefront of women's protection in law enforcement.[2] However, the PPA Unit is not representative of broader attitudes and practices in the police force. Women seeking to report domestic violence generally report to the *Sentra Pelayanan Kepolisian Terpadu* (the Integrated Police Service Centre or 'SPKT'), which is the frontline or general police force. Distinctions will be drawn between the practices of the PPA Unit and frontline police throughout this chapter.

During fieldwork I interviewed representatives from the Banda Aceh police and prosecution. The institutional representative of the police was Ibu E – the head of the PPA Unit (Banda Aceh) at the time. Ibu E is a highly respected community figure with over 15 years of experience working with women and children. The institutional representative for the prosecution team (*Kejaksaan Agung*) was Ibu S, who specialised in domestic violence cases in Banda Aceh.

Women's experiences with frontline police

Overall, very few incidents of domestic violence are reported to police. This is because of compounding barriers that prevent or deter women from reporting violence. In an interview, Ibu Commissioner (*Komnas Perempuan*) identified three main obstacles in domestic violence law enforcement in Indonesia. First, the fact that law enforcement officers generally lack an understanding of gender perspectives, reflective of a lack of relevant training. Second, there is a tendency for police to mediate disputes, which involves 'the husband apologising, the wife forgiving the husband, and violence occurring again' (I argue below that such conduct does not constitute authentic mediation). Third, as explained by Ibu Commissioner:

> in law enforcement, victim-blaming often occurs, and this is part of the reason that victims no longer demand their cases be followed up. So, we have a problem whereby the law has advanced, but law enforcement and the culture of the community has not changed. This is a challenge for victims.

Victim interviews support the Commissioner's suggestions that due to gender bias and/or a lack of understanding of the Law, police officers continue to prevent victims from reporting violence. One victim interviewed explained:

> I requested protection from the police. I reported to the police. I, as a citizen, have the right to protection. Then they said that what I experienced was not physical violence but psychological violence. They advised me

> that women should report to P2TP2A instead of the police. Then I experienced all kinds of terror. I didn't live in one house with my husband, he came to my office, he threatened to take my car, he wanted to kill me. I tried again to report it to police, but they would not take action. Then I reported it to the Regional Police with evidence of SMS messages, proof of threats and terror from my husband. But they said that they could not take action due to it being a household problem (*masalah rumah tangaa*), they said 'wait until you already have a court decision [of divorce from the Islamic Court], only then we take action'.

The rejection of reports by frontline police is in direct contradiction to Article 19 of the Law, which states that the police are obliged to immediately investigate after receiving a report of domestic violence. Further, the Law does not require victims of domestic violence to obtain a divorce before reporting to the police. Indeed, to require victims to be divorced before reporting violence would largely undermine the operation of the Law. Therefore, the police officer's refusal to accept the victim's report in the example above has no legal basis. Such conduct would likely be based on a lack of understanding of the Law, informed by the pervasive idea that domestic violence is a 'private' issue.

Another victim interviewed spoke about her experience of police protecting other officers who commit violence against their spouses:

> My husband is a police officer. I experienced violence so I had to be admitted to the hospital. I had experienced violence for a long time but the most serious instance was in 2017. Because my husband is a respected police officer at POLDA [the Provincial Police], my case has not received exposure. I also reported it to the Police Chief in Jakarta … when the case was finally closed, I felt that there was no justice.

Another victim stated that because her husband was an 'important person' who worked in government, she did not report for fear that her case would be dismissed by authorities. Interviews with women's advocates from P2TP2A support victim also accounts of their reports being rejected or mishandled by frontline police. For example, Ibu S (P2TP2A) stated that 'although the Law greatly accommodates women's interests, law enforcement generally does not have sufficient understanding of the Law'. The experiences of these victims are not isolated incidents, nor are such experiences unique to Aceh. Other scholars writing on law enforcement in Indonesia support victims' perspectives of police practices towards domestic violence. For example, Parnohadiningrat (2002) found that, in Indonesia, domestic violence is 'generally regarded by local police as a private matter. In most cases, law enforcement personnel are not responsive to the plight of women victims'. Further, Parawansa (2002) asserts that 'patriarchal values' are embedded in government institutions, including the police.

Multiple respondents also stated in interviews that victim reports were sometimes rejected by frontline police on the basis that the victim had not yet engaged in village level mediation. In the Acehnese context, this stems from a misunderstanding of *Qanun* No. 9/2008 (introduced in Chapter 3).[3] There is, in fact, a Memorandum of Understanding between the Governor of Aceh, the Acehnese *Adat* Assembly (*Majelis Adat Aceh*), and the police that provides for the resolution of 'petty' or 'minor' (*ringan*) disputes at the village level.[4] For 'minor' cases, if the case is resolved at the village level, a copy of the mediation outcome must be sent to the police and, if the case is not resolved, it must be referred up the village chain of command from the Head of the Village (*Geuchik*) to the Head of the Village Collective (*Mukim*), or reported to the police.

Under Aceh Governor Regulation No. 60/2013, there are strict time limits for these 'community policing' arrangements. If the dispute has not been mediated within three days at the village level or referred up to, and resolved at, the *Mukim* level within nine days, the victim can report directly to the police.[5] Further, as outlined in Chapter 3, cases that are considered severe (*parah*) do not have to pass through village mediation processes. In such cases, victims of domestic violence can immediately report to any division of the police, although, as noted by Venning (2010), there may be social consequences for bypassing village mediation processes. 'Community policing' arrangements and police rejection of victim reports in relation to *adat* mediation are not specific to the Acehnese context and has also been documented by Lestarini et al. (2021) in West Sumatra.

When women's accounts of their reports being rejected by police was put to the Head of the PPA Unit, Ibu E clarified that:

> in general, domestic violence cases reported to the PPA Unit are accepted, because we have obligations under Regulation No. 7/2008 concerning the implementation of human rights. The police ***must not reject*** public reports.[6] But they may facilitate, if the case is mild, for it to be passed to the *Geuchik* first because of the [community policing] agreement (emphasis added).

Women's accounts of their reports being rejected by frontline police do not fit the exemption outlined by Ibu E. Based on women's reports, frontline officers are not formally referring cases to mediation (either at the village level or at P2TP2A) but are simply turning women away without investigation, recourse, or protection. Rejection of women's reports are clearly distinguishable from genuine mediation referrals made by police.[7] The failure of police to carry out their roles and responsibilities under the Law is an example of bureaucratic violence. Overall, the interviews indicate that frontline police attitudes towards domestic violence do not substantially differ from the general community understandings outlined in Chapter 4. This is unsurprising as, in lieu of adequate training on domestic violence and the Law, police opinions are informed by the local context.

If a victim's report is processed by the PPA Unit rather than the frontline police, it is likely that her report will not be arbitrarily rejected. In general, PPA

Unit officers generally receive specialised training and have a better understanding of the Law. The problem is that if victims are not accompanied by a women's advocate or lawyer, they are unlikely to report directly to the PPA Unit and would rely on frontline officers to refer them to the PPA Unit (if there is one locally). Further, not all police stations have PPA Units. According to Afrianty (2018), in 2016, there were only '305 PPA units operating across Indonesia'.[8] To put PPA Unit's operation into perspective, the Banda Aceh PPA Unit only handled 12 cases in 2017 and 13 cases in 2018. Keeping in mind the limited number of cases that the PPA Units handles in comparison to frontline police, this next section outlines the PPA Unit's approach and procedures.

Women's and Children's Protection Unit

At the PPA Unit, cases are first screened to determine if the victim has experienced domestic violence, as well as to explain the victim's rights (as required under Article 18 of the Law). In practice, cases that are considered 'not too serious' may be screened out of the system at this point. However, if the victim has experienced 'severe abuse', then the case is likely to proceed through the police process. Although PPA Unit staff are better trained than frontline police, the determination of whether a case is 'serious' or not is still informed by the understandings of domestic violence outlined in Chapter 4. This is consistent with Venning's (2010) study where she found that police are only likely to be involved in 'cases where the victim is seriously injured or the violence becomes visible from outside the home'.

If the screening process reveals that the victim has experienced domestic violence, she will be taken to the SPKT 'front desk' to make an official police report. At the SPKT, if the victim chooses to file an official report, the victim will be asked to meet with a detective to commence an initial investigation and determine which part of the Law applies to the case. After the initial investigation, the case will be submitted to the Director for case allocation. If the Director agrees that the nature of the case is domestic violence, the case is likely to be allocated to the PPA Unit. If the case is allocated to the PPA Unit, a PPA Unit investigator will be appointed to the case.

Within the PPA Unit, the presence of female investigators is recognised as important to improving victim comfort and trust when reporting violence, particularly in cases of sexual violence where victims may find speaking to male officers embarrassing and even a form of secondary victimisation. All PPA personnel receive training to handle cases involving women and children. However, multiple respondents identified high staff turnover at PPA, due to the transfer of officers between police units, as a barrier to improving institutional understanding of women's issues. Therefore, even though PPA staff are better trained than frontline officers, it cannot be assumed that all PPA personnel necessarily have expertise in domestic violence.

Under Articles 44(4), 45(2) and 46 of the Law, physical, psychological, or sexual violence committed specifically between spouses (as opposed to within other family or household relationships) is a *delik aduan* offense. *Delik aduan* can be translated as 'complaint offence', as opposed to *delik biasa* a 'normal offence', which does not require a complaint. This means that the victim themselves must report the crime to trigger a police investigation (or delegate authority to someone to report of their behalf).[9] Essentially, the police cannot take action in cases of inter-spousal physical, psychological, or sexual violence unless the victim supports the report.

The PPA Unit handles all cases in accordance with Police Regulation No. 14/2012 regarding investigation management.[10] The first step in investigating the case is collecting evidence. This process usually takes one to two weeks and may involve getting a warrant, visiting the crime scene, and taking witness testimony. The aim of the investigation process is to secure two pieces of valid evidence.[11] Under Article 55 of the Law, domestic violence prosecutions only require one piece of evidence in addition to the victim's testimony, as the victim's testimony is regarded as a valid piece of evidence. The type of evidence required depends on the nature of the case. For example, in a case of physical or sexual violence, a medical report (*visum*) documenting the physical evidence could be sought from the hospital, while for a case of psychological violence a psychiatrist's report could be obtained.[12] Another example of non-compliance with the Law is the fact that frontline officers often do not regard the victim's testimony as constituting valid evidence, despite the clear wording of Article 55.

In addition to investigation, the police will ask victims who fall into the 'not too serious' category whether they are willing to undertake mediation via referral to P2TP2A. Notably, while all interviews were conducted in Indonesian, Ibu E (head of the PPA Unit) used the English phrase 'restorative justice' to describe these mediation practices. As discussed below, it is questionable whether current mediation practices constitute restorative justice in a substantive sense. The use of the phrase 'restorative justice' is closer in meaning to 'restoring peaceful/harmonious household relations'. Contrastingly, cases which are considered 'severe' are not usually subject to mediation.

In addition to violence being categorised by severity/physicality of violence, a number of assumptions underpinning the PPA Unit's approach were documented during fieldwork. The first is an assumption of reciprocity, that violence is not one-sided and that both parties are culpable to some extent by contributing to negative domestic relations.[13] Second, there is an underlying assumption that the perpetrator's behaviour can change in the absence of therapeutic interventions. For example, perpetrators are often asked to simply 'promise' not to commit violence again, without the provision of support for behavioural change.[14] Third, the PPA Unit's approach implicitly accepts that there are standalone and remediable causes of domestic violence, as opposed to domestic violence being the result of unequal power relations and violence used as a tool by perpetrators to control or subjugate their partners. In focusing on discrete 'causes' of violence, such as infidelity or economic hardship, the police approach implicitly preferences an incident-based (rather than a pattern-based) understanding of domestic violence. This can be compared to the categorisation of domestic violence by Ibu R (P2TP2A/*Balai Syura*) as 'patterns of violence that are closely related to unequal or unbalanced relations (*relasinya yang tidak seimbang*)'. These assumptions illustrate that even though PPA Unit practices are greatly improved compared to frontline policing, there also have limitations and PPA Unit officers are not immune from carrying gender bias and stereotypes about domestic violence into their work.

Memorandum of Understanding between P2TP2A and PPA Unit (Banda Aceh)

Notably, the PPA Unit have a Memorandum of Understanding with P2TP2A ('MOU') which allows victims to be paired with support persons throughout the reporting process. This MOU allows victims to be accompanied by a women's advocate from P2TP2A or a local NGO; less commonly victims are accompanied by a lawyer (paid or pro bono). Against the background of poor police compliance with the Law, the function of women's advocates and lawyers is significant. When accompanying victims, women's advocates play an important role – clarifying to the police that: 'This is a case of domestic violence, this is the relevant law, this is the relevant provision.'

The importance of women being accompanied by women's advocates is also illustrated in the broader literature. For example, in her study of domestic violence in Indonesia, Afrianty (2018) quotes a paralegal saying:

> I took her [the victim] to the police station. When we got there, we were told that the police headquarters does not have a PPA Unit and were asked by a male police officer in that station to go to the provincial police headquarters, which is a long way from the village. But we went there regardless. When we arrived at the police station, our report was taken, then the police officer told us to go to the hospital to get a medical report (*visum*) … When we arrived at the clinic, we were asked to pay a fee [it should be free] in order to receive the report. They insisted that we pay, but neither of us had brought any money. They only waived the fee after I finally told them 'I am a paralegal'.

One the of most significant practices that flows from the MOU is the formal referral of cases from the PPA Unit to P2TP2A for the purposes of mediation. Referrals by PPA Unit officers to mediation conducted by P2TP2A can be distinguished from frontline police informally 'mediating' cases. To clarify, the term 'mediation' used below refers to formal mediation processes conducted by P2TP2A, as contrasted with ad-hoc or informal recommendations made by police that women return home and make peace with their husbands. Informal recommendations are categorised in this book as akin to rejection of a report as opposed to genuine mediation, as they are not facilitated by the police in any way. Further, although in Banda Aceh the PPA Unit is closely partnered with the local P2TP2A to facilitate mediation under the MOU, this does not seem to be a standard practice for PPA Units across Indonesia. For example, in Sukendar et al.'s (2023) study they found that in Central Java, PPA Unit staff directly mediate cases of domestic violence.

Under the MOU, if both parties agree to mediate, the matter is referred by the PPA Unit to P2TP2A to facilitate mediation in coordination with family and *adat* or religious leaders. Victims weigh many different considerations in deciding whether to mediate rather than pursuing a police report. Ibu E explained that many victims prefer to resolve their cases through mediation to preserve family unity, especially if there are children in the marriage. Shame or stigma around the husband going to jail is also a strong factor, as well as the expediency of finalising the issue through mediation as opposed to often lengthy court proceedings. This is supported by Speedian's (2014) study of domestic violence policing in Indonesia which identified barriers including: violence being considered a 'private issue', the victim's love for their partner, shame in reporting, and the presence of children. Ibu E stated that generally P2TP2A mediation referrals result in 'reconciliation and reunion'. That is, that the cases do not return to the police. However, this does not necessarily mean that perpetrators cease using violence in all cases.

Upon referral, P2TP2A assist the victim and perpetrator to produce a 'settlement letter' (*surat perdamaian*). These letters include both parties identifying what they feel are triggers for violence in their relationship in order to avoid these in the future. For example, in a case of economic violence, the letter may state 'I want my husband to provide economic maintenance (*nafkah lahir*)'. If the husband has the means to provide maintenance (*nafkah*), terms for the provision of *nafkah* owed by the husband to the wife will be included in the settlement letter. A notable outcome of the cooperation between the PPA Unit and P2TP2A is that it allows victims to request, and potentially secure, an economic outcome in terms of maintenance. This is unique as in the criminal justice context fines are generally paid to the State rather than directly to the victims. Police referrals to mediation therefore have the potential to provide a broader range of outcomes for victims than would be available through traditional criminal law avenues, in particular the payment of *nafkah*. The significance of this is evident in cases studies in Chapter 7, as the *Pengadilan Negeri* generally only imposes carceral sentences and, for a number of reasons, incarceration of the perpetrator may not meet the victim's needs.

Once mediation has been conducted, P2TP2A informs the police of the outcome. If mediation is 'unsuccessful' and the victim elects to proceed with their report, the case will be referred back to the police. The victim can also be referred to the Islamic Courts to apply for a divorce at this juncture, if relevant. If a settlement letter between the husband and wife is made, but the husband later breaches the agreement, for example by not providing *nafkah* (maintenance) as promised, or by committing physical, sexual, or psychological violence, the wife can report the breach of the agreement directly to the PPA Unit.

In best case scenarios, mediated settlement letters can act as equalising instruments that place the police and the Law on the side of the victim to encourage the perpetrator to change their behaviour or else face the case continuing to criminal prosecution. However, if there is a breach of an agreement post-mediation this will only be brought to the attention of the police if the victim reports it herself, as there are no follow-up or monitoring procedures in place. If the agreement is breached and the victim reports that breach to the PPA Unit, the case can continue directly to prosecution because, according to Ibu E, 'he promised not to do it again and he did it again, so we did not have "restorative justice"' (that is, a restoration of peaceful marital relations).

At this stage, the investigation can be intensified including by using coercive methods under the Criminal Code, such as calling witnesses. With respect to investigation of domestic violence cases, interviewees from P2TP2A (Ibu S and Ibu A) highlighted difficulties in collecting evidence due to the private nature of domestic violence cases and the associated lack of witnesses. This is consistent with the broader literature, for example Hudson (2002) who states that many criminal cases fail due to a lack of evidence as 'most cases occur in private, so there are no witnesses'.

Even if a case is 'not severe', if the victim does not want to engage in mediation, or does not 'forgive' the perpetrator during mediation, the case can continue to prosecution. It appears that women's perspectives are given meaningful weight during PPA Unit procedures, in that, even if violence is not considered 'severe' from a police perspective, the victim can still choose whether to mediate or pursue their report. On the other hand, a victim may request to withdraw their complaint at any time in the investigation before the case progresses to the prosecutor. While PPA Unit officers allow victims to choose whether to mediate or pursue their report, there is tangible frustration from law enforcement when victims drop their case but later seek help after violence occurs again. Ibu E explained how if the police investigate (including interviewing witnesses and collecting evidence) only to have the victim revoke their report, in such circumstances, officers often feel that their time has been wasted.

The nature of domestic violence means it is common for victims to make and withdraw reports, or otherwise leave and return to perpetrators, multiple times before reporting or leaving the relationship with any finality. Police frustration with victim withdrawal from cases is somewhat incongruous in the context of a system that actively promotes mediation and reconciliation. It also overlooks the broader, compounding barriers to reporting experienced by women, including economic dependency and fear for children's safety. As discussed in Chapter 4, women may also be pressured not to report or to withdraw reports, by perpetrators, family, and/or community members. Women may also be discouraged or victim-blamed by police, leading to the withdrawal of their report. Even where service providers are supportive, help-seeking is not linear and victims may engage with, and withdraw from, help-seeking processes over time.

Despite such barriers, many institutional stakeholders identified victim withdrawal as one of the biggest 'obstacles' to prosecution. Ibu E explained that 'sometimes the victim does not want to continue her case to court even though the violence experienced is quite severe'. For example, in a case study shared by Ibu K – a victim was beaten using a beam and received 12 stitches, the victim returned to the police station two days after her husband was arrested to ask for her husband to be released because she did not have any money and was economically dependent on him. This example illuminates the tension between victimhood and agency in the context of policing. While there is a preference for prosecution in cases of 'severe abuse', as interspousal violence is a *delik aduan* (complaint) offence police cannot force victims to report violence.

Police protection function

In addition to investigation, police also have a protection function. Once the victim has made a complaint, within 24 hours the police must provide temporary protection to the victim (Article 16(1) of the Law). Temporary protection can be provided for up to a maximum of seven days (Article 16(2) of the Law). Article 16(3) of the Law states that the police must also immediately request a protection order from the court. Under Article 28 of the Law, within seven days of receiving the application for protection, the court must issue a ruling unless there is a justification for not doing so. Court-ordered protection orders may be provided for a period of up to one year and can be extended by a court ruling (Article 32 of the Law). Although under the Law there is scope for protection orders to be granted, there is a lack of consistency in the provision of temporary protection, including – as explained in Chapter 1 – the fact that there are currently no operational safe houses in Banda Aceh.

Further, if a woman reports violence or otherwise seeks to leave the relationship, perpetrators may use threats of violence or actual violence against the victim. Therefore, in circumstances where police are not proactive in providing protection, women may feel afraid of reporting or continuing with a report in the face of police ambivalence (or police non-compliance with the victim's rights under the Law). Bapak S (Lawyer) explained 'it's very difficult if the victims are afraid of their husbands. There are some who do not receive direct protection from the police … they will surely be afraid that they will be beaten or killed by their husbands'. Police failure to quickly process reports and the lack of reliable interim protection for victims prevents engagement with the criminal justice system in cases where victims fear violent retaliation from perpetrators. Due to this gap in the policing protection framework, in practice, village leaders, women's NGO or P2TP2A staff are more likely to provide temporary protection for victims.

Domestic violence prosecution

The prosecutor interviewed (Ibu S) explained that the criminal prosecution process commences when the police notify the prosecution that the investigation has begun (by letter of notification – *Surat Pemberitahuan Dimulainya*

Penyidikan – 'SPDP').[15] A week after the SPDP is sent, the case file must be sent to the prosecutor. The prosecutor then has two weeks to examine the case. If any further information or evidence is required, the prosecution will return further instructions to the police. After the police complete the relevant requests for the prosecutor, the prosecution has another 14 days to examine the file. Once the prosecutor is satisfied that the police investigation is complete, they will issue a notice called a 'P21'. A 'P21' is a form that the prosecutor issues to confirm that the case has been formally accepted for transfer from the police. After the P21 has been issued, the police and prosecutor coordinate to hand over all the evidence. The case then becomes the responsibility of the prosecutor to prepare for trial. After receiving the evidence from the police, the prosecution has a time limit of 20 days to bring the case to court for its first mention.

One of the primary differences between the police investigation and prosecution stages is that the victim is no longer able to withdraw the case once it proceeds to prosecution, as the victim becomes a witness for the prosecution. The victim is then referred to as a *mitra* (partner) in the criminal justice process as opposed to a *korban* (victim). Ibu S explained that once the case been delegated to the prosecutor's office:

> if the case fulfills formal and material elements, we will still take it to the court even if [the relationship] is peaceful, because peace does not abolish the crime … no one will be let off from a domestic violence case that has been delegated to the prosecutor's office except … if we cannot satisfy the evidence, then a SP3 will be issued. The SP3 aims to stop the case if there is insufficient evidence.

Prosecution in Indonesia has been described by Wicaksono (2018) as rigid and positivistic. Prosecution in domestic violence cases could even be described as mandatory prosecution as there is little discretion for a prosecutor to terminate a case, with the only grounds for cessation being insufficient evidence, double jeopardy, or the death of a defendant. When prosecuting domestic violence cases, Ibu S stated that what is important are the actions of the perpetrator rather than their motivations. The circumstances of the crime are taken into consideration during sentencing rather than in deciding whether to prosecute. The prosecutorial approach can be contrasted to the approach of other actors in the community and criminal justice systems who focus more on the perceived causes of (or, even, justifications for) domestic violence.

Conclusion

This chapter illustrated that, in the policing context, when domestic violence victims report to frontline police there are substantial barriers to access to justice due to gender bias and a lack of understanding of the Law. Victim accounts of their reports being rejected by frontline officers are supported by women's advocates, P2TP2A, and *Komnas Perempuan*, as well as in the broader Indonesian literature.

The failure of frontline police to comply with their responsibilities under the Law creates a bottleneck for victims in terms of receiving State protection, as well as constituting bureaucratic violence against victims in certain circumstances. The exception to this is the PPA Unit which specialises in women's and children's cases. Although the PPA Unit handles a very small number of cases per year, better training for officers within this unit makes a difference to the processing of domestic violence reports.

Further, this chapter provided insights into PPA Unit processes in the case study context Banda Aceh, in particular with respect to community policing arrangements and referrals to P2TP2A mediation. The MOU between the PPA Unit and P2TP2A provides a potential model that other PPA Units could adopt across Indonesia. The high level of cooperation between the PPA Unit and P2TP2A reduces the likelihood of victims falling between the cracks of the two institutions, which can be contrasted against the lack of coordination between the religious and criminal jurisdictions.

Last, this chapter briefly outlined prosecutorial processes. Understanding how the police and prosecution approach domestic violence cases and the barriers and limitations of these processes is essential to understanding the *Pengadilan Negeri* processes explored in the next chapter.

Notes

1 See, for example, reports by Rahmawati (2015) and the International Crisis Group (2012) and policy brief by the Indonesian Ministry of Women's and Children's Empowerment and Protection (2011).

2 Article 6 of Regulation No. 10/2007 regarding the organisational structure of the PPA Unit states that the Unit is tasked with 'providing protection for women and children who are victims of crime and law enforcement against perpetrators'.

3 For a discussion of *Qanun* No. 9/2008, see Chapter 3.

4 *Keputusan Bersama Gubernur Aceh, Kepala Polisian Daerah Aceh dan Ketua Majelis Adat Aceh*, No. 189/677/2011 regarding *Adat* Justice in Aceh.

5 Article 17(5) of Governor Regulation No. 60/2013 regarding the Implementation of Dispute Resolution via Customary and Traditional Avenues.

6 The interviewee is referring here to Article 13(2) of Police Regulation No. 7/2008 regarding the Implementation of Human Rights: 'Every member of the police is prohibited from: (a) rejecting reports or complaints from the public without a valid reason; (b) refusing a request for help from someone who needs help or seeks justice without a valid reason'.

7 Note that in Venning's (2010) research conducted in Bali, she documented police-conducted 'mediations' in response to reports of domestic violence. Such mediations resulted in a signed agreement to the effect that the husband 'would not influent violence on his wife or children again'.

8 PPAs units can be distinguished from *Ruang Pelayanan Khusus* (Special Service Rooms – RPK) which, under Article 13 of the Law, need to be established at every police station.

9 See Articles 51–53 of the Law, noting that economic violence in the Law is not a *delik aduan* offence. See Article 26 of the Law for an example of delegated authority.

10 Note that this regulation outlines general police procedure and is not specific to domestic violence cases.

11 Article 183 of the Criminal Procedure Code (KUHAP): 'A judge may not impose criminal liability on a person unless he has been convinced with at least two pieces of valid evidence that a criminal act has truly been committed and it is the accused who is guilty of committing it.'.

12 Under Article 21(b) of the Law, health workers must prepare a written report or medical certificate on the results of the victim examination at the request of the police investigator.

13 Note that scholar Stubbs (2002) argues that constructing domestic violence as a 'relationship problem' as opposed to a criminal act compromises victim safety.

14 As discussed in Chapter 1, perpetrator rehabilitation programmes are not currently available in Aceh.

15 The procedures described in this paragraph are set out in Chapter IV 'Police Investigator and Public Prosecutor' and Chapter XIV 'Investigation' of the Criminal Procedure Code (Law No. 8/1981), see specifically Articles 7, 8, 14, 109 and 110.

Bibliography

Abdurrachman, Hamidah, 'A Culture of Neglect: A Study of Indonesian Court Judgements Regarding Victims of Domestic Violence' (2017) 55 *International Annals or Criminology* 26–39.

Afrianty, Dina, 'Agents for Change: Local Women's Organizations and Domestic Violence in Indonesia' (2018) 174 *Bijdragen tot de Taal-, Landen Volkenkunde* 24–46, 39.

Butt, Simon and Tim Lindsey, *Indonesian Law* (Oxford, 2018).

Hudson, Barbara, 'Restorative Justice and Gendered Violence: Diversion or Effective Justice?' (2002) 42(3) *British Journal of Criminology* 616–634.

Indonesian Ministry of Women's and Children's Empowerment and Protection, 'Violence Against Women: Domestic Violence and Human Trafficking' (Policy Brief, 2011).

International Crisis Group, *Indonesia: The Deadly Cost of Poor Policing* (Report, 2012).

Lestarini, Ratih, Dianwidhi Pranoto, and Tirtaweng Tirtawening, 'The Fault in Traditional and Formal Approaches to Domestic Violence: A Call for Reform in West Sumatra' (2021) 22(1) *Journal of International Women's Studies* 152–165.

Memorandum of Understanding between the Governor of Aceh, the Acehnese Adat Assembly, and the Police (*Keputusan Bersama Gubernur Aceh, Kepala Polisian Daerah Aceh dan Ketua Majelis Adat Aceh*, No. 189/677/2011 regarding *Adat* Justice in Aceh).

Munir, Lily, 'Domestic Violence in Indonesia' (2005) 2(1) *Muslim World Journal of Human Rights* 1–37.

National Coalition Against Domestic Violence, 'Why Do Victims Stay?' https://ncadv.org/why-do-victims-stay

Parawansa, Khofifah Indar, 'Institution Building: An Effort to Improve Indonesian Women's Role and Status' in Kathryn Robinson and Sharon Bessel (eds), *Women in Indonesia: Gender, Equity and Development* (ISAS, 2002) 68–77.

Parnohadiningrat, Sudjadnan, 'Prologue' in Kathryn Robinson and Sharon Bessel (eds), *Women in Indonesia: Gender, Equity and Development* (ISAS, 2002).

Rahmawati, Eka, 'Long Road to Equality and Gender Mainstreaming in the Indonesian National Police' (Report, 2015).

Saraswati, Rika, 'Gender Bias in Indonesian Courts: Is Perma No. 3 of 2017 the Solution for Gender-Based Violence Cases?' (2021) 10(2) *Laws* 1–16.

Speedian, Hadi, 'Peran Kepolisian dalam Melindungi Hak Istri Sebagai Korban Penelantaran Keluarga' (Research Paper, 2014).

Stubbs, Julie, 'Domestic Violence and Women's Safety' in Heather Strang and John Braithwaite (eds), *Restorative Justice and Family Violence* (Cambridge University Press, 2002).

Sukendar, Muhammad Saifullah, Priyambudi Sulistiyanto, Luthfi Rahman and Hasan Asy'ari Ulamai, 'Women's Access to Justice: Mediation for the Victims of Domestic Violence in Central Java, Indonesia' (2023) 7(1) *Samarah: Jurnal Hukum Keluarga dan Hukum Islam* 602–628.

Triana, Nita, 'Progressivity of Judges in Domestic Violence Disputes Settlement in the Case of Divorce in the Religious Court' (2018) 2(1) *Jurnal Studi dan Penelitian Hukum Islam* 1–29.

Venning, Philippa, 'Marrying Contested Approaches: Empowerment and the Imposition of International Principles: Domestic Violence Case Resolution in Indonesia' (2010) 46(3) *The Journal of Development Studies* 396–416.

Wicaksono, Adi Hardiyanto, 'Reposition of Local Wisdom Based on Pancasila on the Function of the Prosecution of Attorney as a Legal Enforcement Component in Indonesia' (2018) 1(1) *Asian Journal of Law and Jurisprudence* 23–31.

Laws and regulations cited in Chapter 6

Law No. 23/ 2004 regarding the Elimination of Domestic Violence (*Undang-Undang tentang Penghapusan Kekerasan Dalam Rumah Tangga*).

Law No. 8/1981 Criminal Procedure Code *(Kitab Undang-Undang Hukum Acara Pidana – KUHP)*.

Police Regulation No. 10/2007 regarding the Organisation and Work of the Women's and Children's Protection Unit.

Police Regulation No. 7/2008 regarding the Implementation of Human Rights.

Police Regulation No. 14/2012 regarding Investigation Management.

Governor Regulation No. 60/2013 regarding the Implementation of Dispute Resolution via Customary and Traditional Avenues.

Interviews cited in Chapter 6

Interview with Ibu A (Head of P2TP2A) (Banda Aceh, 17 January 2018).

Interview with Ibu Commissioner (*Komnas Perempuan*) (Jakarta, 12 January 2018).

Interview Ibu K (academic and Head of Faculty) (Banda Aceh, 15 December 2017).

Interview with Bapak S (Lawyer) (Banda Aceh, 15 December 2017).

Interview Ibu S (P2TP2A) (Banda Aceh, 21 December 2017)

Interview Ibu S (Prosecutor) (Banda Aceh, 25 September 2018).

Interview with Ibu E (the head of the Women's and Children's Protection Unit) (Banda Aceh, 24 September 2018).

Interviews with victims of domestic violence (Banda Aceh, 19 January 2019).

7 Domestic Violence at the *Pengadilan Negeri*

Introduction

This chapter analyses a sample of 70 cases of domestic violence heard by the *Pengadilan Negeri* in Banda Aceh between 2013 and 2017. To put these cases into perspective, each victim is likely to have first mediated her case before the *Geuchik* at the village level. She may also have sought help from local women's organisations or P2TP2A and/or may have applied for a divorce at the Islamic Courts, in addition to reporting her case to the police and cooperating with prosecution. The cases studied cannot be viewed in isolation from the journey that the victims undertook to get to this point and the compounding barriers to justice that each victim overcame in doing so. The case data outlined in this chapter provides insight into how judges approach and apply the Law. However, there is also an obvious gap in the data between the prosecution pursuing a case and the court handing down a decision and sentencing – that is, the trial process. As court proceedings are closed for domestic violence cases in Indonesia, I was not able to gather data on the trial process.[1] Nevertheless, since it is well established in the broader literature that the trial process for domestic violence cases can traumatise or re-victimise victims, it is safe to assume that this is also the case in Aceh and throughout Indonesia.[2] While the trial process falls outside the scope of this chapter, it should be noted as part of the legal process that victims must negotiate in seeking to assert their rights under the Law.

Overview of *Pengadilan Negeri* jurisdiction

As previously mentioned, the *Pengadilan Negeri* has direct jurisdiction over domestic violence cases under the Law. According to Chapter VIII (Articles 44–49) of the Law, domestic violence has three primary elements:

1 Anyone ('*setiap orang*' – identity of the perpetrator);
2 Who commits violence ('*melakukan perbuatan kekerasan fisik*' – act of the perpetrator);
3 Within the household ('*dalam lingkup rumah tangga*' – nature or relationship of the perpetrator with respect to the victim).

DOI: 10.4324/9781032613642-7

Depending on the charge brought by the prosecutor there may also be a fourth element, namely 'resulting in serious injury'. For example, it is common for the prosecution to present Article 44(2) (where the perpetrator's act causes the victim to sustain an illness or serious injury) and Article 44(4) (where the perpetrator's act does not bring about illness or obstruction of livelihood/daily activities) as alternatives. The court's interpretation of the first and third elements (outlined above) was consistent across the 70 cases studied, namely that:

1 'Anyone' means a legal subject who is capable of being held criminally responsible (that is, there are no extenuating circumstances that mean the defendant is not fit to stand trial);
2 The relevant relationship 'within the household', for the purposes of this analysis, is of husband and wife. To satisfy this element, the prosecution had to prove to the court that the defendant and victim had a registered marriage (for example, by submitting their marriage certificate into evidence).

This chapter focuses on the second, and most contentious, element – what the court recognises as 'violence' and how the court treats different types of domestic violence. The fourth element will also be discussed in relation to sentencing.

Compared to the Islamic Courts discussed in Chapter 5, the *Pengadilan Negeri* receive relatively few domestic violence cases per year. The reasons for attrition have been covered in previous chapters, including: a lack of community awareness about domestic violence and the Law, community stigma, distance, time and financial barriers, preference for divorce via the religious (civil) jurisdiction, negative experiences with police when reporting, and evidentiary barriers to successful prosecution. Of the cases that do make it to the *Pengadilan Negeri*, the overwhelming majority concern physical violence (approximately 90% of cases studied between 2013 and 2017). In terms of 'non-physical' violence, cases of household neglect (4%), psychological violence (8.5%), and sexual violence (1%) constituted a small percentage of the court's caseload during the case study period.

Overview of case data

In 2013, 20 cases were prosecuted under the Law at the *Pengadilan Negeri* Banda Aceh. All the perpetrators were male, except for one who was the mother-in-law of the victim (Case 4/2013). In other words, 95% of defendants were male. All of the male perpetrators in 2013 were husbands, except for one case where violence was perpetrated by a father against his daughter (Case 13/2013). Overall, in 90% of cases (18 out of 20) the husband was accused of perpetrating domestic violence against his wife. Cases 4 and 13 are excluded from the analysis as they fall outside the scope of this book.

In 2014, 10 domestic violence cases were prosecuted. In every case, the perpetrators were male/husbands accused of committing domestic violence again their wives. Similarly, in 2015, 17 cases of domestic violence were brought before the court. In all cases, the perpetrator and victim were husband and wife. However, in two of the cases, the defendant was the wife and the victim was the husband (Cases 10 and 17/2015). These cases are distinguished within, but have not been excluded from, the analysis. In Case 10/2015, the wife (defendant) had previously been a victim of domestic violence and her husband (victim) had previously been convicted of perpetrating domestic violence against her. This raises the distinction between reciprocal violence and self-defence in domestic violence cases (discussed further below). Further, in Case 17/2015, the wife (defendant) was the victim of domestic violence perpetrated by her husband (victim) in Case 16/2015. Case 17/2015 (discussed below) raises the question of whether the court in this case was complicit in perpetuating violence against the wife, with the legal system being used as a tool by the husband to continue to exercise control over his spouse (i.e. legal systems abuse). The statistics from 2015 remain consistent with previous years with husbands being accused of perpetrating violence against wives in approximately 90% of cases.

In 2016, all cases prosecuted involved husbands who allegedly perpetrated domestic violence against their wives. Notably, Case 12/2016 was the only case studied in which the defendant was found not guilty. Case 12/2016 related to an allegation of economic violence (discussed below). Lastly, in 2017, 10 cases were prosecuted, with 90% of defendants being male and 80% of cases involving marital violence. Cases 5 and 6/2016 involved a mother and father who committed violence against their son (excluded from the analysis). Of the remaining cases in this year, all cases conformed to the gendered trend of husbands committing violence against their wives. In total, over 90% of cases between 2013 and 2017 are consistent with broader trends of domestic violence overwhelmingly being committed by husbands against wives.

In the period 2013–2017, the average length of the perpetrator and victim's marriage – calculated from the date of marriage to the date of the reported domestic violence incident – was between seven to eight years. The longest marriage was 28 years and the shortest only six days. The variation in length of marriage illustrates how domestic violence can occur at any stage of a relationship. Perpetrators were on average 37–38 years old, with the youngest perpetrator 19 and the oldest 52 years old. All perpetrators (besides one Christian) were Muslim, which is not surprising considering the demographic context of Aceh.[3] Further, most perpetrators identified as '*swasta*' or '*wiraswasta*', which is a non-descript term meaning that they are self-employed or do not work for the government. Twenty percent of perpetrators worked for the government as civil servants, government-owned company employees, or police officers. Case demographics reflect the fact that domestic violence can occur in any marriage, regardless of whether the couple is young or old, poor or wealthy, professional or working class.

In the first part of this chapter, the charges laid under the Law will be analysed. In the second part, the sentencing approach of the court will be analysed and in the third part, the gendered nature of mitigating and aggravating factors in sentencing is analysed.

Part I. Approach of the court to different charges

The court's approach towards cases of physical violence

All domestic violence cases in 2013 at the *Pengadilan Negeri* were prosecuted under Article 44 of the Law (physical violence). In four cases the prosecution presented Article 351 of the Criminal Code (maltreatment) as an alternative charge. However, these cases were ultimately prosecuted under Article 44 and the court did not substantively consider the alternative charge. Two cases included additional charges relevant to violence against children and in one case the prosecution pursued a charge of sexual violence in addition to a charge of physical violence.

In 2014, 80% of cases were prosecuted under Article 44 (physical violence), with Article 351 of the Criminal Code presented as an alternative in two cases. In one of these cases the defendant was convicted under the relevant Criminal Code provision (although it was not explained in the case why the court convicted under the Criminal Code rather than under the Law). In 2015, approximately 80% of cases were prosecuted under Article 44 of the Law. Article 351 of the Criminal Code was presented as an alternative in half of these cases. In two cases the defendants were convicted under the Criminal Code because their marriages were unregistered. In the words of the court, these were cases of '*nikah siri*' (secret marriage). As mentioned in Chapter 5, if a couple's marriage is not registered with the State this can preclude women from protection under the Law. Although there are differences in the scope and content of the Law and the Criminal Code, in cases of physical violence the prosecution seems willing to strategically bring alternative charges under the Criminal Code to pursue a conviction whether or not the couple's marriage is formally registered. In contrast, in two other cases the court convicted under the Criminal Code provisions despite valid marriage certificates being entered into evidence. The court did not provide reasons for convicting under the Criminal Code and there were no shortcomings in the prosecution's arguments or evidence presented noted in the judgment. It is therefore likely that the court simply preferred to apply the Criminal Code as it is a more familiar piece of legislation.[4] The remainder of the cases were prosecuted under Articles 45 (psychological violence) and 49 (economic violence) of the Law.

In 2016, every case was prosecuted under Article 44 (physical violence), except for one case prosecuted under Articles 45 and 49. In one other case, the prosecution brought charges of physical and psychological violence together. Similarly, in 2017, every case was prosecuted under Article 44 – an alternative charge was presented in one case, but it was not considered by the court. In total, across the case study period, 90% of cases related to physical violence. This is not to say that physical violence is necessarily more prevalent in real terms than other forms of violence, however, it reflects greater community understandings of physical violence as a 'wrong'. The community's understanding of physical violence as a crime influences the likelihood of victims reporting violence, both with respect to their awareness of their legal rights and the support or stigma they may experience when coming forward.

Criminal cases require two pieces of evidence to prosecute.[5] In most cases the victim sought medical attention which resulted in a medical report (*visum*) documenting their injuries for evidentiary purposes within one week after the incident. The majority of cases illustrate that producing a *visum* is critical to the success of the case. Generally, for domestic violence prosecutions the victim is also expected to testify. However, this is not a blanket rule as in one case the victim did not attend court and the perpetrator was convicted based on the victim's police statement. If necessary, the judge has discretion to make orders to protect victims when giving testimony and counselling with a psychologist is available for the victim to support the witness to give testimony.[6] In addition to the victim's statement, the prosecution in most cases presented testimony from at least one other witness. The second witness was not necessarily an eyewitness but was often someone to whom the victim later recounted the assault, or who witnessed the victim in an injured state. In some cases, the prosecution successfully relied solely on the victim witness' testimony and the *visum* (as per Article 55 of the Law).[7] Evidence from the scene, such as weapons used or clothes worn at the time of the assault, were also commonly presented by the prosecution as physical evidence at trial.

Context of violence

It is important to distinguish between the underlying cause of most domestic violence (being gender inequality and patriarchy – as established in Chapter 3) and triggers for violence specific to couples' circumstances. This section will analyse the context of, and triggers for, incidents of violence.

HISTORY OF VIOLENCE OR MULTIPLE INCIDENTS OF VIOLENCE

Domestic violence can occur or commence at various stages in a marital relationship. However, in practice, the court rarely identified whether domestic violence had occurred prior to the first reported incident ('the prosecuted incident'). A history of domestic violence was only explicitly or implicitly noted by the court in 25% of cases between 2013 and 2017. As the court's decision only provides a snapshot of the couple's relationship, circumstances, and history, it cannot be said that there was not a history of domestic violence simply because it is not identified on the court record. Statistically speaking it is more likely that most victims *would* have experienced a history of domestic violence before reporting violence. As outlined in Chapters 4 and 6, there are compounding barriers which deter or prevent women from reporting violence to the police. Further, many victims interviewed indicated that they waited long periods of time before reporting, usually until a strategic event (for example, children going to boarding school or university) opened an opportunity to safely report or escape.

The court's illustrated lack of engagement with the broader context of domestic violence (namely, the lack of identification of a history of violence in 75% of cases) is largely due to the criminal jurisdiction taking an incident-based approach towards prosecution. One consequence of this is that histories of domestic violence are not deemed relevant to prosecution. As discussed later in relation to sentencing, it is only if there has been a previous conviction for a similar offence that the perpetrator's history is treated as relevant during sentencing as an aggravating factor. The exception to this is where there are multiple incidents of violence temporally close enough to be prosecuted together (which occurred in 9% of cases studied).

In the 25% of cases where the court identified a history of domestic violence, in 15% of these cases the court merely alluded to it, speaking in euphemisms such as: the couple 'often disagreed', the relationship was 'previously not harmonious', there had previously been 'quarrelling', 'frequent differences of opinion' or 'fights between the defendant and victim'.[8] I categorise these phrases as alluding to a history of violence because, as outlined in Chapter 3, domestic violence is characterised by a pattern of coercion and control, which makes it highly unlikely that a single incident of physical violence would have occurred in isolation from other types of domestic violence. Further, it is common for domestic violence to be described as a 'disagreement' or 'disharmony' as a way of minimising the seriousness of domestic violence or implying reciprocity – as opposed to explicitly identifying coercive and controlling patterns of behaviour. In contrast, in the other 10% of these cases, the court explicitly identified previous incidents or patterns of violence (as in Table 7.1).

Notably, in earlier years (such as 2013 and 2014) there are no examples of explicit identification of a history of domestic violence. In more recent years, the court took a more direct approach approximately 20% of the time (9 out of 40 cases between 2015 and 2017). There is therefore a slight trend towards the court explicitly recognising a history of domestic violence. In addition to

Table 7.1 Histories of violence

Case	*Examples*
Case 12/2015	D beat V on more than one occasion.
Case 2/2016	D previously mistreated V.
Case 3/2016	V testified that D had repeatedly persecuted her.
Case 4/2016	V testified that during their marriage D often beat her.
Case 8/2016	D had frequently committed violence in the household.
Case 10/2016	Before this incident D often abused V.
Case 1/2017	Previously D often used violence against V.
Case 2/2017	V's mother testified that it was 'noisy every day'.
Case 8/2017	D had previously committed violence against V.

Source: Author's own.

identifying previous incidents of physical violence, the identification of patterns of controlling, threatening or coercive behaviour is imperative. This is because it is common for abusers to use threats to enforce compliance and create an atmosphere of fear. Therefore, it is inadequate for the court to treat domestic violence as a series of isolated, physical incidents. The failure of the courts to interrogate histories of violence, and broader contexts of control and coercion, likely stems from a lack of judicial education on the nature of domestic violence. Conventional criminal law approaches which treat violence as 'incident-based' demonstrate a need for more specialised training.

SEPARATION/POST-SEPARATION CONTEXT

In approximately 20% of cases prosecuted between 2013 and 2017, incidents of violence occurred in a context where the couple were already separated or in the process of getting divorced. This percentage only includes cases where it was explicitly identified, or clear from the context of the case, that the couple was separated or separating. As discussed in previous chapters, the risk of domestic violence greatly increases in separation or post-separation contexts. 'Post-separation contexts' identified here do not include where couples officially divorced via the Islamic Court before the prosecuted incident of violence occurred. Violence in that context would no longer fall under the Law unless violence occurred prior to divorce (as in Case 2/2015). 'Post-separation contexts' include where the couple are separated (physically but not legally) or where the husband has already '*talak*-ed' (religiously divorced) the wife, but the divorce has not been processed by the Islamic Court. For example, see Table 7.2.

Table 7.2 Context when prosecuted incident of violence occurred

Case	*Examples*
Case 1/2013; Case 15/2013	Couple were in the process of getting divorced.
Case 2/2013	V had recently sued D for divorce.
Case 3/2015	V met with D to discuss divorcing when the violence occurred.
Case 5/2013; Case 18/2013	D had already *talak*-ed V.
Case 2/2014	Couple were living in separate places by order of the *Geuchik*.
Case 3/2014; Case 7/2017	D and V had been sleeping in 'separate beds'.
Case 2/2015; Case 6/2015	D and V had been living separately.
Case 1/2016	D married another woman (via illegal polygamy).
Case 10/2016	D had contacted V's father to 'return her to him'.

Source: Author's own.

In addition to the occurrence or escalation of violence being statistically more likely during separation or post-separation, in contexts where the marital relationship has already broken down the victim may be in a safer or more strategic position to report her husband to the police. While women may report domestic violence to police and cooperate in prosecution in contexts where the couple are separated or where reconciliation is not possible, it is important to note that this is not always the case. Women also commonly reported violence while they were still married and, in some cases, the couple later reconciled. As the remaining 80% of cases occurred in contexts where the couple had not separated, it cannot necessarily be assumed that victims who pursue protection through criminal law avenues will also seek divorce (on the other hand, it is impossible to know how many couples subsequently divorced post-criminal case). Many victims want men to be held accountable for violence, for men's behaviour to change, and for violence to stop, as opposed to wanting to leave the relationship. On this point note that reconciliation, peace, and forgiveness are important themes that influence the exercise of judicial discretion when sentencing (discussed in Part III below).

TRIGGERS FOR VIOLENCE

The 'triggers' for violence (identified in the analysis below) cannot be understood as distinct from the broader context of the couple's relationship. For example, if the couple is separated or there is a history of violence, this naturally provides context to the 'trigger'. 'Triggers' identified when analysing the cases included: men's authority being challenged, jealousy, economic pressure, and custody disputes. There may be multiple 'triggers' in a case and categories are not mutually exclusive. For example, one case may involve both economic pressures and jealousy. Importantly, any identified 'trigger' should not be understood as the *cause* of violence and certainly not as an excuse or justification for violence. The cause of violence is always the perpetrator's decision to commit violence. The identification of a trigger provides the reader insight into the reason why – from the perpetrator's perspective – they chose to use violence. The reasons provided by perpetrators provide a partial answer to the question of 'why do men use violence?' However, this does not excuse men's violence morally or legally. Importantly, triggers should not be understood as legally relevant provocations justifying violence. This can be contrasted to cases of self-defence where there is a legal justification for violence.

As seen in the analysis below, the line between moral and legal justifications for violence sometimes becomes blurred in the exercise of judicial discretion. In one interview, when asked how the judges consider the context and triggers of violence – a judge replied:

> The considerations are, first, what type of violence has the accused committed, some for example commit domestic violence as a method

> to educate … related to religious teachings. People here are very religious, so when the accused commits violence to the victim, ***the accused might only be using violence to educate, or for other religious purposes***. So, the judge will analyse and investigate ***the extent of the relationship between the perceived educative purpose that the accused used*** … and how this was perceived by the victim, meaning, whether the victim accepts this or not, even if the effect is to cause injury to the victim (emphasis added).

The judge specifically identified violence as an educative tool, as discussed in Chapter 4. The fact that judges even consider the relationship between the educative purpose and the violence perpetrated lends itself towards potentially minimising or excusing men's violence, or even implicitly blaming the victim for provoking violence in the first place.

AUTHORITY CHALLENGED

In cases where violence was male to female and husband to wife violence, the most common factor which triggered violence in the cases studied was perceived disrespect of a husband's authority over their wife. In approximately 40% of cases, the trigger appeared to be the wife-victim challenging the husband-perpetrator's authority as the head of the household. This statistic does not take into account indirect challenges to authority such as jealousy or economic pressure, discussed below. Most cases include multi-faceted triggers; therefore, coding of triggers is based on the most dominant or emphasised aspects outlined in the record of the court's decision. As mentioned above, the court's decision is only a partial record of the broader circumstances of the case. Keeping in mind these limitations, it is still significant to note that the triggers cited in cases for men's violence are densely gendered. Examples of what the trigger of 'authority challenged' means in practice can be seen in Table 7.3.

What a 'challenge to authority' means in practice varies broadly depending on the case. Examples range from what appear to be extremely petty challenges to perceived 'male authority' – such as women not answering the phone or wanting to use the phone – to women exercising autonomy over their own lives or bodies (for example, wanting to work or take contraception). What an individual man perceives to be within his 'authority' reflects broader gender norms at play. Men who believe that their wife needs permission to use the phone align with conservative interpretations of gender norms that construct men's authority as the head of the household as all-encompassing and absolute, in contrast to more gender equal constructions of norms. In other words, where men believe that they are *entitled* to have absolute authority – and correspondingly absolute compliance – any deviation from this is viewed as a challenge to their authority as the head of the household. This links back to the patterns of power and control, characteristic of domestic violence.

Table 7.3 Trigger code – authority challenged

Case	*Examples*
Case 1/2013; Case 2/2013; Case 14/2013; Case 13/2015; Case 10/2016	V did not want to talk to or go somewhere with D.
Case 5/2013	V complained about D's nephew always eating the food she cooked at the house without her permission.
Case 12/2013	V declined an invitation to visit D's parents as she still had work to do at her office.
Case 16/2013	D wanted V to stop taking contraception and 'demanded a baby boy'. V refused to stop taking contraception.
Case 19/2013	V locked D out of the house because D had not come home for two days.
Case 4/2014	V was working at the mall. D did not want V to work.
Case 6/2014; Case 9/2014; Case 9/2016; Case 13/2016; Case 10/2017	V did not listen to her husband. E.g. in Case 9/2016 D asked V to put the porridge in the fridge and V did not put the porridge in the fridge as it was still hot.
Case 1/2015; Case 6/2016	D wanted to take the couple's child(ren) somewhere. V did not want the child(ren) to go.
Case 3/2015; Case 14/2015; Case 3/2016	D called V and V did not pick up the phone.
Case 8/2015	V went to talk to the *Geuchik* about D using narcotics in the home of a widowed woman.
Case 11/2015	V wanted to use the phone without D's permission.
Case 1/2016	V reported D to his boss for not providing her *nafkah* (maintenance).
Case 2/2017	V asked D why he was home later than usual.

Source: Author's own.

The construct of 'authority' in these cases has two aspects: first, the husband feels that he is entitled to receive something he believes is part of his gender role (that he *deserves* respect or obedience) and does not receive this. Second, the husband chooses to use violence to enforce his wife's compliance with her gender role (that she *should* be obedient or listen to him). Some gendered ideas centring around how a woman should behave according to her gender role present in these cases, include that women: should listen to/obey their husbands; should cook; should not complain or criticise their husband; should not smoke; should not ask for money; should not work (or in some cases should work more); should take care of the children; should make sure children are never sick, crying or disobedient; and should generally be amenable to their husband's requests. The pattern emerging from the analysis of these cases is that men feel entitled to use violence to enforce their own interpretations of gender norms to 'correct' women's behaviour.

In addition, there are several instances of women being assaulted when they attempt to assert their rights or seek help. As outlined in Chapter 4, women reporting violence can, in itself, be perceived as a challenge to men's authority or entitlement to use violence. For example, in Case 3/2014 the couple were summoned to the *Geuchik*'s office for the purposes of reconciliation. D became 'emotional' during the *Geuchik*'s intervention and assaulted V. Similarly, in Case 8/2015, the husband assaulted the victim in response to her reporting his behaviour to the *Geuchik*. Further, in Case 1/2016, D asked V, 'Why did you report me to my boss?' V answered, 'I was just asking for my rights…'. D replied, 'You don't have rights anymore' before assaulting her. In other cases, the wife seeking to divorce or separate from her husband was, in itself, interpreted as a challenge to male authority. The triggers documented in the case study illustrate that when husbands feel like they are 'losing control' of their wife, they are more likely to use violence to try to maintain control or otherwise punish their partners. The fact that women pursuing their rights is often interpreted by men as a challenge to authority – which has been established as a trigger for violence – also sheds light on the predicament for women balancing pursuing their rights against ensuring their safety and the safety of their children.

JEALOUSY

Twenty-nine percent of cases were triggered by male jealousy or possessiveness, including but not limited to allegations of adultery or cheating by the husband against the wife. A further 6% of cases were triggered by wives confronting their husbands about having an affair and the husband responding with violence. Within the category of 'jealousy' there are several sub-categories, with jealousy in some cases presenting as general possessiveness. For example, in Case 3/2015, when V did not answer D's call, D later asked to see V's phone to check who she had been calling. When V resisted giving him her phone, D forcibly took it – twisting her arm and fracturing the bone, and later said she was 'insolent and did not respect me as [her] husband'. There is an apparent overlap between jealousy and the previous category of 'authority challenged'. Jealousy as a trigger produced some extreme reactions, such as in Case 10/2013 where the defendant accused his wife of having an affair with his brother and, when she denied this, physically assaulted her and then kidnapped his brother's child and held him for ransom.

In some cases, jealousy triggered immediate violent reactions. However, the use of violence in circumstances of jealousy cannot accurately be understood merely as a 'reactive' or 'emotional' response. Men also used violence strategically both to induce fear, and therefore reinforce control over their wives, and to coerce 'confessions'. For example, in Case 9/2017, when D accused V of cheating on him, V replied that she had not cheated on him. D then told her to confess. When V denied it again, D took a machete and put it at V's back saying, 'Admit it, or I will kill you'. V said, 'just kill me then'. This is important to note because the court sometimes excused or justified men's violence – to an extent – with language such as 'D was angry' or 'D became emotional'. The analysis of triggers in the case study illustrates, however, that men's use of violence is not usually random or episodic but, in most cases, is part of a pattern of coercion and control.

Further, there may be a tendency for people to think 'maybe the victim was actually cheating on the defendant which led to him becoming overwhelmed by emotion'. Case 4/2014 is a useful example illustrating why allegations of cheating should be taken with a grain of salt. In the case study, allegations of adultery were almost the 'go to' excuse to justify men's violence stemming from insecurity-related jealousy. In Case 4, V was working at the mall; D called her and asked to meet. When D arrived, he said 'I already know everything'. D 'became angry' and pulled V's headscarf, accusing her of cheating on him, which V denied. Further context to this incident, as elaborated through testimony at trial, reveals that the full explanation as to why D assaulted V was that she 'did not fulfil D's request to stop working at the mall'. Working meant that she was sometimes out late during night shifts and sometimes interacted with other men at the place of business, and it was in this context that D was jealous and accused her of cheating on him. Other reasons that D did not like V working at the mall included that she sometimes could not mind their child and that D was intimidated by his wife's independent wage. In this case, the court did not seem to seriously engage with the husband's allegations. However, as mentioned above, the court may view the perpetrator as being justified, at least morally, in cases where there are accusations of infidelity.

That is not to say that there are not cases where the wife was, in fact, having an affair. However, in the vast majority of cases it is not clear-cut, and jealousy as a trigger was more often related to possessive or controlling behaviour. For example, in Case 6/2014, D said that he felt jealous because he saw V walking with another man whom D did not know. However, from the perspective of an eyewitness to the attack, D 'without a clear reason immediately hit V in a barrage'. Lastly, there were several cases which involved polygamous marriages. Where women's relationships with other men outside of marriage were more likely to be conceptualised as 'alleged adultery', men's extra-marital relationships were generally legitimised under the umbrella of polygamy (albeit the informal/illegal variety).

ECONOMIC PRESSURE

Fifteen percent of cases directly identified economic pressure as a trigger for violence. Economic pressure was often raised in interviews as a cause for violence, feeding into the stereotype that women from lower socio-economic experience higher rates of violence. While domestic violence can occur in families from any type of socio-economic background, women from lower socio-economic backgrounds can face greater barriers to reporting or leaving abusive relationships where they are financially dependent on their husbands. Further, the Marriage Law and *Compilation of Islamic Law* specifically identify husbands as the head of the household and require them to provide financially for their households.[9] This creates a rigid gender expectation – both 'moral' and legal – that men must provide for their families. 'Moral' here meaning according to the dominant religious interpretations.

The social constructions of masculine gender are as fragile as they are rigid. This means that if a husband perceives his wife to be saying 'you are not masculine enough' or 'you are not conforming with your gender norm', men may choose to use violence to re-assert their dominance or masculinity. Such responses, sometimes termed 'humiliated fury' in domestic violence literature, are evidenced in cases where economic pressure is a factor. For example, in Case 9/2014, when the wife criticised her husband's inability to provide for the family – and therefore fulfil masculine gender norms – the husband chose to perpetrate violence against his wife. On the other hand, there are also cases where abusers demand money from their victims (see Table 7.4).

Some of these cases overlap with, but were not prosecuted as, instances of economic violence (discussed below). The trigger described in this category is therefore less about whether husbands did, in fact, provide for their families and more about the pressure they felt to do so.

Table 7.4 Trigger code – economic pressure

Case	*Example of economic pressure*
Case 6/2013	V asked D for money for shopping. D said he felt 'ashamed' because V asked for money in front of his co-workers.
Case 9/2013	D and V disagreed over a cabinet being sold. D wanted to sell the cupboard without informing V because he had no money and no work.
Case 20/2013	D complained about bearing the family's economic burdens – V objected because she also worked and contributed to household expenses.
Case 1/2014	D demanded money from V to pay D's debts.
Case 8/2014	D charged his debts to V (in V's name).
Case 9/2014	D bought a new phone. V said to him 'you can buy a new phone (for yourself), but you can't provide *nafkah* (maintenance)?'
Case 7/2015	V asked D for money to go to her brother's funeral. D did not give her money as he had 'no money and outstanding debt'. V asked him 'how come there is no money, where is your salary?'
Case 8/2017	D was often angry with V, especially when D had no work. D had previously committed violence against V 'due to economic problems'.

Source: Author's own.

Table 7.5 Trigger code – custody disputes

Case	*Examples*
Case 3/2013	D forcibly took their son from the house. When V tried to prevent D from taking the child, D struck V.
Case 2/2014	D broke down the door and forcibly took their child.
Case 2/2015	There was a dispute over their child, D forcibly took the child.
Case 6/2015	V went to pick up their son from school. When she arrived, she was informed that D had already picked him up. She later found D and the child at her brother in law's house. D separated V from the child and took the child inside.

Source: Author's own.

CUSTODY DISPUTES AND THREATS RELATED TO/VIOLENCE AGAINST CHILDREN

Concerns expressed by victims of domestic violence in interviews (Chapters 4 and 5) about the safety of their children were reflected in the reality of how children were sometimes used or abused by perpetrators. For example, in Case 3/2013, the victim in this case was physically assaulted when trying to prevent her husband from taking their son during divorce negotiations, see Table 7.5.

Custody disputes as a trigger for violence substantially overlap with the category of 'threats related to/violence against children', therefore these two categories will be discussed together. Victim concerns about the safety of their children play out visibly in the cases studied. This includes children witnessing violence, children intervening to protect their mother, mothers defending their children, and children being threatened to coerce compliance by mothers (see Table 7.6).

ALCOHOL AND OTHER DRUGS

Lastly, alcohol and other drugs were identified as a trigger for violence in only three cases. This factor is not as significant as in other contexts where alcohol and drug use have been linked with increased rates of domestic violence (for example, World Health Organization, 2014). This is likely because in Aceh drinking alcohol is banned under Article 15 of *Qanun Jinayat*. Narcotics are banned under Law No. 9/1976. Substance abuse is therefore notable for its under-representation in the Acehnese context. The absence of alcohol and other drugs as a trigger for violence highlights that the underlying cause of domestic violence is patriarchy and the entitlement to use violence. In other jurisdictions (such as Australia), alcohol and drug use are commonly invoked by perpetrators as an excuse for committing domestic violence and to avoid taking accountability for their behaviour. By way of comparison, the case study (where the perpetration of violence was rarely accompanied by alcohol or drug use) suggests that while the use of alcohol and other drugs might increase disinhibition, the underlying causes of domestic violence remain the same.

Table 7.6 Trigger code – threats related to/violence against children

Case	*Examples*
Case 20/2013	D hit V in the head with a kitchen tray, as well as with his hands. When their son intervened, D hit the child as well. The child fled from the house, D threatened to kill the child. D continued to severely assault V. The next day D beat both victims again.
Case 9/2015	During the assault V called out to their son for help. When the child arrived, he tried to calm D so that D would not hit V again. D hit and kicked the neck, head, and body of V, and accidentally punched the child.
Case 16/2015	D threatened to kill V saying: 'I will kill you … I will kill our child … and I will kill myself'.
Case 3/2017	D came to V's house and called his son (who was sick) to open the door. When D came inside, D scolded the child for not going to Qur'an class. The child looked at D 'unpleasantly' and cursed him. D became 'emotional' and pulled the child's hair. V tried to break up the dispute between D and the child, but D punched her several times in the head and then kicked their child.
Case 7/2017	D beat V and their two children.

Source: Author's own.

Incidents of violence

This section provides in-depth information on the types of physical incidents of violence that were prosecuted in the court. As mentioned earlier, the majority of cases focused on a single incident of physical violence. 'Physical violence' is defined by Article 6 of the Law as an act which results in pain, illness, or serious injury. The court adopted the definition of pain and illness from general criminal law jurisprudence, namely an unpleasant feeling (such as pinching, slapping, hitting, or punching) or being unable to carry out daily tasks or work. A serious injury includes one from which there is no hope of recovery, the loss of one of five senses, or severe disability.[10] What constitutes incidents of physical violence varies substantially between cases and, in addition to physical assaults, other elements of the crimes include threats to life, stalking, and use of a weapon.

PHYSICAL VIOLENCE AND THREATS TO LIFE

Threats to life (Table 7.7) provide further context to assaults and illustrate that the seriousness of a physical assault should not be determined solely according to physicality or resultant injuries. While the physical impacts of some of the assaults listed in the table below may be limited to pushing or a single punch, the psychological impact is generally far greater than the physical impact. It is well

Table 7.7 Incident code – threats to life

Case	*Examples*
Case 16/2013	D pulled V's blouse until she fell to the floor dragged her across the room and said 'Now you will burn yourself alive' while showing her a bottle of gasoline.
Case 2/2015	D came to V's house and threatened to beat her to death. V tried to prevent D from entering the house, but D overpowered her.
Case 9/2015	The couple's child (witness to the assault) testified that D threatened to kill V.
Case 12/2015	D beat V on more than one occasion, between 2014 and 2015 D slapped V, threatened to poison her and chased/choked her.
Case 16/2015	D threatened to kill V saying: 'I will kill you … I will kill our child … and I will kill myself'.
Case 4/2017	During the assault D threatened to kill V.
Case 9/2017	D accused V of cheating on him. D then threatened her with a machete saying, 'admit it, or I will kill you'. V replied, 'just kill me then'.

Source: Author's own.

known that abusers often use violence strategically to punctuate threats, enforce compliance, and create an atmosphere of fear. Therefore, the seriousness of domestic violence does not directly correlate with physicality (or visuality) of an assault.

PHYSICAL VIOLENCE AND CHOKING

A further example of when an assault may be life threatening or cause significant psychological distress but may not cause substantial visible damage is in cases of choking. Choking has been recognised as a risk factor for violent escalation and spousal homicide. In fact, in Australia, choking has been recognised as an independent offence due to the serious implications of the offence which may otherwise not be recognised as 'serious' under other laws such as assault.[11] Choking was noted in 12% of prosecuted domestic violence cases as shown in Table 7.8. Elements, such as threats and choking, did not receive any interrogation or critical attention by the court in the cases studied.

PHYSICAL VIOLENCE AND STALKING

Stalking is another example of intimating and controlling behaviour which, when considered in combination with physical assaults, increases the seriousness of domestic violence. Although only explicitly identified in a minority of cases, the impacts of stalking are notable in terms of causing fear or anxiety for

Table 7.8 Incident code – choking

Case	*Examples*
Case 12/2013	D slapped V in the face then strangled/choked her before pushing her to the ground.
Case 15/2013	D hit V, choked her, and dragged her to the ground.
Case 19/2013	When D entered the house he choked V, hit her, and pushed her to the ground.
Case 5/2015	D slapped V in the face, punched her then pushed her so she fell onto the bed. D then choked her.
Case 12/2015	D beat V on more than one occasion, between 2014 and 2015 D slapped V, threatened to poison her, and chased/choked her.
Case 5/2016	D slapped V in the face once. V wanted to get out of the car but D held her inside. Later D beat V and choked her.
Case 13/2016	D hit V and choked her.
Case 4/2017	D strangled V, hit her in the face and pulled her hair. D also banged V's head against something and twisted her right hand.

Source: Author's own.

victims, particularly in Case 7/2015 and Case 8/2016 (Table 7.9). Note that while in Case 8/2016 stalking elements were prosecuted under Article 45 (psychological violence), psychological violence was not presented as an additional or alternative charge in Case 7/2015. Stalking also raises the issue of police and judicial cooperation to ensure women's safety in cases of non-custodial sentences, and the imposition of restraining orders (or lack thereof, as discussed below).

Table 7.9 Incident code – stalking

Case	*Examples*
Case 7/2015	The day after D initially assaulted V, he followed her on her way home from work. He stopped the motorcycle she was on, pulled her from the motorcycle, grabbed her and took her phone and smashed it. Later, unbeknownst to V, D continued tailing her. Once again he pulled her off her motorcycle and tried to force her into his car. A few weeks later, V was at a karaoke bar with friends. D suddenly entered the room and slapped her twice.
Case 13/2015	V left the house, D followed her and monitored her from a distance of about 10 meters behind. D saw that there were many people in the house V went to (as it was used as a meeting space) and D saw V sit next to a man. After the man left, D returned home – where he later assaulted V when she returned home.
Case 8/2016	D often 'followed' V and forced her to accompany him, every time she left the house she was afraid that she would run into D. D would also often come to V's place of work and harass her.

Source: Author's own.

PHYSICAL VIOLENCE AND USE OF A WEAPON

While only six cases involved the use of weapons (Table 7.10), the use of a weapon may relate to threats to life and/or premeditation of the crime. Cases that involved the use of makeshift weapons, such as blocks of wood or metal poles, are not included in this discussion. As will be discussed later in this chapter, the court does not appear to explicitly consider these factors in sentencing.

Remarkably in Case 7/2017, the assault was so severe that it led to an active police intervention. The context to this case is that beforehand V had denied D access to the house. When D returned to the house, he beat V and their two children with his belt, he then took a racket and hit V with it four times on the head. D accused V of having an affair. When V denied this, D hit her with an electrical cable. D then beat the children again. The assault was so severe that one of the children jumped from the second floor of the building to escape and ran to find help. D then used his hands and a piece of wood to beat V in an extended assault. D told V to remove all her clothes and demanded that she leave the house without wearing any clothes, threatening her with a machete. The police then arrived and intervened – which is the only active police intervention recorded in the cases studied. As mentioned in Chapter 6, the potential for protective policing practices is, as yet, largely unrealised.

Table 7.10 Incident code – use of a weapon

Case	*Examples*
Case 7/2015	D went and grabbed a machete, V tried to flee but was chased by D. D slashed V with the machete and she fell, her head bleeding.
Case 9/2015	D beat V two times in the head. When V called out to their son for help, D took a knife from under the mattress and pointed it at V. V struggled to get free, and was cut by the knife held by D.
Case 16/2015	D took a machete and directed it to just above V's head threatening to kill her. Later he stuck the machete in the mattress in front of V.
Case 7/2017	D told V to remove all her clothes and then demanded that she leave the house without wearing any clothes, threatening her with a machete.
Case 9/2017	D took a machete and immediately approached V swinging it and putting it at V's back.

Source: Author's own.

WIFE-DEFENDANT/HUSBAND-VICTIM

The last case to be analysed in this section is Case 10/2015, in which the defendant was the wife and the husband was the victim. In this case the husband-victim picked up his son from school as he had a nosebleed. Later, the wife-defendant came to pick up the child. The husband said, 'I want to take the child to the doctor and tomorrow I will drop him at school'. The wife replied, 'But he's not sick and you have no right to [keep] the child'. She said this because previously, when the couple filed for divorce at the Islamic Court, that court had ruled that the mother had sole custody of the child. The defendant-wife then tried to enter the house to retrieve the child, however, the husband obstructed the wife's entry to the house. Effectively, there was a physical 'tug of war' over the child. It was alleged that the defendant-wife deliberately 'ran into' the husband and hit the husband-victim once in the face. An eyewitness and the defendant-wife testified (contrary to the testimony of the husband-victim) that the wife only 'poked' her husband in the face, it was also alleged that the husband-victim kicked and verbally abused the defendant-wife.

The fact that domestic violence is a form of gendered violence which is, statistically, perpetrated by husbands against wives, does not mean that domestic violence is never perpetrated by wives against husbands. However, broader studies of domestic violence have established that female violence against males in spousal settings rarely fits a 'control and coercion' cycle of domestic violence.[12] In other words, when a wife commits violence against a husband it is much more likely to be defensive violence or reciprocal violence. In this case, the husband-victim had previously been convicted of perpetrating domestic violence against the defendant-wife. In these circumstances, it could reasonably be implied that the defendant-wife's violence was defensive in nature. Even if the violence was not defensive, the facts support violence being reciprocal, in that multiple witnesses stated that both parties used violence in the physical scuffle over the child. At a minimum, Case 10/2015 raises questions about the court's understanding of the nature of domestic violence as a pattern of coercion and control as opposed to isolated incidents of physical violence, as well as raising issues regarding the enforcement of court-ordered custody arrangements. Further, there is broader evidence cited by *Komnas Perempuan* (2011) in their report that supports critiques of the Law's implementation in some cases as 'criminaliz[ing] women who are in fact defending themselves or their children'.

The court's approach towards cases of psychological violence

In 2013, only cases of physical violence were prosecuted. In 2014, two cases were prosecuted under Article 45 (psychological violence): Cases 2/2014 and 5/2014, with the former also including an alternative charge under Article 333 of the Criminal Code (deprivation of liberty). In Case 2/2014, the couple were living separately at the time of the incident by order of the *Geuchik*. D went to the house to take their child. D knocked on the door, but V did not open it as she was afraid. D then broke down the door and forcibly took the child. D asked V for their family card[13] but she did not have it. D then ordered her to leave the house, she said to him 'I don't know where to go, the *Geuchik* gave me permission to stay at this house'. In response, D then forcibly locked V *inside* the house and nailed the front and back doors shut from the inside so V could not leave. D then ransacked the entire house looking for the family card before exiting the house through the front window and nailing the window shut from the outside. He then nailed all the other windows shut from the outside and left. V was later rescued by neighbours who crowbarred the doors and windows open. The prosecution presented an expert report from P2TP2A with respect to the psychological injury suffered by the victim in this case. Case 2/2014 provides an example of cooperation between prosecution and P2TP2A to provide evidence of psychological harm.

In Case 5/2014, V was about to enter D's shop. D said, 'Don't enter my shop, if you go into my shop I will hit you – I will kill you'. D was holding a piece of wood and chased V away from the shop saying 'Go home … I'll beat you later'. A witness intervened and took the wood from D to protect V. This incident caused V to be so afraid that she reported it to the police. In this case, an expert report was not entered into evidence and the conviction was based on witness testimonies. The way psychological violence has been conceptualised in the broader literature – with respect to cycles of control and atmospheres of fear – evidently does not align with the reality of how it is prosecuted in the cases studied. Cases 2 and 5/2014 illustrate that prosecuted cases of psychological violence in Aceh are more akin to cases of threatened physical violence or other traditional crimes (i.e. false imprisonment). First, these cases were both incident-based as opposed to focusing on longer-term histories of psychological mistreatment. Second, these cases were based on the use of force, albeit indirect or threatened.

Similarly, in 2015, two cases were prosecuted under Article 45 – Cases 4/2015 and 16/2015. Case 4 involved allegations of both economic and psychological violence. With respect to the latter, the victim testified that, during a quarrel, D had threatened to burn down their family home, which caused psychological suffering to V. In this case, P2TP2A provided an expert report from a psychologist. In Case 16, on one occasion D tried to burn the house down by pouring kerosene in the lounge room. He then went looking for a match but could not find one. On another occasion, D took a machete and directed it to just above V's head threatening to kill her, saying:

> What do you want now, do you want to destroy our family, if you destroy it, do not do it half-heartedly … I will kill you … I will kill our child … and I will kill myself … we better destroy it all.

Later he stuck the machete into the mattress in front of V. On another occasion, D did not allow V into the main room of the house and did not allow her to see her child. A psychological examination conducted by P2TP2A stated that as a result of D's behaviour, V became afraid of D and felt depressed. In both of these cases there were also histories of domestic violence, indicating that a charge of psychological violence may have been brought strategically by the prosecution to capture the dynamics of coercive control more holistically. This strategy may be particularly helpful where abuse spans several years but the victim has not previously sought medical attention or otherwise obtained a *visum* to evidence physical injuries. In such cases, a psychological examination is an alternative avenue to enter a history of domestic violence into evidence.

In 2016, two cases were prosecuted under Article 45: Cases 8 and 12/2016. In Case 8, a charge of psychological violence was presented to the court alongside a charge of physical violence. The prosecution led evidence that D often stalked V and forced her to accompany him so that V was afraid every time she left the house. D would also frequently come to her workplace and harass her. For example, one day when V was about to leave work, D was waiting outside and forced her to go home with him on his motorcycle. V realised that D was taking her somewhere else (instead of taking her home) so V asked D to stop the motorcycle. D did not stop the bike and squeezed V's thigh so hard that it caused bruising. After this, V jumped from the motorcycle and ran. D ordered V to get back on the motorcycle, then dropped her home. As a result of D's actions, V was so afraid of seeing D again that she could not go to work for several days. In the other case, Case 12, the defendant was found not guilty (discussed below).

In the scheme of the cases studied, few cases brought dual charges of physical and psychological violence even where it was documented on the court record that D's behaviour had caused psychological injury to V. However, bringing a standalone or accompanying charge of psychological violence has the potential to strengthen the prosecution's case by providing broader context to the relationship and patterns of abuse. The low prosecution rate for psychological violence reflects a limited understanding of the Law at every stage of criminal prosecution. Improved criminal justice stakeholder education on why the identification of psychological violence matters could be a strategic avenue to deepen understandings of patterns of control and coercion within domestic violence relationships.

The court's approach towards cases of sexual violence

The perpetrator in Case 18/2013 was charged under Article 46 of the Law (sexual violence) in addition to Article 44. In this case, D had already '*talak*-ed' V. D then started to pressure V to have sex with him, but V refused as D had already religiously divorced her. In this context, V considered sex to be *haram* (forbidden) or *zina*. D sexually assaulted V resulting in physical injury. Case 18 is the only case of sexual violence prosecuted in the cases studied. The fact that the couple in this case were religiously divorced but had not processed their divorce through the Islamic Court means that the case falls both within Islamic religious understandings of sex outside of marriage being forbidden and within the parameters of the Law. This can be contrasted to marital rape where the couple of are both religiously and legally married. The sexual violence in this case therefore did directly relate to marital rape which remains a taboo subject in Indonesia despite it being explicitly criminalised by Articles 5 and 8 of the Law.

The court's approach towards cases of economic violence and 'household neglect'

Out of all of the domestic violence cases studied, the jurisprudence on Article 49 is arguably the most clearly influenced by gender norms and biases. Article 49 states that spouses must 'provide livelihood, treatment or care for an individual which he/she is obliged to provide *according to prevailing law*'. While the article only requires spouses to fulfil their marital obligations as required by 'law', in practice spousal obligations are interpreted broadly by the court and influenced by religiously constructed gender norms. Only three cases of economic violence were heard by the *Pengadilan Negeri* during the period studied – Cases 4/2015, 17/2015 and 12/2016.

In Case 4/2015, it was alleged by the wife that, for 'no apparent reason', D suddenly stopped financially supporting his wife and child. According to D, he stopped providing for the family as their home situation was 'not harmonious'. The court reasoned that according to Article 34 of the Marriage Law, 'Husbands are obliged to protect their wives and provide all the necessities of family life in accordance with their abilities'. In addition, Article 80(3)–(4) of the *Compilation of Islamic Law* stipulates that – subject to the husband's financial capacity to do so – the husband is responsible for providing *nafkah* (maintenance) to his wife, cover household expenses for his wife and child/ren, and education costs for any child/ren. As D had not provided *nafkah* to his wife from September 2014 until the time of the hearing, and had the financial capacity to do so, he was found guilty of household neglect.

In Case 12/2016, the couple had one child together and divorced in 2016. As part of the divorce settlement, the Islamic Court ordered that D pay *nafkah* during the *iddah* period, however, it was alleged by the wife that nothing had been provided by D. After undertaking some forensic accounting, the court determined that D had, in fact, provided the required *nafkah* to the Registrar of the Islamic Court. The Islamic Court also made an order that D must provide child maintenance. However, the implementation of the child maintenance arrangement was contingent on a meeting of both parties with the *Geuchik* – which V's family refused to attend. In coming to the not guilty verdict, the court also highlighted that as D was still undertaking a Masters' degree his financial capability was limited. This case illustrates that where husbands have the financial capacity to provide *nafkah* but refuse to comply with relevant obligations (whether under an Islamic Court order or not), husbands could be prosecuted under the Law. Prosecution would not lead to *nafkah* monies owed being paid, however, as mentioned in Chapter 6, the threat of prosecution (during the policing stage) could lead to a mediated agreement between the parties for the payment of *nafkah*.

These cases can be contrasted to Case 17/2015, in which the defendant was the wife, and the victim was the husband. It was alleged that the wife abandoned her husband within the scope of the household as 'according to the law in force, or because of an agreement, she was obliged to provide livelihood, care or maintenance to that person'. The court held that she was guilty under Article 49 in the following ways:

- Since May 2012, the wife-defendant did not want to 'serve' the husband – in particular, when the husband invited her to have intercourse the wife-defendant always refused 'on the grounds that [her] genitals were sick', so the husband invited her to attend a health check. The result of the obstetrician's examination was that the wife-defendant's genitals had 'no disease or abnormality'.
- In 2013, when the husband invited the wife-defendant to have intercourse, she would 'shout for help' and act as if he was not the wife-defendant's husband.
- Further, the wife-defendant often left the house 'without asking permission or without [the husband's] permission', and since March 2014, the wife-defendant no longer lived at home with the husband.
- As a result of the wife-defendant's actions, the husband felt that he was 'not respected' and 'unappreciated' as her husband.
- The husband also alleged that the wife-defendant had an affair with one of her superiors at work. The wife-defendant denied that she was having an affair. The husband provided 'photographic evidence' of the wife and her colleague being 'close' to the court, although it was not specifically mentioned in the decision what the photos depicted. The court held that the breakdown of the household was 'due to the closeness and presence of a third party as the trigger for the problem arising'.

The exact wording used by the court was that the wife-defendant 'abandoned' the husband by not providing 'inner maintenance' (interpreted by the court as including sex) which was the duty of a wife to her husband. Further, the court stated that the wife-defendant made a commotion every time her husband requested contact with her body and she refused to 'serve him' (that is, have sex).

The Law states that a person is prohibited from neglecting people within the scope of the household if 'according to law' they are obliged to care for them. The court in this decision did not cite any relevant source of law to support the contention that women are legally obliged to have sex with their husbands. Article 83 of the *Compilation of Islamic Law* provides that 'the main obligation of a wife is to be loyal to and be devoted physically and spiritually to her husband as permitted by Islamic law'.

Further, under Article 84(1) of the *Compilation of Islamic Law* it is stated that a wife may be considered '*nushuz*' if she does not comply with the obligations under Article 83 unless there is a valid reason.[14] The court's decision focuses largely on 'internal maintenance'. There is no formal, legal definition of 'inner maintenance' and Article 83 above refers broadly to the content of spousal obligations as based on 'Islamic law'. Interpretations of religious law vary broadly depending on the specific context and the interpreter. Therefore, the court's decision with respect to a wife's obligation to 'sexually serve' her husband is likely informed by their own interpretations of religious gender norms. In fact, the court explicitly stated that: 'The defendant's actions are very contrary to the nature (*kodrat*) of a wife who should be obliged to serve her husband'.

The analysis in this book has established that the content of a woman's *kodrat* is highly contested even within the Acehnese context. Explicit reference by the court to women's *kodrat*, combined with the absence of any reference to legal provisions to establish the precise content of a wife's marital obligations, creates legal uncertainty in the court's reasoning. This can be contrasted to the legal provisions explicitly cited in the above cases prosecuted under Article 49 of husband-wife household neglect. No analysis is provided by the court to support the conclusion that wives are *legally obliged* to have sex with their husbands. I argue that such an interpretation negates women's ability to consent and is tantamount to legitimising marital rape. Such a contention also potentially contradicts the Anti-Domestic Violence Law with respect to prohibitions on sexual violence in Articles 5 and 8.

Another issue is that if the court has defined the content of women's marital obligations based on the implied content of women's *kodrat*, this may be contrary to the rule of law.[15] In the words of the same court in Case 12/2016, an act can only be criminal if 'it meets elements which are formulated in applicable laws and regulations' and 'formally or legally an act is illegal if someone violates a statutory provision then it is against the law'. These statements correlate to Article 1(1) of the Criminal Code: 'No action may be punished unless on the basis of regulations with legal power that exists prior to the existence of the action'. If the content of women's marital obligations is not clearly promulgated in the law, it is impossible for women to know in advance what their legal obligations are. The reasoning in Case 17/2015 therefore creates a risk that women can be held to 'marital obligations' based on different interpretations of gender norms, which – as established in Chapter 4 – are often fluid and arbitrary as opposed to being based on clearly promulgated laws or regulations. The court's interpretation of Article 49 of the Law appears to criminalise the failure of wives to fulfil amorphous or idiosyncratic marital obligations or, in other words, for being '*nushuz*'.[16] Due to the legal uncertainty that this interpretation would create, the relevant question should not be whether the wife-defendant was *morally* right or justified in her actions, but whether she is *legally* culpable in a criminal capacity. This case raises the distinction between 'moral wrongs' and 'legal wrongs' and the muddling of these categories in domestic violence jurisprudence.

On this point, the court's inclusion in its decision of the wife-defendant 'leaving the house without asking permission' clearly illustrates a conflation of legal and moral obligations with respect to the interpretation of wives' marital duties or women's *kodrat* more broadly. Further, while the husband-victim may have presented evidence of *ikhtilath* (closeness) between the wife-defendant and her colleague to the court, this conduct could be prosecuted separately under Article 25 of the *Qanun Jinayat*. A question remains as to whether it is appropriate for allegations of *ikhtilath* to be criminally prosecuted as a form of domestic violence under Article 49 of the Law – I would argue that it is not appropriate to do so.

The outcome of this case is especially egregious when considered against this case's extended background. The court handed down a guilty verdict on the above basis, even though the judges also recognised that there had been disharmony in the household since 2010, including 'frequent quarrels and disputes' between the spouses. Further, the husband-victim in this case was convicted of perpetrating psychological violence against his wife in Case 16/2015. In Case 16, evidence was presented that between 2011 and 2014, the husband tried to burn down the family home by pouring kerosene in the living room, threatened to kill the wife and their child with a machete, restricted the wife's access to just a small part of the house, and limited contact between the wife and their child. This caused the wife to be afraid of her husband and suffer from depression. It is extremely difficult to comprehend how the court could justifiably convict the same woman of domestic violence in the form of, essentially, not having sex with her husband, when her husband had been convicted – by the same court – of committing psychological violence against her. Further, under Article 84(1) of the *Compilation of Islamic Law*, a wife will not legally be considered *nushuz* if there is a 'valid reason' for not complying with her obligations under Article 83. Domestic violence being perpetrated against her by her husband is a valid reason for not complying with such obligations under these same laws.

Such an egregious failure of the court to carry out its role and responsibility under the Law to protect genuine victims of domestic violence constitutes bureaucratic violence. In this case, it appears that the court was complicit in further perpetuating violence against the wife in the form of a criminal conviction and sentence. On my interpretation of this case, the legal system was used as a tool by the husband to continue to exercise control over aspects of his wife's life and punish her after she sought to separate from him and exercise her rights under the Law. The risk of the court being used as a tool of control by abusers is known as 'systems abuse' and often relates to misidentification of victims as perpetrators. This case calls into question the court's understanding of domestic violence dynamics. At a minimum, the content of 'marital obligations' for wives under the Marriage Law and *Compilation of Islamic Law* urgently needs to be reviewed in relation to household neglect as a form of domestic violence to avoid any more cases being prosecuted based on this flawed line of reasoning.

Summary with respect to charges laid under the Law

The cases studied above illustrate the gendered nature of domestic violence: in 90% of cases, violence was perpetrated by husbands against wives. Further, 90% of cases concerned incidents of physical violence. This statistic directly reflects community and State stakeholder understanding which over-emphasise and prioritise physical violence over other forms of domestic violence. The context and triggers of violence were analysed in each case. In 25% of cases, the court implicitly or explicitly identified a history of domestic violence preceding the prosecuted incident of physical violence. The court's general approach of not engaging with the broader context or history of the relationship stems from an incident-based approach towards criminal prosecution. I would argue that such an approach is not appropriate as most domestic violence relationships involve patterns of violence over a long period of time. The need for a deeper understanding of the nature of domestic violence in the judiciary calls for continuing and specialised training. Further, 20% of cases occurred in contexts where the couple had separated or were in the process of separating, highlighting the escalated risks faced by women who seek to leave an abusive relationship. On the other hand, a significant proportion of women also reported domestic violence, and were witnesses for the prosecution, while remaining in the marriage. The dilemmas faced by women who seek accountability for men's violence and changed behaviour through criminal prosecution are considered further below.

This chapter also analysed various 'triggers' for violence. While I stressed the distinction between *causes* and *triggers* of violence (with the cause of violence being the perpetrator's choice to use violence), judges interviewed conflated triggers of violence with moral justifications for violence. In the words of a judge, 'the accused might only be using violence to educate, or for other religious purposes'. The most common trigger for violence was men's authority being challenged – noted in 40% of cases. The challenges to men's authority in the case studies correlate with varying interpretations of women's gender norms or *kodrat*. This category in particular, reflected the gendered tensions underlying violence against women who exercised their autonomy and rights often being perceived by men as challenging their authority. More specific triggers, which can be considered extensions of the 'challenge to authority' category, included jealousy, economic pressure, and custody disputes.

Analysis related to incidents of violence highlighted that even in cases of physical violence, there were numerous surrounding factors that may be significant but were rarely interrogated by the court. Such factors include threats to life, choking, stalking, and the use of a weapon. I argue that such factors should be taken more seriously by the court, challenging the court's predominant focus on the physicality or visibility of violence. The last section in my analysis of the court's approach to physical violence presented a case study of a wife-defendant/husband-victim case. This case illustrated how the failure of the court to engage with the broader context of the relationship and the couple's history of violence potentially puts women at risk of being convicted of physical violence in contexts of self-defence.

Cases of psychological violence were also prosecuted in an incident-focused way with a focus on physical force albeit indirect or threatened – which is a limited use of this provision. However, the cases studied also revealed the potential strategic value of bringing psychological violence charges (either alone or in combination with another charge) where the prosecution seeks to enter more holistic evidence of domestic violence dynamics via an expert report. However, overall, the psychological violence provision is underused, likely due to a lack of understanding of this kind of violence among criminal system stakeholders. There was only one case of sexual violence prosecuted, which demonstrated that prosecutions for sexual violence are, at least, possible, despite substantial barriers to victims of sexual violence reporting due to stigma.

Finally, analysis of economic violence or household neglect showed that prosecutions of husbands who abandon their wives and children are dependent upon the husband's legal obligations and practical capacity to financially provide. In contrast, in the prosecution of a wife who 'neglected' her husband, the court's interpretation of the content of women's marital obligations did not clearly identify the relevant legal source, relied on idiosyncratic religious interpretations of *kodrat*, and blurred moral and legal obligations. This next part of this chapter will analyse sentencing in these cases.

Part II. Sentencing study

This section investigates the judicial approach towards sentencing of domestic violence by the *Pengadilan Negeri* in the 2013–2017 cases. The first section outlines the sentencing options under the Law. The second provides an overview of sentencing trends, including an analysis of sentence type and length, as well as the provisions under which sentences are handed down. The analysis in this section reveals that there are major inconsistencies in the way the court has interpreted the relevant provisions across the cases studied. In addition, the interaction between sentencing and pre-trial detention is analysed.

Sentencing framework

Articles 44–50 of the Law set out the sentencing thresholds for domestic violence (Appendix 2). In addition to the imprisonment and fine thresholds outlined in Appendix 2, judges may impose additional sentences for any kind of violence in the exercise of their discretion. These include restraining orders or injunctions which limit certain rights of the perpetrator (Article 50(a)) and court-mandated counselling (Article 50(b)). There are four non-carceral sentencing options: (1) suspended sentences and probationary periods; (2) restraining orders; (3) fines; and (4) court-mandated counselling. First, as explained by the prosecutor interviewed, suspended sentences and probationary periods are often imposed in less 'severe' cases:

> The defendant is sentenced for six months on the condition that he does not commit a criminal offence for one year, this means that during the next year he may not commit any crime, if he does commit a crime, he will be imprisoned for six months. We do this because sometimes the action is not too heavy (*berat*).

Second, restraining orders – known as being a 'city prisoner' (*tahanan kota*) – involve the limitation of the perpetrator's movement in relation to the victim.[17] Restraining orders have the potential to improve victim safety. However, in cases where the perpetrator exhibited threatening behaviour – such as stalking, in Cases 7/2015, 13/2015 and 8/2016 – there was nothing on the court record to indicate that restraining orders were requested or issued. It is also significant to note that the average time between offending and the commencement of pre-trial detention across the cases studied was approximately three months. The fact that restraining orders are not routinely issued during the pre-trial period to provide interim protection for victims of domestic violence illustrates a potentially dangerous oversight in the current system. As mentioned in Chapter 5, in the context of child custody and housing arrangements, the lack of State protection for women and children during interim periods (such as, post-reporting and pre-prosecution/detention) leaves victims vulnerable to an increased risk of violence. As explained in Chapter 1 in relation to bureaucratic violence, if State justice system stakeholders do not give effect to protections that women are entitled to under the Law, they are not merely being negligent but are also placing the victim at an exacerbated risk of violence. Noer and Agustanti's (2024) study of restraining orders in domestic violence cases found that despite the legal mechanisms in place under the Law, restraining orders are rarely applied or adequately enforced against perpetrators. Noer and Agustanti recommend the enactment of implementing regulations to encourage the police to more consistently apply restraining orders in domestic violence cases, alongside further training and education for criminal justice system stakeholders.

Third, although the imposition of fines is available in theory – this type of sentence is rare and was only used in one instance in the cases studied.[18] Last, as explained in the Elucidation to Article 50, counselling is intended to complement suspended sentencing, with the purpose of educating the perpetrator and keeping households intact. The Elucidation implies that counselling is conditional upon the sentence being suspended and where parties have reconciled. The Elucidation to Article 50(b) states that this article is 'intended to provide freedom to the judge passing probationary sentencing with the purpose of conducting guidance for the perpetrator and maintaining household intactness'.

When sentencing, judges generally take into account a number of aims including punishment, education, and rehabilitation of the offender, specific and general deterrence, and legal and social justice. For example, in Case 5/2014, the court stated that:

> the objective of the conviction is not solely revenge, but to create a *deterrent effect* and in imposing the said punishment on the defendant the Panel of Judges pays attention to the *proportionality principle* (or imprisonment according to the level of error of the defendant) and to fulfill the goals of punishment which must be *corrective, preventive* and *educative*, as well as seeing the good and evil nature of the defendant as required by Law No. 4/2014 concerning Judicial Power, so that the punishment is felt fairly by both the defendant and by victims or the community (emphasis added).[19]

The prosecutor interviewed also identified reconciliation as a secondary aim of the criminal justice system. This challenges the assumption that if prosecution is pursued in the context of domestic violence, then the marriage is or will be dissolved, an assumption that is further interrogated later in this chapter. In addition, when calculating sentences, judges must deduct the length of time the defendant spent in pre-trial detention (if any) from any sentence of imprisonment imposed (Article 22(4) of the Criminal Procedure Code).

During sentencing, judges exercised their discretion to consider factors which, although not legally exculpatory (*pemaaf* – finding the defendant not guilty) or justifying the perpetrator's act (*pembenar* – a positive defence), provide context and contribute to reducing (or increasing) the sentence. This section analyses judicial approaches towards sentencing across the cases studied as well as identifying inconsistencies and disparities in sentencing.

In this sentencing analysis the length of the sentences imposed are measured against the statutory minimum and maximum sentences (if relevant) and the prosecutor's recommended sentence, in combination with whether the court has adequately justified its approach towards the mitigation and aggravation of sentences. It should be noted that there are several factors that are taken into account by the court when sentencing, some of which are subjective aspects (such as a defendant's demeanour in the courtroom), which are not fully reflected on the court record. Therefore, while at its core this book seeks to promote perpetrator accountability, it is often difficult to say that a sentence should be harsher or longer in a particular case due to various considerations, including the victim's wishes and the lack of prison-based rehabilitation options. Further, this book does not promote a carceral approach for dealing with domestic violence per se for reasons discussed below.

Overview of sentencing trends

Type of sentence

A carceral sentence was imposed in 83% of the cases studied. In cases where imprisonment was ordered, it was common for judges to also order defendants to remain in detention (unless the entirety of the sentence had been served during pre-trial detention). In addition to sentences, defendants were ordered to pay the court fees (Rp 2000 or approximately AUD $0.20). In 2013, 38% of sentences were in the form of probationary periods and suspended sentences. In all other years, the prosecution rarely sought this form of punishment, except in Cases 16 and 17/2015. In addition to these cases, suspended sentences were handed down in Cases 5/2014 and 4/2015. Cases 5/2014 and 4/2015 are also notable because the court did not adopt the prosecution's recommendation of a sentence of imprisonment. Contrastingly, in approximately 97% of cases, the court adopted the same type of sentence as recommended by the prosecutor, although, the court's sentence was usually somewhat lighter than that sought by the prosecutor.

It is not clear why the prosecution recommended suspended sentences and probationary periods so sparingly after 2013.[20] The significance of this shift in approach is that court-mandated counselling for perpetrators is intended to complement suspended sentencing. The potential of court-mandated counselling is therefore, at present, unexplored due to the prosecution and court's preference for carceral sentences, among other reasons. Even in cases where a probationary sentence was imposed by the court, these were not accompanied by orders for counselling. This is likely because, at present, no court-adjacent rehabilitation or counselling programmes for perpetrators have been established. Therefore prosecutors and judges do not consider counselling to be an available sentencing option. Even if the infrastructure for such a system was created, there would remain a need for judicial training regarding the role and importance of counselling for breaking cycles of violence.

During an interview, a *Pengadilan Negeri* judge highlighted the need for co-operation between criminal justice stakeholders in order for additional orders, such as restraining orders and counselling, to be implemented. The judge confirmed that perpetrator counselling services had not been established by the government in Banda Aceh, and, as a consequence, judges have never handed down such orders. According to judges interviewed, the responsibility for establishing such services lies with institutional stakeholders outside the courts, however, no budget has yet been allocated. Services for court-mandated counselling are therefore another example of the implementation of the Law falling through the cracks of institutional responsibility – an iteration of bureaucratic violence. As with the failure to establish operational safe houses (discussed in Chapter 1), the failure to establish a court-adjacent counselling system for perpetrator rehabilitation as required under the Law is not merely negligent but has negative consequences for the safety and protection of domestic violence victims undermining the operation of the Law.

In a number of cases, the court stated that sentencing should aim to be 'corrective therapy for the defendant so that the defendant can realise the consequences of the deed he did and not repeat [such actions] again in the future'. However, the reality is that court-mandated counselling programmes targeted towards perpetrators are currently non-existent. In Aceh, there is also no evidence of any domestic violence-related rehabilitation programmes being implemented in State prisons. However, it should be noted that in some parts of Indonesia there are NGO-run intervention programmes that violent men may attend voluntarily (for example, programmes run by *Rifka Annisa* in Yogyakarta). Ibu R (P2TP2A/*Balai Syura*) explained that currently, 'if the husband goes to prison, after getting out there will [likely] be more violence because there is no education for the offender … and he may feel [he was] unfairly imprisoned'. As identified by Ibu R, without therapeutic intervention, it is common for perpetrators to conceptualise themselves as the 'victim' of criminal prosecution.

While the content of the Law is promising in its inclusion of counselling for perpetrators, substantive barriers remain to successful implementation of these provisions. In Aceh, it is currently not possible for such orders to be executed in practice. The lack of a system implementing, or making functional, the powers given to the court to impose counselling under Article 50(b) of the Law is particularly concerning considering that contemporary, international approaches towards domestic violence generally promote inclusion of rehabilitation pathways for perpetrators instead of solely punitive approaches.[21] This is therefore a critical area for reform.

Length of sentence

In 2013, the average length of imprisonment was approximately three months, however this ranged from one month to two years. Excluding Case 18/2013 (a two-year sentence) as an outlier, the average sentence was less than two months. Case 18/2013 involved sexual violence and was one of the longest sentences imposed by the court of the cases studied. In 2014 and 2015, the average length of imprisonment was four months, ranging from 20 days to two years. Excluding Case 3/2015 (two-year sentence, where D broke V's arm) as an outlier, the average sentence in 2015 was closer to three months. In 2016, the average sentence was three and a half months, ranging from 20 days to a year. In the case where a one-year sentence was handed down, D repeatedly beat V while she was pregnant (Case 3/2016). If this case is excluded, then the average sentence was two and a half months. In 2017, the average sentence was almost five months, ranging from 20 days to a year and a half in Case 3/2017 (where D harmed his wife and child, with V harmed while protecting the child). However, if Case 3/2017 is excluded, the average sentence in 2017 was less than three months, making the sentencing average across the cases studied consistently around three months (excluding the most severe cases) or four months (including those cases).

Further, in approximately 87% of cases, the sentence handed down by the court was less than the sentence sought by the prosecution. In 6% of cases the sentence was the same and, in the remaining cases, one sentence was increased and two sentence types were changed from a recommendation of imprisonment to a suspended sentence. I do not seek to suggest that the court must adopt the prosecutor's recommended sentence, as it is the judge's role to exercise their discretion in sentencing taking into account a range of factors. In saying this, the prosecutor's suggested sentence is a useful benchmark from which to consider the judge's reasons for mitigating or aggravating a sentence. Further, as documented in Assegaf's (2020) study of sentencing in Indonesia, it is common for judges to follow prosecution sentencing recommendations to avoid appeal.

At first instance, an average sentence of three (or even four) months appears to fall at the lower end of sentencing – if compared to the statutory maximum of five years for (general) physical violence or three years for (general) psychological or economic violence (refer to Appendix 2 for sentencing ranges). However, to draw a clearer conclusion, it is necessary to look at the specific provisions cases were prosecuted or sentenced under. Take, for example, the various subsections for physical violence in Table 7.11.

Each of these subsections broadly correlates to the level of violence perpetrated or the injuries sustained by the victim as a result of the perpetrator's violence. Article 44(1) is, arguably, the catch-all provision from which a charge can be mitigated under subsection (4) or aggravated under subsections (2) or (3). However, the court's interpretation of the scope of subsection (1) varies, as discussed below. Notably, the 'limited' form of physical violence only applies where the defendant and victim are spouses.

Table 7.11 Physical violence provisions

Article of the law	*Type of violence*	*Maximum sentence*
Article 44(1)	'General' physical violence	5 years
Article 44(2)	'Aggravated' physical violence resulting in 'serious sickness or injury'	10 years
Article 44(3)	Physical violence resulting in 'death of the victim'	15 years
Article 44(4)	'Limited' physical violence- between spouses;- *not* resulting in 'sickness *or* obstructing the performance of work or daily activities'	4 months

Source: Author's own.

In 2013, the perpetrators in every case were sentenced under Article 44(1), except for Case 18/2013, which was prosecuted under Article 46 (sexual violence). In several cases, Article 44(4) was presented as an alternative charge, however, all sentences for physical violence in 2013 were handed down under the general provision subsection (1). In cases where subsection (4) – 'limited' physical violence between spouses – was presented in the alternative, the following acts of violence and resulting injuries were held to be sufficient to fulfil Article 44(1) – 'general' physical violence (see Table 7.12).

Further, in Case 14/2013, the prosecution charged the defendant under Article 44(2) – 'aggravated' physical violence, with Article 44(1) in the alternative. In this case, D pulled V's hand causing V to fall. D then dragged V and banged her head against the wall causing blunt force trauma. As a consequence, V was hospitalised and temporarily could not carry out work. Despite the submission of medical evidence from the hospital, the court did not classify V's injuries as 'serious injuries' under subsection (2) on the basis that V did not sustain an injury that 'could not heal'. The defendant was sentenced under Article 44(1) in the alternative. This interpretation is based on the definition of 'serious injury' in the Criminal Code as 'falling ill or sustaining an injury that does not have any hope of being healed, or that poses a danger of death', that renders the victim 'incapable of continuing to carry out work or livelihood duties', or otherwise results in the 'loss of one of the five senses, severe disability, paralysis, impaired thinking for more than four weeks, or infertility' (Article 90 of the former Criminal Code). It should be noted that the interpretation of Article 44(1) in these cases is broadly defined to include where the victim experiences 'pain', as defined in ordinary criminal law jurisprudence. In later cases, the scope of Article 44(1) is interpreted more restrictively.

Case 4/2014 is the first of the cases studied to be sentenced under the limited physical violence provision (Article 44(4)). The court's decision stated only that the 'level of violence' committed by D did not fulfil the requirements of Article 44(1) – see Table 7.13. This line of reasoning will be explored further below.

Table 7.12 Acts held to fulfil Article 44(1) in 2013

Case	*Court's reasoning*
Case 7/2013	D pushed the victim causing her to fall then slapped V's left cheek two times so that it caused bruising on V's cheek.
Case 11/2013	D beat V causing V to have a bump on her forehead and cheek.
Case 12/2013	D slapped V two times on the right and left cheeks and pushed V so that she fell and hit the TV rack. As a result, V experienced swelling and bruising.

Source: Author's own.

Table 7.13 Acts held to satisfy Article 44(1) or (4) in 2014

Case	*Court's reasoning*
Case 4/2014	D slapped V once on the left cheek. Article 44(1) not satisfied. Alternative charge of Article 44(4) proven.
Case 8/2014	D pulled the victim and slammed her to the floor so that her head hit the floor. The Court held that this level of violence satisfied Article 44(1).

Source: Author's own.

For psychological violence there are two relevant subsections, distinguished by the defendant's actions and the resulting harm caused to the victim. Under Article 45(1) – 'general' psychological violence – the maximum sentence is three years. Under Article 45(2) – 'limited' psychological violence (defined as between spouses and not resulting in illness or the obstruction of work or daily activities) – the maximum sentence is four months. In Case 5/2014, the defendant was prosecuted under Article 45(1), with Article 45(2) in the alternative. The court stated:

> The defendant was angry and emotional and threatened the victim-witness by using a piece of wood saying "If you enter my shop, I will hit you, I will kill you," then the defendant was interrupted by a witness … The defendant threatened to beat and kill the victim-witness, the victim-witness became afraid and reported the incident to the police for further investigation.

The court held that the actions of the defendant did not fulfil Article 45(1), as the psychological violence committed did not 'cause illness or obstruction to carry out work, livelihood or daily activities'. Therefore, the defendant was sentenced under the alternative charge of Article 45(2). There is a shift in logic between previous decisions and the court in Case 5/2014 regarding the distinction between general and limited violence. This case inverts the reasoning so that, arguably, Article 45(1) can only be satisfied if the victim's injuries results in illness or obstruct her work or daily activities. This interpretation potentially narrows the scope and application of Article 45(1). Under this interpretation, in any case where the victim's injuries cannot be proven to result in illness or obstruct her work or activities, the court will likely prefer the charge of *limited* violence. This shift in logic becomes more apparent in cases discussed below.

In 2015, there were three cases (Cases 2, 10 and 15/2015) where the perpetrators were convicted under Article 44(4) (limited physical violence). Taking physical violence as an example, Table 7.14 illustrates how the court's

Table 7.14 Acts held to satisfy Article 44(1) or (4) in 2015

Case	*Court's reasoning*
Case 2/2015	D threatened to beat V to death. There was a dispute over their child and D wanted to take the child. D tried to trap V in a room by closing the door on her. V managed to get out of the room but was injured while doing so. While trying to retrieve their child (who D was trying to take), D harshly closed a gate on V's feet. The court held that although D's actions caused pain for V, the pain 'did not create obstacles in carrying out daily activities'. Therefore Article 44(1) was not satisfied, and D was convicted under Article 44(4) in the alternative.
Case 10/2015	The wife-defendant was trying to pick up her child from the custody of the husband during a dispute over custody. The husband-victim obstructed her from entering the house. The wife-defendant was 'angry and emotional' and hit the husband-victim on his right cheek one time. Convicted under Article 44(4), similar to Case 4/2014 above.
Case 12/2015	D punched V in the ribs, and as a result V felt pain. D's actions, in hitting V, were carried out more than once. Namely in 2014 to 2015 by slapping V, threatening to poison V, and chasing V. Convicted under Article 44(1).
Case 15/2015	D slapped V's cheek one time. Convicted under Article 44(4), similar to Cases 4/2014 and 10/2015 above.

Source: Author's own.

interpretation of Article 44 begins to shift in 2015, like the court's interpretation of Article 45 in 2014.

There is a noticeable split in the interpretation of Article 44 in 2015. On one hand, in Case 12/2015 the court followed the same reasoning as in 2013, focusing on the severity of the assault and pain caused to the victim by the defendant's actions, while in Case 2/2015, the court held that subsection (1) was not satisfied on the basis that the pain caused by the defendant's actions 'did not obstruct the victim from carrying out work or daily activities'. The interpretation in Case 2/2015 echoes the distinction in Case 5/2014, which interpreted Article 45(1) in a similarly narrow way.

The split in the court's interpretation becomes even more noticeable in 2016. In 2016, eight cases (Cases 1, 2, 5, 7, 8, 10, 11 and 13/2016) were prosecuted under Article 44(4) (limited physical violence) instead of Article 44(1) of the Law. In Table 7.15, the reasons for this split are analysed.

The court's shift in interpretation is made explicit in Case 1/2016:

> Considering that the physical violence meant in this element [Article 44(1)] is violence which ***results in the victim suffering injuries that cause obstruction in doing work***; …

Table 7.15 Acts held to satisfy Article 44(1) or (4) in 2016

Case	*Court's reasoning*
Case 1/2016	D slapped V's cheek once and kicked her thigh once, which caused bruising. Article 44(1) not satisfied, D convicted under Article 44(4) in the alternative.
Case 2/2016	D slapped V on the cheek twice, verbally abused her and threw her phone. Article 44(1) not satisfied, D convicted under Article 44(4) in the alternative.
Case 5/2016	D held V's hands tightly so that V could not escape and as a result of the struggle, V's neck and both wrists were reddish and bruised but as a result of D's actions V was not interrupted in her daily activities. Article 44(1) not satisfied, D convicted under Article 44(4) in the alternative.
Case 7/2016	D committed violence by beating V on the face, which resulted in V suffering from a reddish bruise above her eye. D also threw a backpack at V, resulting in V suffering a bruise on her left leg. The result of D's actions did not cause V to be hindered in carrying out her daily work. Article 44(1) not satisfied, D convicted under Article 44(4) in the alternative.
Case 8/2016	D waited outside V's place of work and forced V to go home with him on a motorcycle, V was afraid of D. D took V in a different direction (not towards her home). V asked to be dropped off, but D refused to let her off the motorcycle. D squeezed V's left thigh so hard it caused bruising. After this V got off the bike and ran away. D ordered her to get back on the motorcycle. As a result of D's actions, V was traumatised and 'did not come to work for four days'. However, the court found that because the *physical* injury V suffered did not prevent her from carrying out work or daily activities, Article 44(1) was not satisfied. D was convicted under Article 44(4) in the alternative as well as under Article 45.
Case 10/2016	D elbowed V three times then kicked V twice so that V fell and hit the door. The injuries suffered by V did not prevent her from carrying out her daily activities. Article 44(1) was not satisfied, D convicted under Article 44(4) in the alternative.
Case 11/2016	D hit V once in the head causing her to faint. Article 44(1) not satisfied, D convicted under Article 44(4) in the alternative.
Case 13/2016	D choked V around her neck, then D held her and hit her in the head once, before hitting her in the left arm so that the V felt ill. Article 44(1) not satisfied, D convicted under Article 44(4) in the alternative.

Source: Author's own.

> Considering, that because in this case the result of the defendant's actions only caused the victim-witness to suffer a bruise and not be obstructed in carrying out work or daily activities and [she] continued to work as usual, the Panel of Judges was of the opinion that this element was not satisfied by the defendant's actions.
>
> (emphasis added)

This interpretation is even narrower than in previous cases where it was held that the violence needs to *either* cause illness *or* obstruct work, livelihood, or daily activities to meet the subsection (1) threshold. In Case 1/2016, these requirements were collapsed into one another.

Similarly, in Cases 5, 7 and 8/2016, the court stated that as the physical violence occurred between a husband and wife, and did not cause the victim to be unable to perform daily work or activities, Article 44(1) was not satisfied. Notably, the level of violence committed in Cases 10 and 13/2016 was similar to earlier cases where Article 44(1) was held to be satisfied (that is, the violence was not a single slap or punch but a more extended assault). It is particularly concerning that the court's limited interpretation of Article 44 appears to classify choking as 'not serious' – or a 'limited' form of violence – on the basis that 'the pain experienced by the victim-witness did not prevent the victim-witness from carrying out her daily activities' (Case 13/2016). This not only overlooks the seriousness of choking as a form of physical assault (as mentioned earlier in this chapter) but also potentially undermines the utility of Article 44(1) by focusing too myopically on the consequences of physical violence on a victim's ability to carry out work post-assault. Similarly, in Case 2/2015, the court convicted the defendant under Article 44(4), despite the defendant threatening to beat the victim to death during the assault.

The court's approach also does not seem to take into account the psychological impacts that a physical assault may have on a victim's 'ability to carry out daily activities'. Case 8/2016, in particular, illustrates the potential consequences of adopting an overly strict interpretation of Article 44(1). In this case, the court acknowledged that 'as a result of the defendant's actions, the victim-witness cannot carry out daily activities and cannot work'. The court elaborated that the victim was afraid of the defendant because the incident of physical violence (in Table 7.16) was part of a broader pattern of stalking and intimidation by the defendant, including at the victim's place of work. Despite this, the court held that Article 44(1) was not satisfied, because the physical injury (namely, the bruise suffered by the victim) – considered in isolation from the psychological violence – 'did not prevent her from carrying out work or daily activities'. Although the defendant in this case was also convicted under Article 45 (psychological violence), the court's treatment of physical and psychological violence in total isolation from one another illustrates a lack of understanding of the dynamics of domestic violence, especially since, in this case, the defendant's actions meant the victim was traumatised and 'did not come to work for four days'. Luckily in this case, the prosecution brought a charge under Article 45 alongside Article 44 which is not always the case.

In domestic violence contexts, where threats of violence or use of limited physical violence may be used to exert control over the victim, physical and psychological violence should not be viewed in isolation from each other. As in Case 8/2016, the use of physical violence may not necessarily be intended to seriously harm the victim but to instil fear in the victim or coerce compliance. The limitations of the current approach are arguably a consequence of the focus on physicality (and visibility) of violence identified in Chapter 4 in the court's understandings of domestic violence, and a lack of judicial education to remedy this misunderstanding. I argue that psychological harm caused by, or suffered in relation to, incidents of physical violence should be treated by the court as equally valid as visible bruises or lacerations, or at least not be artificially considered as occurring in isolation from physical violence. As such the court's current approach hinders the implementation and effectiveness of the Law.

The impact of such a limited interpretation is evidenced by the sharp increase in cases where convictions were imposed under subsection (4) of Article 44 in 2016, compared to prior years. However, the same cannot be said of 2017, where every case was sentenced under Article 44(1) (general physical violence), except for Case 10/2017 which was sentenced under Article 44(4) (limited physical violence) – see Table 7.16.[22]

Overall, the court's approach in 2017 tended to favour a broader interpretation of Article 44 compared to in 2016. This indicates that the trend towards a narrow interpretation is not linear and is not necessarily becoming increasingly narrow over time. However, the court's interpretation of the scope of general

Table 7.16 Acts held to satisfy Article 44(1) or (4) in 2017

Case	*Court's reasoning*
Case 2/2017	D slapped V on the cheek twice. Then D punched V in the head and clawed at her eyelids. Article 44(1) satisfied.
Case 4/2017	D strangled V and hit her the face several times. D then held V by the hair and banged her head against the floor. D also twisted V's right hand while sitting on V so that she could not move and threatened to kill V. Article 44(1) satisfied.
Case 8/2017	D kicked V and hit her in the head and body multiple times. Article 44(1) satisfied.
Case 9/2017	D pressed a machete against V's back and threatened to kill her. Article 44(1) satisfied.
Case 10/2017	During a verbal argument D 'reflexively' slapped V's left cheek once. D was sentenced under Article 44(4) in the alternative to Article 44(1).

Source: Author's own.

and limited violence was, again, split between two distinct approaches. Therefore, the analysis illustrates a persistent inconsistency in judicial interpretation of these provisions across the cases studied, leading to conviction and sentencing under different provisions across cases.

It is critical that prosecutors and women's advocates engage actively with, and respond to, this split in the court's interpretation, especially in terms of satisfying a potentially heightened evidentiary burden under Article 44(1). Importantly, in Abdurrachman's (2017) study of domestic violence in Indonesia, he also documented the narrower interpretation of Article 44(4) of the Law being applied by courts. To satisfy the narrower interpretation of Article 44(1) adopted by some judges, prosecutors must present specific evidence illustrating the impact of the assault on the victim's ability to perform daily activities or work. Even if the victim's ability to carry out such activities was, in fact, obstructed, it is another question whether evidence of such an impact was collected at the time of the assault or presented at trial. If the prosecution are aware that some judges tend to adopt a narrower interpretation of Article 44(1), the prosecution may need to request that police collect further evidence relevant to the impacts of injuries on a victim's ability to work.

As well as creating uncertainty in the court's approach, the significance of such a split in interpretation is that the maximum sentence under Article 44(1) is five years as compared to four months under Article 44(4). Although, in theory, the sentencing range varies significantly between the general and limited provisions, in practice there are many factors that influence sentencing discretion. The provision under which the defendant is prosecuted is, therefore, not necessarily determinative of the ultimate sentence handed down. In other words, an act prosecuted under Article 44(1) may only receive a sentence of a month, and a defendant convicted under Article 44(4) may receive a sentence of four months. Nevertheless, the provision under which a sentence is handed down is a relevant factor, as it directly impacts the sentencing range and is therefore worthy of analysis. Having distinguished between sentences based on the specific provisions under which they were prosecuted or sentenced, the question of whether the average sentence of three, or even, four months, in fact, falls at the lower end of the sentencing range can be answered in the affirmative. This is consistent with the findings of Abdurrachman's study, where he concluded that 'punishment for the perpetrators is quite moderate compared with the suffering of the victims'.

As pointed out by a judge of the *Pengadilan Negeri*, in addition to receiving adequate training and guidance to correctly interpret the law, judges must *want* to apply the law in a way that protects women's rights. The judge continued:

> Most cases only receive a minimum sentence, even if the case is extraordinary ... Sometimes we [judges and lawyers] argue over definitions. They [lawyers] once argued that the definition of 'confinement' was limited [to being] tied up for more than 24 hours. While in that case [the victim] was

> not tied up but [she] could not go anywhere, her cellphone was dead, and the door was locked [from the outside]. So I say, besides [judges] being smart and understanding, [they] also have to be *creative in developing the law* (emphasis added).

The point made by the judge resonates with respect to the interpretation of the scope of Article 44(1) and the interaction between Articles 44 and 45 analysed above. Even if judges received adequate training, the entrenched attitudes and values held by certain judges towards women, and their misconceptions about domestic violence, may continue to thwart the application of the Law in a way that protects women and holds perpetrators accountable. At present, an overly narrow (or obtuse) approach towards the interpretation of Articles 44 and 45 threatens to undermine the utility of these provisions for securing justice for victims.

Multiple charges

As mentioned above, an accompanying charge of psychological violence in addition to a charge of physical violence can potentially strengthen a prosecutor's case by providing broader context for the relationship and patterns of abuse. However, only a few cases in the study involved dual charges of physical and psychological violence, even where the victim had clearly suffered trauma from, or related to, an incident of physical violence. In cases where the court adopts a narrower interpretation of the scope of Article 44(1), hinging on the impact that a victim's injuries had on her daily activities and work, then a complementary charge of psychological violence may strategically open an avenue for entering into evidence the psychological impacts of violence. Entering such evidence could assist in illustrating the impact of violence on a victim's ability to carry out activities, even in cases where the physical injuries of the assault are limited. As in Case 9/2017, where the defendant used a machete to threaten the victim. Although the victim did suffer a physical injury (a laceration and bruising where the machete was pressed against her), evidence was also presented by the prosecution related to the trauma the victim suffered from the defendant's actions. On the other hand, in Case 8/2016 (discussed above), bringing dual charges reflecting both psychological and physical violence did not shift the court's focus when sentencing to the broader dynamics of domestic violence and, in that case, domestic violence was approached by the court as an isolated incident of physical violence.

Noting that Indonesia is a civil law system and therefore has no system of precedent, the prosecution can still learn from Case 9/2017 how to frame arguments to clearly explain the interrelationship between psychological and physical violence for the benefit of the court. Even if the court followed the line of reasoning in Case 8/2016 (which I argue contains a logical fallacy by artificially separating psychological and physical violence), a dual conviction under Articles 44 and 45 is likely to result in a sentence that more accurately represents the severity of the perpetrator's actions instead of focusing solely on the victim's physical injuries, or – even more restrictively – solely on the impact of those physical injuries on the victim's ability to undertake work or other activities.

Pre-trial detention

Pre-trial detention is measured from when the defendant is first incarcerated to the date that the sentence is handed down. When the sentence is handed down the perpetrator will either be released (for example, on probation with a suspended sentence) or start their official sentence of imprisonment (from which any period of pre-trial detention is deducted as time served). Defendants generally served pre-trial detention, except for in four cases. Excluding these four cases as outliers, the average period spent in pre-trial detention was between three and a half and four months. The longest pre-trial detention period served was over a year (14 months in Case 7/2013) and the shortest time – excluding the cases where no pre-trial detention was served – was 29 days. In most cases where pre-trial detention was served, the perpetrator was incarcerated until the date of trial. The average period of pre-trial detention correlates approximately to the average sentence handed down by the court, which means that many perpetrators did not spend further periods incarcerated but were released based on time served.

The average time between the date of the offence and date the court decision was handed down was approximately five and a half months (including four cases which had significant delays of a year or more, or just under five months excluding these cases).[23] This is somewhat surprising, considering that delay in prosecution and/or long processing times are common reasons given for victims not wanting to report domestic violence to police. In fact, instances of violence reported to the police in the cases studied were generally investigated, prosecuted, and sentenced within a five-month period. Although this timeframe may seem relatively short, as mentioned earlier, if perpetrators are not detained pre-trial this may be an extremely dangerous period for domestic violence victims, especially considering that restraining orders are rarely implemented. Further, victims may face continuing or exacerbated risks of violence when perpetrators are released. For example, Hudson (2002) states in her study that 'If the offender is acquitted or is not given a custodial sentence, [victims may] fear more violence, aggravated by the perpetrator's anger at being prosecuted'. Considering that many perpetrators are released shortly after trial and alternative sentencing options (such as counselling or restraining orders) are currently underused, it becomes apparent why many victims of domestic violence do not feel that pursuing criminal prosecution will ensure their safety.

Summary with respect to the court's approach to sentencing

The Law sets out a range of carceral and non-carceral sentencing options. However, due to substantive barriers, as well as institutional stakeholder preferences, carceral sentences are overwhelmingly handed down in domestic violence cases. The case analysis illustrates that carceral sentences handed down are generally at the lower end of the sentencing range. This is due both to the provisions under which domestic violence is prosecuted and sentenced (with respect to the statutory maximum sentences) and the exercise of judicial discretion in sentencing. Inconsistency in judicial interpretation of Articles 44 and 45 should urgently be addressed as it potentially leads to disparity between like cases.

In terms of court-mandated counselling or other avenues for perpetrator rehabilitation, the court's current approach seems to solely rely on specific deterrence flowing from prosecution and conviction to prevent future abuse. In Abdurrachman's (2017) study, he argued that the light sentences generally handed down in domestic violence cases do not effectively deter perpetrators. Further, carceral approaches alone – without rehabilitation and re-education – is highly unlikely to meaningfully address domestic violence and end the cycle of violence. In the worst-case scenario, prosecution and conviction of a perpetrator without complementary behavioural intervention may result in the perpetrator conceiving of themselves as the 'victims' of prosecution, leading to an increased risk of retaliation against victims and their children. In the words of the prosecutor interviewed for this study 'many [perpetrators] who get out of prison get worse. So the system needs to be reviewed'.

In terms of reform opportunities, the first major area for reform identified in this section is with respect to non-carceral sentencing pathways in domestic violence cases, in particular, the potential of court-ordered counselling programmes and restraining orders. The fact that 80% of victims did not seek to separate from the perpetrator at the time of the court decision makes the importance of non-carceral pathways clear. That is not to say that perpetrators should not serve carceral sentences, but that carceral sentences may not always meet victim needs (namely, for violence to stop or in terms of continuing economic support) or keep women and children safe long-term. The first step in resolving this issue is to address the lack of funding allocated to perpetrator rehabilitation programmes, which is required so that counselling is a viable sentencing option.

Secondly, there is a need for further judicial education as evidenced by inconsistency in judicial interpretations of the Law between cases, largely based on misunderstandings about domestic violence dynamics. In particular, the current judicial emphasis on the physicality of violence and an incident-focused approach limits the utility of the Law. A shift towards a more contextual consideration of domestic violence would require re-training within the police, prosecution, and judiciary, as the court's consideration is, to an extent, limited by the collection of evidence by the police and presentation of evidence by the prosecution, as well as the specific provision that the perpetrator is charged and/or sentenced under. Further, controlling, threatening, or coercive behaviour continues to be under-recognised. Poor understandings of the dynamics of domestic violence relationships with respect to the non-physical – but equally serious – elements also affect the gravity of sentencing. Continued judicial education about the severity of non-physical violence is imperative to ensure that sentences fit the crime and not only the physical elements of the crime.

It can be concluded that current criminal justice processes do not adequately protect women and their children. In some cases, current practices exacerbate risks to women's safety. An urgent area for reform is the State's failure to establish functional perpetrator rehabilitation programmes. Criminal justice stakeholders must ask themselves what, beyond an arguably empty 'moral victory', do women gain from participating in criminal prosecution? Women are called '*mitra*' (partners) in the criminal justice system. However, it is at best a lopsided partnership, with women cooperating with prosecutions at great personal risk, with little tangible protection in return. I argue that, at a minimum, criminal prosecution should adequately protect victims from further harm – for example from violence during pre-trial and post-trial periods, not to mention harm associated with the trial process itself (which are beyond the scope of this chapter's analysis). Women are currently not adequately protected due to the under-use of alternative sentences (namely, restraining and counselling orders) and the overreliance on (short) carceral sentences imposed by the court. A fairer 'partnership' between criminal justice stakeholders and victims would require changes in police and prosecutorial practices, as well as greater coordination between police, prosecutors, and the courts.

Part III. Mitigating and aggravating factors in sentencing

In addition to the under-use of restraining and counselling orders and inconsistency in judicial interpretations of Articles 44 and 45 of the Law, analysis of the cases also illustrated that sentencing discounts are often affected by gendered norms that sway the court towards lower (or higher) sentences for perpetrators. This section analyses judges' sentencing considerations. In every case, the court noted sentencing considerations under the headings of 'Mitigating' and 'Aggravating' Factors.[24]

First, the court's approach towards mitigating factors is analysed. Relevant factors highlighted by judges and prosecutors in interviews, as well as by judges throughout the cases studied, include the husband's role as the head of the household (in terms of being the primary economic provider) and the impact of reconciliation and victim wishes on sentencing. The second section analyses the court's approach towards aggravating factors, including the husband's role of the head of the household (in terms of an obligation to protect the family), as well as the type, severity, frequency, and impact of violence. This analysis illustrates that despite some evident inconsistencies in the application of mitigating and aggravating factors across cases, there are some promising opportunities for reform and advocacy.

The court's approach towards mitigating factors

In an interview, a *Pengadilan Negeri* judge highlighted both the role of the husband as the 'breadwinner' in the family and reconciliation as factors relevant to sentencing. The judge stated that:

> If the victim feels regretful for reporting the husband due to the hardship that she faces as no one is providing for her, sometimes the victim proposes to the judge to not give a long period of imprisonment to the perpetrator, if necessary or possible, to directly free the accused without jail time ... However, if the victim does not want to be together anymore, here, judges can consider that fact to give heavier punishment.

The role of the husband in the family and the integrity of the family unit were, in fact, dominant re-occurring themes in sentencing across cases. These will be considered alongside broader mitigating factors.

Role of the husband in the family

Over 45% of cases cited a mitigating factor related to the role of the husband in the family, including the husband being the 'backbone' of the family, the family being financially dependent on the husband, or the husband having family responsibilities. The role of the husband in the family, as conceptualised by the court, is two-fold: as the primary economic provider (*economic reliance*) and as the head of the household (*religious and cultural position*). The second limb of this categorisation will become clearer in the discussion of Aggravating Factors below.

The role of the husband in the family was conceptualised by the court as follows:

- D is the backbone (*tulang punggung*) of the family or D's wife and/or children are dependent on him;[25]
- D has family responsibilities or D's children need the presence of a father figure.[26]

In addition to the first limb – economic reliance – being raised by the judges in the above quotation, the prosecutor interviewed also raised the consideration of whether the husband is the 'backbone' (*tulang punggung*) of the family. That is, whether the husband has a continuing obligation to provide *nafkah* (maintenance) to his wife and/or children. For such an obligation to be continuing, this would generally imply that the husband and wife are not divorced. As outlined in Chapter 5, the husband's obligation to provide maintenance to his wife is temporally limited to the *iddah* period post-divorce. Although the husband's obligation to provide child support continues, in theory, until the child is no longer dependent, in practice, once a couple is divorced husbands commonly neglect to provide child support even if there is an Islamic Court order to this effect.

It is commonly assumed that if reporting violence, women also seek to separate from their abusive spouse, with 'leaving' the relationship positioned as the only, and/or ultimate, exercise of agency in an abusive relationship. However, the cases studied illustrate that it is not a sound assumption that women necessarily seek to divorce perpetrators when pursuing or cooperating with criminal prosecutions. Approximately 80% of couples in the cases studied were not separated or separating at the time of the court's decision, although it is impossible to know how many subsequently divorced. As illustrated below, at least some victims participating in criminal prosecutions indicated that they did not want to leave the relationship but wanted their abusers held accountable for violence and wanted violence to stop.[27] In cases where women maintain their relationship with the perpetrator, non-carceral options such as rehabilitation pathways become even more important.

The fact that women who report their abusive husbands to the police are not necessarily divorced or want to divorce leads to a moral and practical tension in prosecution and sentencing. As explained by the prosecutor interviewed:

> On one hand, the man has the responsibility to provide for his children and if we continue prosecution, what if his wife doesn't work? We feel sorry for the children as there is no one who can support them and they may end up neglected. But … if the case is very heavy (*berat sekali*), we must continue prosecution aiming for incarceration. However, if the consequences of his actions are not so heavy (*tidak begitu berat*) on the victim sometimes the perpetrator will not be incarcerated.

This tension was often mentioned by respondents, as imprisonment is, at present, overwhelming imposed when sentencing under the Law. If the husband is sent to jail, then the wife and child may suffer economic consequences. For example, Bapak S (Lawyer) stated: 'If a wife reports her husband and her husband goes to jail, who will give her family food? How will they live if the wife does not work?' Bapak S emphasised the importance of alternatives to imprisonment in cases where a period of incarceration would effectively punish or render the victim and her family destitute. However, due to the current lack of implementation of alternative orders, current domestic violence sentencing practices often do not serve victim needs nor break the cycle of violence. This highlights the need for the expansion and strengthening of alternative sentencing outcomes in domestic violence cases.

It should also be noted that consideration of economic reliance is not relevant to all cases and was only applied by the court on a case-by-case basis. Abusive husbands may have already economically abandoned their wives and families or be economically abusive and coerce money from their wives. Further, in many cases, the victims were financially independent or also working and contributing to household expenses. However, the dilemma for some victims of domestic violence (who are not financially independent and/or unable to work) is that the incarceration of an abusive spouse can lead to impoverishment for her and her children – highlighting that a 'harsher' carceral sentence does not always reflect victim needs.

Women who do not have a financial safety net and/or are financially dependent on their husbands may face greater barriers to reporting or leaving abusive relationships. As criminal prosecution of domestic violence does not occur in a vacuum, initiatives for economic empowerment of women from lower socio-economic backgrounds and other welfare avenues must also be developed alongside legal interventions. While women's NGOs run economic empowerment initiatives, there is no comprehensive State welfare system for domestic violence victims. The absence of such a State 'safety net' means that kinship and community support play an even greater role. However, as discussed in Chapter 4, limited community understanding of the Law and continuing stigma mean that women may not receive family or community support when reporting domestic violence. A lack of support for victims – both social and economic – is one of the many dilemmas faced by victims when deciding whether to report domestic violence, and if so, via which avenue (if any).

Reconciliation and 'making peace'

As mentioned above, a secondary aim of domestic violence prosecution in Indonesia is 'reconciliation'. *Pengadilan Negeri* judges interviewed stated that:

> During the trial, sometimes the husband and wife forgive each other and bring their children … the judges are also human, seeing the human side … that children need the love of a father. But, if the victim is no longer willing to be in the relationship, the judge can see the facts – this is something that is burdensome [an aggravating factor], so in carrying out domestic violence decisions, the judge looks at it case by case.

In fact, approximately 70% of cases highlighted reconciliation as a relevant mitigating factor, ranging from crediting attempts to reconcile to citing formal or written 'peace agreements'. The Court considered the following factors with respect to reconciliation:

- V had forgiven D or V has apologised for D's actions;[28]
- D and V have made peace/reconciled or a peace letter/agreement has been made;[29]
- D has apologised or tried to apologise to V.[30]

The court noted in approximately 55% of cases that the couple had 'made peace' but what exactly does 'making peace' mean in domestic violence contexts? It is clear that 'making peace' does not necessarily equate to the couple reconciling. For example, in Cases 1, 2 and 3/2013 the facts state that the couples were in the process of divorcing yet the mitigating considerations state that the victims had 'forgiven' the perpetrators or the couple had 'made peace'. On the other hand, in mitigating sentences, some judges cited the fact that: 'the relationship between D and V has been re-established', 'D and V live together again', or 'D and V want to rebuild their household'.[31] Other cases cited peace settlements officiated by the village *Geuchik* (for example, Cases 6 and 8/2013 and Case 12/2015).

There is an obvious tension between prioritising and respecting the agency of victims and acknowledging the substantive barriers that women face when exercising agency in abusive contexts, such as stigma, social isolation, economic reliance, threats to personal safety or safety of children, and the psychological impacts of abuse. As outlined in Chapter 4, interviews with domestic violence victims revealed multifaceted decision-making processes when exercising agency. Insights from domestic violence victims complicate the false dichotomy between 'staying' and 'leaving' found in some literature – or in the language of sentencing, the dichotomy between 'making peace' and 'not making peace'. Women's reasons for choosing whether to 'make peace' cannot realistically be judged by outsiders – who cannot possibly know the intricate circumstances and immense pressure under which women are making such decisions. Notwithstanding these difficulties, in practice, the judges interviewed identified the victim's wishes as a primary consideration in sentencing.

The balancing of these factors is illustrated in Case 16/2013, where D assaulted V and threatened to burn her alive in response to V choosing to take contraception. The court stated:

> [O]n one hand such an act of the defendant is essentially a crime against human dignity or an act that is demeaning of human dignity, especially women … [O]n the other hand the defendant as the perpetrator and the witness-victim are a husband and wife that have been married for more than six years and married life is a facility to achieve true happiness both physically and spiritually.
>
> In other words, the ultimate goal of married life is to achieve a peaceful life (*sakinah*), as well as to love each other. Therefore, the panel of judges decides that punishment that has the nature to take away the freedom of the defendant (such as imprisonment) will obviously separate them … [Therefore] the punishment that is appropriate to be given to the defendant is a suspended sentence.

While identifying domestic violence as a crime against human dignity, the court mitigated the perpetrator's sentence primarily on the basis that the couple had made peace. As the couple had reconciled, the court opted for a non-carceral sentence (a five-month suspended sentence with a 10-month probationary period). Further, the victim and children in this case were financially dependent on the perpetrator. Such a case illustrates the dilemmas that prosecutors and judges face when approaching sentencing in domestic violence cases.

While in many cases it was a mitigating factor that the victim and perpetrator reconciled, in at least one case a legal divorce between the parties was also considered to be a mitigating factor (Case 2/2015). Considering the judges stated in interviews that relationship breakdown was an aggravating factor, it is not clear why in Case 2/2015 a divorce was cited as a mitigating factor. In the same case, the fact that the couple had not made peace was also cited as an aggravating factor. Although each case must be considered on its own facts, there also appear to be inconsistencies in the exercise of judicial discretion in sentencing illustrated in the case study.

Trial demeanour

Another relevant sentencing consideration was the defendant's demeanour during the trial. In almost every case, defendants were described as remorseful, polite, or cooperative among other things. The court considered the following factors:

- D was polite/courteous during the trial/in court;[32]
- D regretted/acknowledged or admitted his actions; felt guilty; or promised not to reoffend;[33]
- D gave clear testimony in court or was forthright in court expediting the trial process.[34]

There was also some inconsistency in the consideration of this factor. For example, in Case 8/2014, where the court described the perpetrator as polite and contrite, the facts stated: 'D denied the statements given by the witnesses, arguing that he did not push V but that the victim fell because she was wearing high heels'. It is not clear why the court gave mitigatory credit to the defendant for contrition if, at the same time, he denied his actions and contested the claims of the victim regarding violence.

In a handful of cases judges also mitigated sentences if the defendant pleaded guilty.[35] In the Indonesian system, pleading guilty does not speed up the court process and even if a defendant admits to the offence the defendant and victim-witness are still subjected to the trial process. It is common knowledge that the trial process is itself traumatic for victims – whether or not the perpetrator is cooperative.[36] Comparatively, in a common law system like Australia, a guilty plea would end the need for a trial and the case would proceed straight to sentencing.

Other mitigating factors

Other mitigating factors include: the defendant having no prior convictions, the youth of the perpetrator, and the age of the perpetrator's children (associated with the responsibility of caring for young children). Further, there is a tendency for male violence to be (morally) justified, leading to the mitigation of sentences even where is no legal basis for doing so. As mentioned earlier in this chapter, judges stated that they considered whether the accused used violence 'to educate' the victim or if the accused used violence 'straight away out of emotion'. In some cases, this meant that triggers for violence were implicitly accepted by the court, to an extent, as 'justifying' the offender's behaviour. For example, in Case 5/2013, the court placed blame on the victim when discussing mitigating factors. In this case, the court stated that the acts were not the 'absolute errors' of the defendant but also partly 'the victim's fault'. In this case, the victim and the defendant were having a verbal argument. The defendant testified that the victim then slapped him and that it was in response to the slap that the defendant hit, choked, and dragged the victim to the ground. The victim did not testify. In mitigating the defendant's sentence, the court implicitly classified the violence as reciprocal and invoked ideas of provocation (which can be contrasted to cases of self-defence discussed below).

The court's approach towards aggravating factors

Role of the husband in the family

In over 40% of cases, judges considered it an aggravating factor if men did not act in accordance with their role as head of the household (including to be a role model or set an example for their family).[37] Notably, many judges conceptualised domestic violence in general as being intrinsically contradictory to men's gender roles as the head of the household, due to that fact that the perpetrator committed violence against someone who he 'said he loved' and 'who he should have protected'.[38] This type of reasoning strikes a chord with constructions of caring masculinities that try to challenge toxic masculinities built on shame and violence. Positive framings of masculinity based on non-violence (as opposed to the use of violence to exercise power and control) are increasingly being recognised as an important aspect of combatting domestic violence.[39]

In Indonesia, where interpretations of Islam firmly position men as the head of the household, it is generally not considered pragmatic to directly challenge men's position as the head of the household but instead to re-define the content of such a position. Significantly, the conceptualisation of male gender roles (as an aggravating factor in sentencing) attaches responsibilities to men's position as the head of the household – particularly an expectation of non-violence, instead of an unfettered privilege of holding such a position without accountability. As discussed above, the fact that some judges raised the perceived entitlement of men to use disciplinary violence during interviews make discourses that re-define the content of men's gender norms towards non-violence especially important. This is supported by Mahmood's (2018) study which identifies the use of the 'responsible husband' figure in feminist Islamic interpretations to promote 'reciprocal and complementary duties' for men in the context of marriage.

In an interview, a victim of domestic violence stated that 'I need a head of the household, but I don't need *you* [her husband]'. She went on to explain that although in her interpretation of Islam she believed that the husband should symbolically be the head of the household, if her husband did not meet the expectations of this role (that is, if he perpetrated violence) then he loses the privilege of respect associated with that position. Conceptualising such privileges as contingent on the performance of responsibilities in line with constructs of caring masculinities is a promising approach to open discussions within Indonesian Islam about men's gender roles including non-violence as a core tenet. Such an approach should be further explored in future as discussed in Chapter 8.

This chapter has shown that gendered norms relating to men as the head of the household affect the exercise of judicial discretion in sentencing in two important ways. First, in terms of economic reliance and, second, as a cultural and religious position, imbuing men's role as the head of the household with obligations as well as privileges. While there are many instances of implicit gender bias in the approach of the court towards domestic violence, the latter construction of gender norms illustrates at least some potential for masculine gender norms to be re-conceptualised in a way that promotes non-violence.

Type, severity, frequency, and impact of violence

The type, severity, frequency, and impact of violence are generally considered in sentencing. Judges are much more likely to impose non-custodial sentences in cases where violence is not considered to be '*berat*' (heavy or severe). The impacts of the defendant's actions on the victim are also considered, including whether pain or trauma are suffered and if so, whether these issues are acute or ongoing. In an interview, a *Pengadilan Negeri* judge stated that if the perpetrator has committed violence repeatedly then a heavier sentence is likely to be handed down. With respect to the frequency of violence, it must be recalled how rarely the court considers a history of domestic violence. The fact that most judges take an incident-based approach partially explains why courts tend to hand down light sentences. On the other hand, if the court more holistically considered domestic violence within relationships, this may support the imposition of heavier sentences since the 'frequency of violence' is an aggravating factor.

Further, in terms of severity of violence, the fact that the court generally continues to treat physical violence more seriously than other types of violence means that controlling, threatening, or coercive behaviour remains under-recognised. Limited understanding of the dynamics of domestic violence relationships with respect their non-physical elements continue to affect the gravity of sentencing. This is supported by Abdurrachman's (2017) study which found that 'many judges still regard domestic violence as a less serious offence, especially in regard to psychological intimidation'.

Community expectations

In several cases, the court relied on the concept of 'community expectations' to aggravate a perpetrator's sentence. The consideration of community expectations in criminal sentencing is often a vexed exercise. This is particularly so in the sentencing of domestic violence in a context where the broader community may not recognise domestic violence or may otherwise minimise or justify the use of violence. Putting to one side the potential biases introduced into domestic violence sentencing by community expectations, the consideration of community expectations as an aggravating factor in the cases studied operated to condemn acts of domestic violence as going against community expectations of non-violence.

In some cases, the 'shame' or 'unrest' caused by the perpetrator's violence was seen as an aggravating factor (implying that the community condemns the use of violence). For example, in Case 3/2016 – where V was pregnant at the time of the assault – D's actions were considered to be aggravated as they 'unsettled the community'. Further, in Case 8/2016, where D not only assaulted V but repeatedly stalked her outside of her workplace, D's actions were held to have 'disturbed the community'. In other cases, the court considered community's expectations that civil servants or police should model non-violent and law-abiding behaviour. The court's comments included that:

- D's actions have caused shame to V in the eyes of the public (Case 4/2015);
- D's actions have unsettled/disturbed the community (Case 12/2015; Case 12/2015; Case 3/2016; Case 8/2016; Case 11/2016; Case 2/2017);
- D is a Civil Servant who is supposed to be an example to the community (Case 5/2014);
- D is a member of the National Police who should be an example to the community (Case 10/2014; Case 17/2015); and
- D is a government employee who should be an example for others (Case 10/2015).

Trial demeanour

In most cases, perpetrators did not object to the statements of witnesses and cooperated with the court and, to varying extents, took responsibility for their actions. However, in some cases perpetrators denied or refuted the charges and victim claims. Perpetrator denial had an aggravating impact on sentencing. The court's considerations included that:

- D did not admit to beating the defendant (Case 17/2013);
- D was convoluted in giving information during the trial (Case 18/2013; Case 13/2016); and
- D did not admit to his act and was not forthcoming (Case 6/2015).

In saying this, even if perpetrators did not outright deny that they committed violence, many still attempted to minimise or justify their behaviour.

Other aggravating factors

Additional aggravating factors cited by judges included that peace had not been achieved between the defendant and victim,[40] the defendant was a recidivist,[41] and that D's actions were 'acts of vigilante violence' (*tindakan main hakim sendiri*).[42] By condemning vigilantism, the court made a clear statement about the entitlement of men to judge the behaviour of women and to use violence to enforce their interpretations of socially acceptable norms, regardless of whether their wife's behaviour was, in fact, 'morally problematic'. The aggravation of an offence based on vigilantism is a strong condemnation of men's moral justifications or excuses for choosing to use violence. For example, in Case 6/2014, the court aggravated the defendant's sentence due to vigilantism, stating:

> [T]he defendant beat the victim-witness because the defendant at the time was upset with the victim-witness for smoking ... because the defendant saw the victim-witness walking with other men, and because the victim-witness did not want to listen to the defendant.

Although this factor was only explicitly cited as an aggravating factor in four cases, it is important to note because it frames men's moral justifications for violence as irrelevant and holds perpetrators legally accountable. Significantly, the condemnation of vigilantism challenges the prevalent idea that men are entitled to use violence to enforce gender norms. This line of reasoning can be used to combat justificatory rhetoric that minimises the seriousness of violence in contexts where the 'intention' of the perpetrator was to 'educate' the victim (including judge's justificatory rhetoric discussed earlier in this chapter).

There is potential for the 'vigilante violence' approach to be emphasised by reformers and women's advocates to demonstrate that making an exception for morally 'justified' violence is untenable. The cases studied illustrated that, at times, the line between moral and legal justifications is blurred by criminal justice stakeholders. Against this background, the aggravation of sentencing based on 'vigilante violence' holds perpetrators accountable despite abusers' justifications for using violence. The strength of this approach is that it emphasises that the perpetrator's subjective moral justifications do not give them the right to use violence.

Summary relating to mitigating and aggravating sentencing factors

The sentencing considerations discussed above reflect the complexity of women's decision-making in domestic violence contexts, in particular, victim wishes related to economic reliance and reconciliation in a context of emotional and financial interconnectedness and dependency. Relatedly, it illustrates the dilemmas faced by judges in sentencing. While acknowledging the complexity of judicial decision-making, I argue that, in the absence of clear sentencing guidelines, judicial discretion is exercised in a densely gendered way which often implicitly (morally) justifies male violence. Further, I argue that sentencing guidelines should be developed to promote judicial transparency and accountability in the exercise of sentencing discretion. The absence of clear guidelines mean that sentencing based on moral (as opposed to legal) justifications is an ever-present risk in domestic violence cases.

Despite contradictions and inconsistencies illustrated in the above analysis, a few pathways for strengthening sentencing practice (and domestic violence advocacy in general) were also identified. In particular, the aggravation of sentencing based on a condemnation of spousal violence as inconsistent with the male's role as head of the household, and of domestic violence as vigilantism, both send a clear message to perpetrators that there is no justification for using violence. Reasoning along these lines should be developed further by women's advocates to strengthen the utility of the Law in delivering justice for victims, as well as for the purposes of public education and prevention.

Moreover, the cases studied highlights the need for institutional stakeholders to reflect on how and why victims engage with the criminal justice system. In other words, what do victims need? And does the status quo effectively engage with and protect women? Despite the many barriers identified in this book that prevent and deter victims of domestic violence from engaging with the State system, the *Pengadilan Negeri* cases studied represent a number of women who, despite compounding barriers to reporting, cooperated with the State to prosecute their abusers. An important question for the State must therefore be: why these women? What enables and motivates these women to engage with a system which, in many ways, does not serve their interests? And how can the State system better serve the needs of victims of domestic violence in the future?

Notes

1 Bapak S (Lawyer) noted that although courts are meant to be closed for domestic violence cases, some judges do not close the court leaving families feeling 'embarrassed'.
2 See, for example, Saraswati's (2021) study in the Indonesian context and Hudson (2002) more generally.
3 As noted in Chapter 3, while this book studies the specific framing of domestic violence and gender in Aceh, Indonesia, domestic violence is in no way unique to Aceh, Indonesian or Islamic contexts and occurs in communities around the world irrespective of religion.
4 In 2017–2019 when fieldwork was conducted, various interviewees indicated that some criminal justice system stakeholders still did not feel confident to apply the Law as it is a relatively 'new' piece of legislation, despite being passed in 2004. This indicates that there remains a need for continued judicial training and education.
5 Article 183 of the Criminal Procedure Code; Article 55 of the Law.

6 Under Article 10(d) of the Law victims are entitled to be accompanied by a social worker and legal aid worker during the examination process.
7 Article 55 of the Law: 'As one of the legitimate instruments of proof, the testimony of a victim witness alone shall be adequate to prove that the accused is guilty, if accompanied with another legitimate instrument of proof'.
8 This can be distinguished from a further 20% of cases where the court noted that the couple 'argued' or 'quarrelled' directly before the prosecuted incident of violence (i.e. where the court was commenting on the immediate context rather than a history of 'arguments' or 'quarrels').
9 Articles 31(3) and 34 of the Marriage Law and Articles 79–80 of the *Compilation of Islamic Law*.
10 Article 90 of the former Criminal Code and Article 155 of the new Criminal Code.
11 For example, s 315A of the *Criminal Code 1899* (Qld) on 'Choking, suffocation or strangulation in a domestic setting'. Further, on this point, see Strack and Gwinn (2011), Douglas and Fitzgerald (2014) and Douglas (2019).
12 On this point, see Chapter 7 of Hill's (2019) book and sources cited therein.
13 An Indonesian 'family card' – or *Kartu Tanda Penduduk* (Residential Identity Card) – is a type of identity card. It is commonly referred to as a family card as it is often issued upon marriage and usually lists members of the family residing with the holder.
14 Regarding the contested interpretation of '*nushuz*', see Chapter 4.
15 The source of the rule of law in Indonesia (the *negara hukum*) is the preamble to the 1945 Constitution, which establishes a State based on law.
16 Alfitri (2020) and Ramadhita et al. (2023) identify the risk of the poorly defined concept of '*nushuz*' being applied inconsistently and arbitrarily against women.
17 The Elucidation to Article 31(1) of the Law further defines it as including 'limitation of movement of the perpetrator, prohibition to enter a joint dwelling, prohibition to follow, watch or intimidate the victim'.
18 A fine was imposed in Case 6/2017, although this case was an instance of violence by a parent against a child and so is excluded from the substantive analysis. The sentence imposed was one month's imprisonment and a fine of Rp 500,000 (or approximately AUD $50). If the fine was not paid, it was to be replaced by an additional one month's imprisonment.
19 For a more complete discussion of sentencing law in Indonesia see Assegaf (2020).
20 In 2018, the prosecution recommended a suspended sentence and probationary period in 38% of cases, whereas from 2014 to 2017, such recommendations occurred only in three cases, that is, at a rate of approximately 6%.
21 On this point see Day et al. (2010) and Bowen et al. (2003). Also note the MenCare+ Gender Justice Pilot Programme run in Indonesia between 2013 and 2015. The pilot found that perpetrator counselling which focused on the transformation of patriarchal gender norms to gender-equitable norms can result in the reduction of domestic violence (Haryanto 2018).
22 In Cases 1, 3 and 7/2017, Article 44(4) was not presented in the alternative. In Case 1, D threw a ceramic cup at V's head, causing a head wound. In Case 3, D grabbed V's hair and hit her, then kicked their child. In Case 7, D beat V with a racket, an electrical cable, and a piece of wood, before threatening her with a machete and demanding she remove all her clothes. D also harmed their child. Other than the fact that Cases 3 and 7 involved relatively serious acts of violence, it is not clear why prosecutors did not bring alternative charges in these cases.
23 Case 3/2013 – 15 months, Case 5/2013 – 23 months, Case 4/2015 – 14 months, and Case 3/2016 – 12 months.
24 As stipulated in Article 8(2) of Law No. 48/2009, in sentencing judges must pay attention to the aggravating and mitigating factors ('good and evil nature of the defendant'), as well as matters listed in Article 197(1)(f) of the Criminal Procedure Code.

25 Case 1/2013; Case 3/2013; Case 5/2013; Case 6/2013; Case 7/2013; Case 8/2013; Case 9/2013; Case 10/2013; Case 11/2013; Case 12/2013; Case 16/2013; Case 17/2013; Case 19/2013; Case 20/2013; Case 7/2014; Case 2/2015; Case 6/2015; Case 12/2015; Case 1/2016; Case 5/2016; Case 7/2016; Case 3/2017; Case 9/2017.

26 Case 2/2013; Case 9/2014; Case 3/2015; Case 4/2015; Case 16/2015; Case 17/2015; Case 4/2017.

27 On this point, Ibu S (Prosecutor) stated in an interview: 'the results [of criminal prosecution] are sometimes unsatisfying for victims, not all who report immediately want their husbands to be imprisoned, some want their husbands to change, those who report sometimes wait for years, even then many [perpetrators] who get out of prison get worse'. This is also reflected in the international literature, see for example Hudson (2002).

28 Case 1/2013; Case 2/2013; Case 9/2013; Case 19/2013; Case 20/2013; Case 7/2017; Case 10/2017.

29 Case 3/2013; Case 6/2013; Case 8/2013; Case 10/2013; Case 12/2013; Case 14/2013; Case 16/2013; Case 1/2014; Case 4/2014; Case 6/2014; Case 10/2014; Case 9/2014; Case 4/2015; Case 5/2015; Case 7/2015; Case 8/2015; Case 9/2015; Case 10/2015; Case 11/2015; Case 12/2015; Case 13/2015; Case 14/2015; Case 16/2015; Case 17/2015; Case 2/2016; Case 5/2016; Case 6/2016; Case 8/2016; Case 10/2016; Case 11/2016; Case 13/2016; Case 1/2017; Case 2/2017; Case 7/2017; Case 8/2017.

30 Case 7/2016; Case 8/2016.

31 Case 12/2013; Case 4/2015; Case 11/2016; Case 2/2017; and Case 7/2017.

32 Case 1/2013; Case 2/2013; Case 9/2013; Case 10/2013; Case 17/2013; Case 18/2013; Case 19/2013; Case 20/2013; Case 1/2014; Case 2/2014; Case 3/2014; Case 4/2014; Case 5/2014; Case 6/2014; Case 8/2014; Case 9/2014; Case 10/2014; Case 1/2015; Case 2/2015; Case 3/2015; Case 4/2015; Case 5/2015; Case 7/2015; Case 8/2015; Case 9/2015; Case 10/2015; Case 13/2015; Case 14/2015; Case 15/2015; Case 16/2015; Case 17/2015; Case 1/2016; Case 3/2016; Case 4/2016; Case 7/2016; Case 8/2016; Case 9/2016; Case 11/2016; Case 3/2017; Case 4/2017; Case 8/2017; Case 10/2017.

33 Case 1/2013; Case 2/2013; Case 3/2013; Case 5/2013; Case 6/2013; Case 7/2013; Case 8/2013; Case 9/2013; Case 10/2013; Case 11/2013; Case 12/2013; Case 14/2013; Case 15/2013; Case 16/2013; Case 17/2013; Case 19/2013; Case 20/2013; Case 1/2014; Case 2/2014; Case 3/2014; Case 4/2014; Case 5/2014; Case 6/2014; Case 7/2014; Case 8/2014; Case 9/2014; Case 10/2014; Case 1/2015; Case 3/2015; Case 4/2015; Case 5/2015; Case 7/2015; Case 8/2015; Case 11/2015; Case 12/2015; Case 13/2015; Case 14/2015; Case 15/2015; Case 16/2015; Case 17/2015; Case 2/2016; Case 3/2016; Case 4/2016; Case 5/2016; Case 8/2016; Case 4/2017; Case 8/2017; Case 10/2017.

34 Case 4/2014; Case 5/2014; Case 10/2014; Case 4/2015; Case 5/2015; Case 8/2015; Case 13/2015; Case 14/2015; Case 15/2015; Case 2/2016; Case 3/2016; Case 5/2016; Case 10/2017.

35 Cases 6 and 9/2014, Cases 16 and 17/2015 and Case 4/2017.

36 See, for example, Saraswati's (2021) study in the Indonesian context and Hudson (2002) more generally.

37 Regarding the role of head of the household including being a role model or example for the family see: Case 1/2013; Case 2/2013; Case 9/2013; Case 10/2013; Case 19/2013; Case 4/2016.

38 Regarding the role of head of the household including to love and protect the family see: Case 2/2013; Case 3/2013; Case 5/2013; Case 6/2013; Case 7/2013; Case 8/2013; Case 11/2013; Case 12/2013; Case 14/2013; Case 15/2013; Case 16/2013; Case 7/2014; Case 9/2015; Case 2/2016; Case 3/2016; Case 5/2016; Case 7/2016; Case 9/2016; Case 11/2016; Case 2/2017; Case 3/2015; Case 9/2017.

39 In the Acehnese context, see Nashriyah and Syahabuddin (2015).

40 Case 18/2013; Case 3/2014; Case 1/2015; Case 2/2015; Case 4/2016.

41 Case 3/2013; Case 18/2013; Case 3/2015.
42 Case 6/2014; Case 9/2014; Case 3/2015; Case 16/2015.

Bibliography

Abdurrachman, Hamidah, 'A Culture of Neglect: A Study of Indonesian Court Judgements Regarding Victims of Domestic Violence' (2017) 55 *International Annals or Criminology* 26–39.

Alfitri, 'Protecting Women from Domestic Violence: Islam, Family Law, and the State in Indonesia' (2020) 27(2) *Studia Islamika* 273–307.

Assegaf, Rifqi, *Criminal Sentencing in Indonesia: Disparity, Disproportionality and Biases* (PhD Thesis, University of Melbourne, 2020).

Bowen, Erica, Len Brown and Elizabeth Gilchrist, 'Evaluating Probation Based Offender Programmes for Domestic Violence Perpetrators: A Pro-Feminist Approach' (2003) 41(3) *Howard Journal of Crime and Justice* 221–236.

Butt, Simon and Tim Lindsey, *Indonesian Law* (Oxford, 2018).

Day, Andrew, Donna Chung, Patrick O'Leary, Donna Justo, Susan Moore, Ed Carson and Adam Gerace, *Integrating Responses to Domestic Violence: Legally Mandated Intervention Programs for Male Perpetrators* (AIC Report, 2010).

Douglas, Heather, 'Victoria's Commitment to a Non-fatal Strangulation Offence will Make a Difference to Vulnerable Women', *The Conversation* (3 July 2019) https://theconversation.com/victorias-commitment-to-a-non-fatal-strangulation-offence-will-make-a-difference-to-vulnerable-women-119743

Douglas, Heather and Robin Fitzgerald, 'Strangulation, Domestic Violence and the Legal Response' (2014) 36 *Sydney Law Review* 231–254.

Haryanto, Sindung, 'Engaging Men: Results of the MenCare+ Gender Justice Program in Indonesia' (2018) 26(1) *The Journal of Men's Studies* 40–55.

Hill, Jess, *See What You Made Me Do: Power, Control and Domestic Abuse* (Black Inc, 2019).

Hudson, Barbara, 'Restorative Justice and Gendered Violence: Diversion or Effective Justice?' (2002) 42(3) *British Journal of Criminology* 616–634.

Komnas Perempuan, *Implementation of ICESCR in Indonesia* (Report, 2011).

Mahmood, Shahirah, 'Adapting Human Rights: Gender-Based Violence and Law in Indonesia' in Mehrangiz Najafizadeh and Linda Lindsey (eds), *Women of Asia: Globalization, Development, and Gender Equity* (Taylor & Francis, 2018) 154–169.

Nashriyah and Khairiah Syahabuddin (eds), *Masculinities in Post Conflict Aceh and Its Impacts on Violence Against Women* (PSW UIN Ar-Raniry, 2015).

Noer, Aleydha Patriana and Rosalia Dika Agustanti, 'The Application of the Restraining Order Mechanism to Domestic Violence Crimes' (2024) 7(2) *Jurnal USM Law Review* https://doi.org/10.26623/julr.v7i2.9416

Ramadhita, Ramadhita, Mahrus Ali and Bachri Syabbul, 'Gender Inequality and Judicial Discretion in Muslims Divorce Indonesia' (2023) 9(1) *Cogent Social Sciences* https://doi.org/10.1080/23311886.2023.2206347

Saraswati, Rika, 'Gender Bias in Indonesian Courts: Is Perma No. 3 of 2017 the Solution for Gender-Based Violence Cases?' (2021) 10(2) *Laws* 1–16.

Soesilo, *KUHP and Explanation* (Politea, 1996).

Strack, Gael and Casey Gwinn, 'On the Edge of Homicide: Strangulation as a Prelude' (2011) 26(3) *Criminal Justice* 32–37.

World Health Organization, 'Intimate Partner Violence and Alcohol' (Factsheet, 2014) https://womensaidorkney.org.uk/wp-content/uploads/2014/08/WHO-IPA-and-Alcohol-Fact-sheet.pdf

Laws and regulations cited in Chapter 7

Law No. 23/ 2004 regarding the Elimination of Domestic Violence (*Undang-Undang tentang Penghapusan Kekerasan Dalam Rumah Tangga*).
Law No. 27/1999 (Former) Criminal Code (*Kitab Undang-Undang Hukum Pidana - KUHP*).
Law No. 1/2023 (New) Criminal Code (*Kitab Undang-Undang Hukum Pidana - KUHP*).
Law No. 8/1981 Criminal Procedure Code *(Kitab Undang-Undang Hukum Acara Pidana – KUHP)*.
Law No. 1/1974 Marriage Law.
Presidential Instruction No. 1/1991 (*Compilation of Islamic Law*).
Qanun No. 6/2014 (*Qanun Jinayat*).

Interviews cited in Chapter 7

Interview Bapak S (Lawyer) (Banda Aceh, 15 December 2017).
Interview with Ibu R (P2TP2A/*Balai Syura*) (Banda Aceh, 19 December 2017).
Interview Ibu S (Prosecutor) (Banda Aceh, 25 September 2018).
Interviews with victims of domestic violence (Banda Aceh, 19 January 2019).
Interview with *Pengadilan Negeri* judges (Banda Aceh, 26 September 2018).

8 Conclusion

Recalling the prologue to this book

October 2018, at home

Ibu Hayati sits on the veranda with her neighbours Ibu Dina and Ibu Risa.

'My husband will never agree to a divorce', says Ibu Hayati.

'You want to get divorced? … For what – to be a *janda* (divorcee)?', Ibu Dina retorts.

'I can't take this anymore', Ibu Hayati responds, 'I keep praying that he will get better.'

'*Allah* would never give you a greater burden than you can bear', says Ibu Risa softly, 'You have to be *sabar* (patient) *Kak*.'

Ibu Hayati nods and responds, '*Inshallah*', excusing herself to go and pick up her eldest child from school.

January 2019, in the village

The *Geuchik* (Head of the Village) sits across from Ibu Hayati furrowing his brow.

'It keeps getting worse', she says, 'I don't know what to do.'

Bapak (Mr) *Geuchik* shrugs. 'It's normal for couples to *cek-cok* (disagree) sometimes', he replies.

'It's not just disagreement though Bapak … I don't feel safe at home anymore and I am worried about the children.'

'You *should* think of your children', the *Geuchik* responds, 'they need a father to provide for them.'

DOI: 10.4324/9781032613642-8

July 2019, at the police station

Ibu Hayati sits next to Ibu Risa at the police station.

'There is nothing we can do', the officer explains. 'We don't have any evidence to charge him.'

'I saw it myself', Ibu Risa offers. 'He threatened to kill her – please, there must be something you can do. She even has texts on her phone, show them *Kak* –'

'It's just', the officer interrupts, 'that this kind of case … it's not that serious (*tidak berat*).

With household problems, it's better to go P2TP2A – they deal with cases like this.'

'Come on let's go', Ibu Risa says, taking Ibu Hayati's hand.

July 2019, at P2TP2A's office

Ibu Hayati hands the forms that she has spent the last hour filling out back to the P2TP2A secretary.

'Do you have anyone that you can stay with?', the secretary asks while looking over the forms.

'No, my mother and father live in a different province', Ibu Hayati replies. 'The *Geuchik* said that he can ask my husband to move out of the house so that my children and I can stay in the *kampung* (village), but I am worried that my husband will not listen.'

The secretary nods, 'It is probably best not to stay there if you think your husband might react badly to the divorce application.'

'He threatened to take the children if I file for divorce, I don't know what to do.'

'I understand, it's hard. But you have rights and it's not okay for him to treat you like this – you have to be strong Ibu.'

December 2019, back at P2TP2A's office

Ibu Hayati sits in the waiting room at P2TP2A, looking at the 'Stop *Kekerasan* (Violence)' poster on the wall. 'Ibu Hayati', the secretary calls, 'Ibu Raihan will see you now.'

'Do you want the good news or the bad news?' Ibu Raihan asks.

Ibu Hayati ignores the question, 'I just need to know when I will be able to see my children again. I need to be with them.'

'The good news', Ibu Raihan continues, 'is that the enforcement proceeding for your divorce case has been listed for next month.'

'What does that mean?', Ibu Hayati asks.

'It means that we will be able to ask the Judge to enforce the original custody arrangement which was made when your divorce was finalised.'

'And in the meantime?'

'You just have to be *sabar* (patient) Ibu.'

(Source for the above: Author's own)

Community (mis-)understandings

In the first instance, Ibu Hayati faced community stigma and the 'taboo' of speaking about domestic violence. Victims of domestic violence often experience significant stigma from their families and communities when seeking help or reporting violence, based on hegemonic gender norms informed by patriarchal religious interpretations. Gender norms influence both community and State actor understandings of domestic violence as being a 'private' issue or 'not sufficiently serious' in cases where severe physical/visual violence is not present (or able to be evidenced). Such understandings, especially as they permeate State institutions, reflect poor understandings of the Law and a lack of adequate training for police, prosecutors, and judges. As illustrated throughout this book, it is common for domestic violence to be ignored, silenced, minimised, normalised, justified or excused, and for victims to be blamed for 'provoking' violence.

Of the domestic violence cases that are reported, the majority are mediated informally through *adat* justice avenues and do not enter the State system. Community understandings of domestic violence as 'normal' or 'justified', in practice, often pressure victims into remaining silent or mediating disputes at the community level instead of pursuing religious (civil) or criminal law avenues. Notably, if a victim were to apply for a divorce and report violence to the police, it is likely that she would have to go through mediation three times: once at the village level; once at the Islamic Court; and once when reporting to the police. Although the latter is not compulsory, in cases where violence is not considered 'sufficiently serious' victims may feel pressured to take part in police mediation (conducted by referral to P2TP2A Banda Aceh).

Mediation

There are currently insufficient safeguards in place to protect victims of domestic violence during mediation. This is of particular concern during *adat* mediation due to power inequalities and a lack of transparency in decision-making, in addition to a lack of community understanding about domestic violence and the Law. Further, in Chapter 5 it was argued that mediation should not be compulsory at the Islamic Courts for cases that involve domestic violence – or, at a minimum, screening processes and relevant training for mediators should be introduced to actively address domestic violence. At least at the policing stage, mediation is, in theory, voluntary and is conducted by referral P2TP2A. However, these referrals are facilitated by a Memorandum of Understanding (MOU) between P2TP2A and the PPA Unit in Banda Aceh. The MOU and associated mediation referral system are not replicated consistently at the provincial level across Indonesia. Indeed, studies mentioned in Chapter 6 have documented police 'mediating' cases themselves (without adequate processes or training in place) or police informally 'referring' cases to *adat* mediation. Informal police referrals, without more, can be more accurately described as a rejection of the victim's report rather than a genuine attempt at mediation or referral.

Islamic Courts

Ibu Hayati's journey then led her to seek a divorce at the Islamic Courts. A jurisdictional divide between the Islamic Courts and the *Pengadilan Negeri* means that victims must seek assistance from two different legal avenues with little cooperation between the two. This lack of institutional cooperation means that victims often fall between the cracks of the State system. Further, due to a lack of clarity regarding jurisdiction, Islamic Court judges consistently fail to engage with, or recognise, domestic violence in determining divorce applications and, in turn, fail to protect victims. In Chapter 5 revealed that since domestic violence directly affects substantive divorce rights, including *nafkah* (maintenance) and custody, domestic violence falls squarely within the Islamic Courts' jurisdiction. As such there is a need to further train Islamic Court judges to improve their understanding of domestic violence. Widespread or mandatory trainings specific to domestic violence have not yet been implemented at the Islamic Courts. The need to implement such training is particularly pertinent, considering that the vast majority of domestic violence cases entering the State system are dealt with by the Islamic Courts as divorce applications. The Islamic Courts' current passivity towards domestic violence not only substantially contributes to perpetrator impunity and a lack of protection of victim rights but also constitutes ***bureaucratic violence***. The exception to this is Islamic Court judges who rely on PERMA 3/2017 to actively engage with domestic violence and make gender equal judgments (discussed in Chapter 5). While some of the barriers faced by Ibu Hayati are specific to domestic violence victims, other challenges, such as the ineffective enforcement of Islamic Court decisions, are systemic issues requiring broader reform. Further, high numbers of unregistered marriages and unauthorised divorces continue to fall outside the State regulatory system, without registered marriages victims of domestic violence are not protected by the Law.

Policing and prosecution

Ibu Hayati also attempted to report violence to the police, but her report was swiftly rejected by the officer at the front desk. As shown in Chapter 6, police rejections of victim complaints are unfortunately common due to poor understandings of domestic violence and victim rights under the Law, particularly where a case does not relate to severe physical or visual violence. Widespread issues with police compliance with the Law mean that women's advocates and lawyers play important roles in protecting victim rights. The lack of police training with respect to domestic violence creates a bottleneck in the criminal law system with very few cases moving onto prosecution, as well as constituting *bureaucratic violence* (discussed below). Current policing practices raise questions about the utility of the law, in particular criminal law, for victims of domestic violence. The exception to police failures to protect victims or hold perpetrators accountable is arguably the PPA unit. PPA officers have more training and greater institutional knowledge regarding domestic violence, however, the impact of their unit is limited due to a lack of referral of cases from frontline officers.

The fact that Ibu Hayati was referred to P2TP2A by the hypothetical police officer who rejected her report is unlikely to be a common scenario. However, when victims are referred to P2TP2A, the organisation plays a significant role in connecting victims to services, such as counselling, as well as acting as victim advocates. P2TP2A provides essential support to victims including when filing their divorce applications or reporting to police. Without such support, victims, who generally do not know their rights under the Law, are unlikely to be properly protected by either religious (civil) or criminal law stakeholders. However, as raised in Chapter 3, the capacity of P2TP2A is limited due to a lack of institutional funding. This means that the services of P2TP2A alone cannot remedy the barriers to access to justice that exist within the State system, nor is P2TP2A always able to act as a safety net when religious (civil) and criminal law institutions fail to protect victims.

As suggested throughout this book, what is required is reform of current Islamic Court and *Pengadilan Negeri* practices, as well as greater cooperation between the two. An alternative avenue would be to create a specialist Domestic Violence or Women's Court with the jurisdiction to resolve all related issues within a single case (see Katjasungkana 2013). The potential opportunities and benefits of creating an integrated judicial avenue is an important area for further research.

In the relatively rare cases where violence is prosecuted, it is likely that the prosecutor will recommend a low to modest sentence and that *Pengadilan Negeri* judges will hand down a slightly lower sentence in a similar range to the prosecutor's recommendation. The *Pengadilan Negeri* failings analysed in Chapter 7 are, therefore, not solely attributable to judges themselves but are also, to an extent, attributable to police and prosecution practices that feed into the court's reasoning via the evidence presented and the arguments made.

Pengadilan Negeri

The analysis of the 70 domestic violence cases decided by the *Pengadilan Negeri* between 2013 and 2017 confirmed much of the literature set out in Chapter 3, such as the distinctly gendered nature of domestic violence and the fact that domestic violence can occur in any marriage, regardless of whether the couple is young or old, poor or wealthy, professional or working class, and so on. In line with community understandings set out in Chapter 4, the court tended to prioritise physical violence and treat non-physical violence as less serious. In addition, the court consistently treated domestic violence as 'incident-based' as opposed to as a pattern of coercive and controlling behaviour. For example, judges rarely considered histories of domestic violence in their decisions.

Triggers for violence were identified in Chapter 7. While triggers are not the *cause* of violence – and certainly not an excuse or justification for violence – these triggers helped explain, to an extent, why perpetrators felt entitled to use violence. Most, if not all, triggers for violence could be related back to the gender norms set out in Chapters 3 and 4. The umbrella category of 'authority challenged' encapsulated a variety of reasons that abusive men felt entitled to use violence against their spouses. Most of these aligned with conservative interpretations of gender norms relating to a man's authority as the head of the household to 'educate' his wife if he perceived her to be non-compliant with her *kodrat* (or his interpretation of what her *kodrat* was). Triggers related to challenges to authority included jealousy, economic pressure, and custody disputes. When interviewed, judges seemed to conflate triggers for violence with moral justifications for violence, for example, when one of the judges stated that 'the accused might only be using violence to educate, or for other religious purposes'. Further, it was argued that the low sentences handed down reflected the mitigation of sentences based on implicit (and sometimes explicit) gender bias.

As discussed in Chapter 7, there were also inconsistencies in the court's reasoning when interpreting Article 44 of the Law (physical violence) regarding whether violence had to result in injury *and/or* prevent victims from working or carrying out daily activities to fall under Article 44 subsection (1). Prosecutors and women's advocates need to actively engage with, and respond to, this split in the court's interpretation, especially in terms of satisfying a potentially higher evidentiary burden. Further, the courts did not substantively engage with several forms of violence that should be treated as 'serious' forms of violence, including threats to life, choking, stalking, and use of a weapon. Notably, none of these factors were explicitly considered as aggravating the nature of the offence in sentencing. The lack of understanding of the dynamics of domestic violence, in particular, the relationship between physical and non-physical violence (such as threats to life or stalking) indicates an urgent need for judicial education on this topic.

While cases of psychological, sexual, and economic violence/household neglect are heard relatively infrequently by the court, the cases studied provided insights into how judges approach non-physical forms of violence. Cases of psychological violence (Article 45 of the Law) were also prosecuted in an incident-focused way, with a focus on indirect or threatened physical force, as opposed to psychological violence more broadly. Importantly in terms of potential reform, the cases studied revealed the potential strategic value of the prosecution bringing a charge of psychological violence to introduce more holistic evidence at trial, including a history of domestic violence. Further, cases of economic violence/household neglect (Article 49 of the Law) illustrate how criminal charges can potentially be brought under the Law where husbands have the capacity to provide *nafkah* (maintenance) but refuse to do so, leading to the neglect of the family, such as where Islamic Court orders are already in place but have not been successfully enforced.

The most problematic of these cases was the application of the 'household neglect' provision in Case 17/2015, where a female victim of domestic violence was convicted of committing 'violence' against her abusive husband, including by refusing to have sex with him. The outcome in this case is egregious, not only because the defendant was a victim of domestic violence at the time but because of the amorphous gender norms which were applied as a criminal legal standard against the defendant without a clear legal basis. This case is the most clear-cut example of gender norms being applied in a discriminatory way by the *Pengadilan Negeri*. It was argued that the reasoning in this case is dangerous because it opens the possibility of the court being complicit in perpetuating violence against victims of domestic violence (i.e. legal systems abuse), which is, itself, a form of *bureaucratic violence* (discussed below).

Drawing on victim perspectives in Chapter 4, the analysis in Chapter 7 showed that often no clear lines could be drawn when it came to victims 'staying' and 'leaving' the relationship or, in the language of sentencing, between 'making peace' and 'not making peace'. With respect to separation and post-separation contexts, the *Pengadilan Negeri* cases studied validated victim concerns that violence may escalate during or post-separation. However, it was also illustrated that the majority of victims reporting domestic violence (even via criminal law avenues) were not separated and did not necessarily seek to divorce their husbands. This evidence challenges the assumption that victims who pursue protection through criminal law avenues necessarily want to 'leave' the relationship, at least at the time of prosecution and/or sentencing. As seen in sentencing considerations, this creates a conundrum for judges who, due to a lack of available rehabilitation programmes, generally hand down either a carceral sentence or a suspended sentence with a probationary period. A victim's wishes to remain with the perpetrator as a family, or the family's economic dependency on the perpetrator, mean that in some cases incarceration of the perpetrator may indirectly punish the victim.

There is currently a lack of options for sentencing. To remedy this, it is crucial to develop operational perpetrator rehabilitation services to address the root causes of violence and attempt to break the cycle of violence. The legal infrastructure for court-ordered rehabilitation programmes as a sentence under the Law is in place, however, facilities and programmes to implement the promises of the Law in practice currently do not exist. It was argued that the failure of the State to establish counselling programmes for perpetrators, as promised by the Law, is another iteration of *bureaucratic violence* (discussed below). It was also noted that even if the infrastructure for non-carceral sentencing was established, there would remain a need for specialised judicial training on domestic violence for *Pengadilan Negeri* judges, including the importance of counselling orders for breaking cycles of violence. The option of creating sentencing guidelines for domestic violence cases was also raised due to the densely gendered way in which discretion is currently being exercised in domestic violence cases.

Non-violence, religion and gender

After reading the horrific accounts of violence in this book, it is tempting to disregard domestic violence as the work of 'monsters', not men. It would be easier to do so than to face the reality that men's violence against women is rooted in the patriarchal social structures currently embedded in our communities. However, the statistics show us that many women each year continue to fall in love with, marry, and start families with men who, at some point, may choose to perpetrate violence against them. Further, female victims of domestic violence often express a desire for men to stop being violent and to remain in their relationships. This book has illustrated that the majority of victims do not seek to leave the relationship at the time of criminal prosecutions or may attempt to leave many times before they finally do so. Therefore, while our legal systems must facilitate access to justice for victims who seek to leave violent relationships, it must also facilitate access to justice for victims who do not believe it is possible, preferable, or tenable to leave their relationships at the time that they engage with the State system. In other words, the State's protection of domestic violence victims cannot be contingent on women first leaving abusive relationships. If women choose to remain in abusive relationships or otherwise cannot leave, our justice systems must continue to support and protect them as far as possible. This means that along with holding abusers to account for violence they have perpetrated, there is an urgent need to establish rehabilitation programmes that seek to prevent future violence. Breaking the cycle of violence must, at some level, involve a positive re-definition of masculinity and respectful relationships, starting with the condemnation of violence as an acceptable expression of masculinity.

Throughout this book, it has been argued that barriers to access to justice arise in the form of patriarchal religious interpretations that influence community understandings of domestic violence, which feed into gender bias and discrimination against victims. Such gender bias informs institutional responses to domestic violence, compounding barriers to access to justice for women seeking support or exercising their legal rights. From the community to the courts, the interpretation and implementation of the Law is affected by gender norms that often operate to discriminate against women, leading to a failure to protect their victim rights or hold perpetrators accountable. From the outset of this book, I sought to be clear that the law does not exist in a vacuum, therefore, initiatives for the empowerment of women and improved understandings of the Law at the community level – for example, the important activities of NGOs and women's advocates – must continue to be developed alongside legal interventions.

As documented in Chapter 4, victims of domestic violence who seek to assert their rights in rarely do so alone. The importance of community member and institutional stakeholders who provide support for victims cannot be underestimated. In addition to experiences of stigmatisation and victim-blaming, victims also highlighted the support they received from their communities and their own sense of empowerment inspired by feminist or gender equal interpretations of Islam. References to alternative or subversive gender norms were woven throughout the book. For example, the idea iterated by victims that men's entitlement to respect as the head of the household is conditional on their performance of responsibilities in line with constructs of caring (or non-patriarchal) masculinities – was also reflected in the sentencing remarks of judges in Chapter 7. Judges who aggravated sentences based on the idea that violence against spouses or children is incompatible with a husband's role as head of the household opens a promising avenue of discussion within the Islamic tradition about the construction of men's gender roles based on non-violence.

Islamically-informed approaches towards combatting the stigma around domestic violence and re-directing stigma away from victims and towards perpetrators to highlight perpetrator accountability for violence should be the subject of further research in the future. Additionally, non-discriminatory interpretations of *hadith* and the *Qur'an* by women's advocates outlined in Chapter 4, such as 'it is shameful if a husband chastises his wife', resonate with the sentencing remarks by some judges that 'vigilante violence' is an aggravating factor. Such an approach could be adopted and developed by women's advocates in order to counter the idea that men are 'morally justified' in using disciplinary or educative violence. In Indonesia, the re-framing of masculinities within an Islamic framework is crucial to its socio-religious legitimacy. Further, more research needs to be done in to the role of men in addressing family violence (for example, Haryanto (2018) highlights the potential of men as 'agents of change').

From the community to the courts, religious interpretations and gender norms continue to be contested within Indonesia. This book has highlighted patriarchal religious interpretations as the source of contemporary hegemonic gender norms. However, as mentioned above, women's advocates and victims also identified alternative ways of defining gender based on non-discriminatory and gender equal interpretations of religious doctrines. Further, while the majority of actors in religious (civil) and criminal law institutions do not sufficiently understand domestic violence, passionate and knowledgeable individuals exist in every part of the system. In the words of Mahmood (2012), there is 'no possibility of "undoing" social norms' without the '"doing" of norms'. This means that the source of oppression, the exercise of agency, and potential opportunities for reform all exist within the same context. In Indonesia, this means that the key to responding strategically to barriers to access to justice, better protecting victim rights, and improving perpetrator accountability for violence is a nuanced understanding of the socio-religious context, in particular, the intersections between religion, gender and law.

Benang merah *(the red thread)*

The *benang merah* of this book is the theory of bureaucratic violence against domestic violence victims. Introduced in Chapter 1 and woven throughout, this theory sought to emphasise the roles and responsibilities of the State to protect victim rights based on the explicit promises that the State has made in the Law. The primary examples that I provided of this was the failure of the State to establish operational safe houses for victims and rehabilitation programmes for perpetrators – critical areas of reform which must be remedied by the State as soon as possible. Further examples of bureaucratic violence were raised throughout the book, including in the current practices of the police and in the flawed approaches of both Islamic Courts and *Pengadilan Negeri* judges towards domestic violence. Throughout this book, it has been argued that due to the failure of the State to fulfil its promises, victims are exposed to an escalated risk of violence as well as a perpetuated risk of violence.

The emphasis throughout this book on State responsibility does not lessen the responsibility of each of us as individuals to seek to address domestic violence. Whether this is by promoting non-discriminatory or gender equal religious interpretations, conducting community education to improve socialisation of the Law, or advocating for law reform – the work of individual men and women to address family violence across Indonesia is deeply important. Put simply, the State is unlikely to remedy gaps in implementation of the Law without consistent pressure from civil society to do so. The State can only be held accountable for bureaucratic violence – in both its failure to protect victims of domestic violence and hold perpetrators accountability – if the people hold it to account.

Bibliography

Haryanto, Sindung, 'Engaging Men: Results of the MenCare+ Gender Justice Program in Indonesia' (2018) 26(1) *The Journal of Men's Studies* 40–55.

Katjasungkana, Nursyahbani, 'The Indonesian family as a Contested Site of Women's Rights: Implementation of the Domestic Violence Act' in Maznah Mohamad and Saskia Wieringa (eds), *Family Ambiguity and Domestic Violence in Asia* (Sussex Academic Press 2013) 169–191.

Mahmood, Saba, *Politics of Piety: The Islamic Revival and the Feminist Subject* (Princeton University Press, 2012).

Glossary

Adat an Indonesian word used in this book to broadly describe 'customary law'.

Allah God

Bapak the Indonesian word for an adult man, the equivalent of the honorific 'Mr', also 'Pak'.

Cerai liar the Indonesian term for a divorce which is conducted in accordance with moral religious law as opposed to formalised by the *Mahkamah Syariah* under State law (literally 'wild divorce').

Fiqh the interpretative process through which *shari'a* (defined below) is derived from the *Qur'an* and *hadith* or, in other words, human interpretation of divine sources to extract norms and rules.

Geuchik the Indonesian word for the Head of the Village, also sometimes '*Kepala Desa*'.

Haram meaning forbidden in Islam (the opposite of *halal*, meaning permissible).

Ibu the Indonesian word for an adult woman, the equivalent of the honorific 'Mrs'; used interchangeably with 'Kak' (short for *Kakak*) among close female friends.

Imam religious leader, also see *ulama*.

Inshallah God willing.

Janda the Indonesian word for a woman who was married but is no longer married. *Janda* can refer to widows, divorcees, or women who have otherwise been abandoned but is used in this book to refer specifically to divorcees.

Kampung the Indonesian word for village, also *kampong* or *desa*.

***Kekerasan dalam rumah tangga* (KDRT)** the Indonesian phrase for domestic violence, literally 'violence in the household'.

Kodrat predetermined nature or fate/destiny of a person depending on their sex. For a discussion regarding the contested content of *kodrat*, see Chapter 3 of this book.

Komnas Perempuan the Indonesian Women's Commission.

Mahkamah Syariah the Acehnese name for Islamic Courts in Indonesia. Indonesian Islamic Court jurisdiction includes Islamic marriage, inheritance, *shari'a* economy and, in Aceh, Islamic criminal law. Also sometimes referred to as: religious courts, *shari'a* courts.

Nikah siri the Indonesian term for a marriage conducted under moral-religious law but not registered with the State (literally 'secret marriage').

Pengadilan Agama Indonesian State religious courts with jurisdiction over marriage and divorce and related civil law rights.

Pengadilan Negeri Indonesian State courts with jurisdiction to apply the criminal provisions of the Anti-Domestic Violence Law.

PERMA Indonesian Supreme Court Regulations.

PPA Unit Women's and Children's Protection Unit (*Bidang Perlindungan Perempuan dan Anak*, known as the PPA Unit).

P2TP2A the Integrated Service Centre for the Empowerment of Women and Children (*Pusat Pelayanan Terpadu Pemberdayaan Perempuan dan Anak*, known as P2TP2A) is the primary organisation tasked with responsibility for coordinating State responses to domestic violence.

Qanun the Acehnese name given to *peraturan daerah* (regional regulations).

Qur'an Islamic holy book.

Shari'a Islamic teachings or values derived from the *Qur'an* (Islamic holy book of revelations) and *hadith* (the sayings of the Prophet). Alternative spelling *Sharia, Shariah, Syariah, Syariat*.

Talak Divorce initiated by Muslim husbands is known as *talak*, while divorce initiated by Muslim wives is known as *khulu* or *cerai gugat*.

Ulama Islamic religious expert or leader, also see *imam*. For more information on the difference between 'white-collar' *ulamas* and '*dayah*' *ulamas*, see Chapter 2 of this book.

Undang-Undang the Indonesian term for 'laws'.

Visum a medical report documenting the nature of the physical evidence sought from a hospital.

Zina extra-marital sex.

Appendices

Appendix 1 Historical timeline of Aceh

Indonesia	*Aceh*
	Pre-colonial Islamic sultanate
	1641–1675 Sultanah Safiatuddin Syah
	1675–1678 Sultanah Naqiatuddin Syah
	1678–1688 Sultanah Zakiatuddin Syah
	1688–1699 Sultanah Kamalat Syah
	1873 Dutch first attacked the Acehnese sultanate
	1874 Dutch captured the Sultan's palace
	1901 Dutch Ethical Policy
	1903 Sultan surrendered and the Dutch declared
	Aceh conquered
	1904 Despite the events in 1903, the war continued
	1913 Dutch conquered Aceh
	1942 Dutch colonial occupation ended
	1942-1945 Japanese occupation
1945	
17 August 1945 Indonesia unilaterally declared independence	
1949	
27 December 1949 Indonesia gained independence	
1949–1957 Soekarno Parliamentary Democracy	**1950** Abolition of Aceh's provisional status **1953**
1957–1965 Soekarno Guided Democracy	Aceh joins Darul Islam movement
1965	**1959** Aceh re-instated as a province and receives special regional autonomy
– 30 September failed coup – Anti-PKI (communist) massacres	**1962** Darul Islam movement ends
1966–1998 Soeharto New Order	**1976** Aceh unilaterally declares independence from Indonesia led by GAM
	1989 Aceh declared an Area of Military Operations (DOM)

(*Continued*)

Indonesia	*Aceh*
1998 *Reformasi* period – **1998–1999** President Habibie – **1999–2001** President Abdurrahman Wahid (Gus Dur) – **2001–2004** President Megawati Sukarnoputri – **2004–2014** President Susilo Bambang Yudhoyono (SBY) – **2014–** President Joko Widodo (Jokowi)	**1998** DOM ends **1999** Military operations escalate **2000** Humanitarian Pause **2002** Cessation of Hostilities Agreement **2003** Martial law reimposed **2004** Boxing Day Tsunami **2005** Helsinki Peace Agreement signed

Appendix 2 Sentencing of different types of domestic violence

Type of violence	*Provision*	*Maximum imprisonment*	*Maximum fine*
Physical violence	Article 44(1) – 'general' provision	5 years	15 million rupiah
Physical violence resulting in serious sickness or injury	Article 44(2) – 'extended' provision	10 years	30 million rupiah
Physical violence resulting in the death of the victim	Article 44(3)	15 years	45 million rupiah
Physical violence – between spouses – not resulting in sickness or obstructing the performance of work/livelihood or daily activities	Article 44(4) – 'limited' provision	4 months	5 million rupiah
Psychological violence	Article 45(1) –'general' provision	3 years	9 million rupiah
Psychological violence – between spouses – not resulting in sickness or obstructing the performance of work/livelihood or daily activities	Article 45(2) –'limited' provision	4 months	3 million rupiah
Sexual violence (8(a)) – forced sexual intercourse	Article 46	12 years	36 million rupiah
Sexual violence (8(b)) – forced sexual intercourse for commercial purposes	Article 47	*At least* four years and *no longer* than 15 years	*At least* 12 million rupiah and *not more than* 300 million rupiah

(*Continued*)

Type of violence	*Provision*	*Maximum imprisonment*	*Maximum fine*
Economic violence – failing to provide livelihood, treatment or care for an individual which he/she is obligated to provide according to prevailing law (9(1)) – bringing about economic dependence by limiting/prohibiting an individual to work thereby placing the victim under his/her control (9(2))	Article 49	3 years	15 million rupiah
Any kind of violence causing the victim to: – sustain a permanent injury; – suffer from a mental or spiritual disorder for at least four weeks continuously or cumulatively; – suffer a miscarriage or the death of a fetus or; – experience dysfunction of reproductive organs	Article 48	*At least* five years and *no longer* than 20 years	*At least* 25 million rupiah and *not more than* 500 million rupiah
Any kind of violence	Article 50	Additional sentences at the judge's discretion	

Index

MIX
Papier | Fördert gute Waldnutzung
FSC® C083411

Kolibri 360 GmbH
Ferdinand-Jühlke-Straße 7
99095 Erfurt, Deutschland
produktsicherheit@kolibri360.de